T0284668

SAINTS and LIARS

SAINTS and LIARS

The Story of Americans
Who Saved Refugees from the Nazis

～

DEBÓRAH DWORK

～

W. W. NORTON & COMPANY

Independent Publishers Since 1923

Manufacturing by Lakeside Book Company
Book design by Brooke Koven
Production manager: Anna Oler

ISBN 978-1-324-02034-9

W. W. Norton & Company, Inc., 500 Fifth Avenue, New York, NY 10110
www.wwnorton.com

W. W. Norton & Company Ltd., 15 Carlisle Street, London W1D 3BS

To Ken

Whom I met thanks to fortuitous circumstances
And whom I love for good reason and just because

CONTENTS

MAPS

CREDIT: Maps by Maël Le Noc, PhD

SOURCES: *Building the New Order: 1938–1945 Dataset,* Michael De Groot. *The CShapes 2.0 Dataset,* Guy Schvitz, Seraina Rüegger, Luc Girardin, Lars-Erik Cederman, Nils Weidmann, and Kristian Skrede Gleditsch. *Japanese Expansion in the Late 19th and 20th Centuries,* Encyclopaedia Britannica. *Virtual Shanghai Dataset,* Christian Henriot and Isabelle Durand.

FREQUENTLY USED ACRONYMS

AFSC	American Friends Service Committee
AmRelCzech	American Committee for Relief in Czechoslovakia
AUA	American Unitarian Association
BCRC	British Committee for Refugees from Czechoslovakia
CFA	Committee for the Assistance of European Jewish Refugees (Shanghai, China)
EastJewCom (EJC)	Committee for the Assistance of East European Refugees
HICEM	Merger of the New York–based Hebrew Immigrant Aid Society (HIAS), the Paris-based Jewish Colonization Association (JCA or ICA), and the Berlin-based emigration organization EmigDirect.
IC	International Committee for European Immigrants (Shanghai)
IGC	Inter-Governmental Committee on Refugees
JDC	American Jewish Joint Distribution Committee
JEWCOM	Jewish community of Kobe (Japan)
NRS	National Refugee Service
OSS	United States Office of Strategic Services
OSE	Oeuvre de Secours aux Enfants
SACRA	Shanghai Ashkenazi Communal Relief Association
UNRRA	United Nations Relief and Rehabilitation Agency

USC   Unitarian Service Committee
USCOM   United States Committee for the Care of European
                     Children
WRB   War Refugee Board

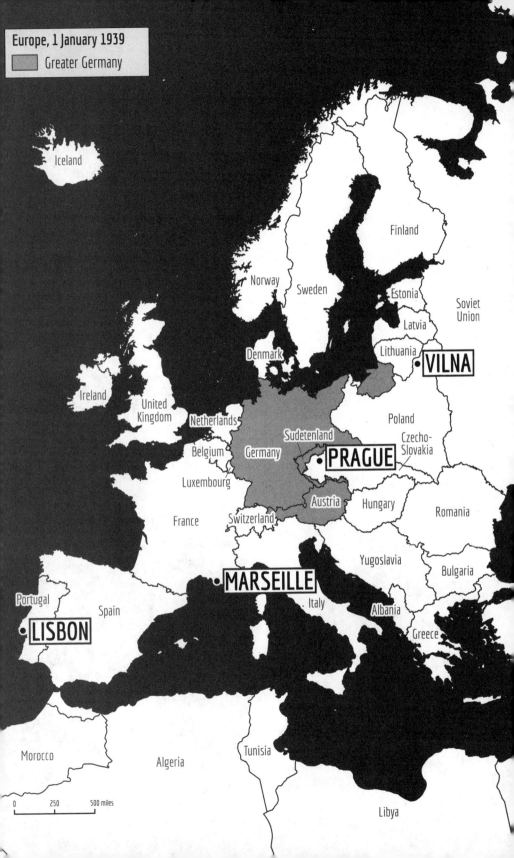

Europe, 1 January 1939
Greater Germany

Iceland

Norway

Sweden

Finland

Denmark

Estonia

Latvia

Lithuania

VILNA

Ireland

United Kingdom

Netherlands

Belgium

Germany

Sudetenland

Poland

Czecho-Slovakia

PRAGUE

Luxembourg

Austria

Hungary

Romania

France

Switzerland

MARSEILLE

Yugoslavia

Italy

Bulgaria

Albania

Portugal

Spain

LISBON

Greece

Morocco

Algeria

Tunisia

Libya

0   250   500 miles

0   250   500 miles

Soviet Union

Tuvan People's
Republic

Mongolia

Manchukuo

Southern
Sakhalin Island

Korea

Japan

Tibet

China

Nepal

Bhutan

SHANGHAI

India

Taiwan

Burma

Thailand

Philippines

French
Indochina

North Borneo

Sarawak

British
Malaya

East Asia, 1 January 1939

Japanese-controlled
territories

Dutch East
Indies

SAINTS and LIARS

INTRODUCTION

AMERICANS
TO THE RESCUE

A HUNDRED ENDANGERED CHILDREN crowded into the Marseille office of the American Friends Service Committee (AFSC) one day in June 1941. They had been selected from thousands of candidates by AFSC staff for a coveted spot on a convoy to the United States. Organized by the United States Committee for the Care of European Children (USCOM), this rescue effort was supported by no less a figure than Eleanor Roosevelt, who served as USCOM's honorary president; the philanthropic department store magnate Marshall Field, who served as president; and a roster of relief agencies. As USCOM's partner on the ground in France, the AFSC chose the children to be offered the opportunity to emigrate as well as the chaperones accompanying them who also needed to flee.[1]

The youngsters and adults walked from the AFSC's Marseille premises to the main train station. "Ragged and disheveled, each child carried a small untidy bundle and a battered valise," Isaac Chomski, a Polish-born physician who worked as a medical officer for the French Jewish philanthropy Oeuvre de Secours aux Enfants (OSE), recalled a few months later. "The white numbered cards which hung from their necks made them look like so much live baggage."[2]

It was bitingly cold despite the spring month. And the children were hungry. Dr. Chomski and his wife, Masha, also an OSE employee, handed them their food ration of three thin slices of bread as the locomotive crawled through southern France. Still, the young refugees looked forward to seeing family members soon. They knew the train had a scheduled stop at the small station of Oloron, close to the Gurs internment camp, and that OSE had persuaded the camp authorities to allow their interned relatives to bid the children farewell. In anticipation, a "youngster timidly displays a photograph of a sweet, comely, young woman. 'Minna,' he explains..., 'my sister. She took care of me.' The snapshot was taken only a year ago," Dr. Chomski noted. "Today, she too is in Gurs."[3]

The children rushed to the windows as the train reached Oloron. "Mothers, fathers, and kin, with the last few ounces of strength in their frail bodies, suddenly tear through the cordon of gendarmes and dash to the doors of the train," Dr. Chomski remembered. "As the children pour out of the train, their parents and relatives hug them tightly." Minna was there, too, "now a living corpse. Thin as a lathe, sallow-faced, she has no strength for words. Instead, she immediately falls upon her little brother's neck and smothers him with kisses."[4]

The children offered their loved ones the currency of the day: bread. "Children of eight and ten, themselves terribly hungry," sought to give their rations to their fathers and mothers. The parents understood the enormity of their gift and "a heart-rending wail bursts from their throats." Touched, the French commanding officer allowed the train to remain in the station for an extra few minutes. Then it clattered away. "Through the doors and windows, the children wave their hands to the group of living dead. The shriveled faces slowly grow less distinct, become distant specks, and then are seen no more."[5] Traveling through Spain, the children arrived in Lisbon, where they boarded the New York–bound Portuguese SS *Mouzinho*, which had been chartered for their journey. They were, as Dr. Chomski noted, "fortunate youngsters on their way out of the hell that is France."[6] And at the same time, they were separating, probably forever, from everyone they loved.

WHO WERE THE AMERICAN QUAKERS who, burdened by the knowledge of what was at stake, selected these children for emigration and worked unflaggingly to secure all the required papers and permissions? What did they accomplish, and how did they manage those feats? This book unearths the history of a number of Americans—Quakers, Jews, Unitarians—who became both saints and liars as they sought to save lives. Traveling to points around the globe to offer aid to targets of Nazi Germany and its allies, they remained to rescue as many as possible when the victims' peril turned lethal. The narrative arcs from one center of activity to another. As one place grew too dangerous and the operatives' scope dwindled, opportunities emerged elsewhere.

Our story opens in 1939 prewar Prague. The Nazis had been in power in Germany since 1933 and had annexed Austria in March 1938. Turning their eyes on Czechoslovakia, they claimed the German-speaking area of Sudetenland. The Nazi regime's control of each territory (Germany, Austria, Sudetenland) created wave upon wave of asylum seekers, particularly political opponents and Jews. As the numbers climbed and conditions deteriorated, American philanthropic organizations already operating in Europe, particularly the American Jewish Joint Distribution Committee (the JDC, or "Joint") and the American Friends Service Committee, directed resources and detailed personnel to provide aid. The unfolding humanitarian disaster prompted the creation of new initiatives as well, such as the Unitarian Commission for Service in Czechoslovakia, which sent two operatives, Martha and Waitstill Sharp, to support relief efforts in Prague. The Germans' invasion of what remained of Czechoslovakia in March 1939 triggered desperation among those pursued by the regime. The Sharps understood: lives hung in the balance. Their focus shifted to rescue; they would

Martha Sharp. (*Courtesy of Artemis Joukowsky.*)

Waitstill Sharp. (*United States Holocaust Memorial Museum, courtesy of Renée Rizzoni.*)

use legal emigration or clandestine flight to move targeted people beyond German reach.

The Germans' acquisition of Austria and the Czech lands was a prelude to their onslaught across the continent. Unleashing World War II, Germany invaded Poland from the west on 1 September 1939 and, by agreement with the German government, the Soviets rolled in from the east on 17 September. Fearing both the Nazis and the communists, Polish Jews streamed across the border to neutral Lithuania. The JDC, with its long record of aid to the 155,000 Lithuanian Jews and to the 85,000 Jews in greater Vilna (previously Polish, now Lithuanian), saw an area of impending need and an arena for constructive action. Established in 1914 to help Jewish communities in Europe and Palestine ravaged by World War I, the JDC stood ready to act. European director Morris Troper sent recently hired Moses Beckelman to the area. Our story continues (chapter 2) with his arrival in October 1939. The Soviet occupation of Lithuania in the summer of 1940 redirected Beckelman's efforts from relief to rescue. Who got help? What pressure was brought to bear, and by whom—and on behalf of whom?

Moses Beckelman. *(NY_16201,*   Laura Margolis. *(NY_16518,*
Courtesy of JDC Archives, New York.)   *Courtesy of JDC Archives, New York.)*

Shanghai (chapter 3) was one of the destinations to which refugees from Lithuania fled, joining German, Austrian, and Czech Jews who had landed there a few years earlier. With some twenty thousand migrants in that Chinese city, the JDC sent its first woman field agent, social worker Laura Margolis, to ease the bottleneck and facilitate further emigration. Thus, she was there when the Japanese attacked Pearl Harbor in December 1941 bringing the United States into the war and, at the same time on the other side of the Pacific Ocean, the Japanese military occupied Shanghai. The refugees were trapped in the city under Axis control, and so was she. Margolis shouldered the even greater need for relief work. The refugees faced critically important immediate demands—food, housing, medical care, education—that stretched into an uncertain future. How was she to keep them alive?

If emigration was no longer possible from Shanghai after the attack on Pearl Harbor, it was the focus of much effort and energy in 1942 Marseille (chapter 4). Drawing upon its tradition of hospitality, France had accepted large numbers of people targeted by the Nazis after they came to power in 1933. Nearly half a million Spanish refugees followed, fleeing over the Pyrenees into France when

General Francisco Franco's forces toppled Republican Spain in 1939. Overwhelmed by the mass arrivals, the French government erected internment camps to house them in the south of the country. These centers gained a new function when war began in September; the authorities filled them with Jewish refugees and other so-called enemy aliens, even if anti-Nazi.

Germany invaded France in May 1940, and Paris fell in June. Embracing an official policy of collaboration with Germany, Field Marshal Philippe Pétain signed an armistice that divided France in two, with a German-occupied zone to the industrial north and an unoccupied "free zone" that covered the grape-growing southern third of the country, where many of the internment camps were situated.

The American Friends Service Committee, founded in 1917 to address humanitarian needs during World War I, had initiated supplemental meal and medical care programs in the internment camps. But conditions deteriorated after the armistice. Relief ini-

Roswell (left) and Marjorie McClelland (second from left) at the General Delegates' Conference in Marseille, June 1942. (Roswell and Marjorie McClelland papers, United States Holocaust Memorial Museum, gift of Kirk McClelland.)

tiatives helped, but hope lay in emigration, as Marjorie and Ross McClelland, two of the Marseille AFSC delegates, well understood. Marjorie was charged with selecting the children to be included in a May 1942 USCOM transport. Again the dilemma of whom to choose, what criteria to apply, gripped the American operative. And if children were at risk, so were adults. The search for the certificates, papers, and tickets that asylum seekers required claimed much of the Marseille office staff's attention. Whom did they deem worthy of that effort? Their quest ended abruptly in November 1942. The Allied invasion of French North Africa sent the Germans over the demarcation line, and neutral Vichy France was no more. The Americans were forced to flee.

By 1943, Lisbon (chapter 5) had gained the popular reputation of "Europe's sole window to the west." Portugal, a neutral if fascist country run by the dictator António de Oliveira Salazar, admitted transients who offered proof of onward passage. The Unitarians had opened an office in 1940 in Lisbon's central square to help refugees from the continent who managed to reach that port to ship out across the Atlantic or the English Channel. With the German occupation of all of France, the Lisbon operation, run by Elisabeth

Elisabeth Dexter. (*Unitarian Service Committee, bMS 16076/11, Harvard Divinity School Library, Harvard Divinity School, Cambridge, Massachusetts.*)

Robert Dexter. (*Unitarian Service Committee, bMS 16076/11, Harvard Divinity School Library, Harvard Divinity School, Cambridge, Massachusetts.*)

and Robert Dexter, expanded its reach. Marseille teemed with refugees, thousands of whom crossed the Pyrenees into Spain and then slipped into Portugal. Many were undocumented and thus "illegals." Others had valid papers but could not get passage out and fell into "illegality."

Danger lurked at all times. Refugees and the aid workers who helped them were constantly watched by an efficient and ruthless political police force as well as the Gestapo, which had agents in Lisbon. Undaunted, American relief workers continued to offer help to refugees in Portugal and to rescue as many as they could. Like the American operatives in Prague, Vilna, Shanghai, and Marseille, they hung on and held out. In their case, however, war's end glimmered on the horizon.

ZOOMING IN on one city, one year, and one person or couple, each chapter offers a microhistory that yields a rich picture lost in a larger frame. The key role of two previously obscured factors emerges. The unpredictable: luck, timing, chance, fortuitous circumstances. And the irrational: human sympathies and antipathies, drives, and desires. Historians have traditionally trained their lenses on social class, occupation, religion, race, age, and gender. But they have shied away from the unpredictable and irrational. Yet these variables loom large in daily life.

This is not to minimize the underlying structures of ideology, policy, and practice. Were it not for Nazi ideology, policy, and practice, the Americans would not have needed to be abroad at all. Yet over and over again, luck, timing, fortuitous circumstance, spontaneous feelings, and irrational impulses shaped individual fates. It might be the fortuitous circumstance of rain when running to a border across an open field, because it prevented guard dogs from picking up the fugitive's scent, impeded the sentries' view, and muffled the noise of crashing through a meadow. Or the timing of slipping across a frontier during the interval of the guards' rounds on the chance that, on that one particular night, the schedule would have changed. Then there might be the unexpected kindness—for an unknown reason or no reason at all—of an official who chose to ignore regulations just that once.

Saints and Liars plumbs factors—feelings, luck, timing, chance—that we know shape our own lives but often get lost in our analyses of the past. Telescoping into the lives of American rescuers in desperate situations across Europe and in Shanghai, *Saints and Liars* amplifies the function of the unpredictable and the irrational. American operatives evinced improbable courage, resourcefulness, and resilience. They were fueled by principles, to be sure. But they were fueled, too, by personal and professional ambition, a taste for adventure, and a frustration with limitations. Social ties and connections counted for a lot with them. Emotions played no small part, as did visceral responses, spurring decisions and actions.

Saints and Liars prompts us to imagine history as a time as full and rich as our own; to reframe the way we think about, analyze, and write about the past. This does not marginalize factors already identified as significant. But it adds a new lens to train on any era, anywhere. A moment in Hanna Sztarkman's life serves as an example. Then about twelve years of age, Hanna lived with her mother and brother Heniek in the German-imposed ghetto in the Polish city of Radom. Hanna recalled what happened on 5 August 1942:

> One night we heard shooting. We went to the window [and] we saw people running and German soldiers shooting. We got dressed and then a couple minutes later, we heard German soldiers in the building yelling "Raus, Raus, Raus." . . . So we all went out and there were masses of people on the street. . . . You could go either to the right or to the left into the middle of the street. We stood there for, I don't know, half an hour. And then they told us to go back into the apartment house.
>
> We didn't know what happened. We found out later: Radom had two ghettos, a small ghetto on one side of the town and the bigger ghetto where we were in another part of town. The Germans sent out everybody from the small ghetto to Treblinka

Hanna Sztarkman, ca. 1935. *(Courtesy of Susan Avjian.)*

[annihilation camp]. They had a few cars, those cattle cars, train cars left. So they needed some more people [to fill them]. So they got all the people from the big ghetto out on the street and they counted how many people they needed. So some of our neighbors who, when they left the apartment, went to the right, were sent to Treblinka that night. And we because we turned to the left, were not sent out. The luck of the draw.

So later on when my brother came home from work and my neighbor's son came, he didn't find his mother and sister. My brother found us. It was just one of those things.[7]

Again, this is not to minimize the importance of ideology, policy, and practice, which forced Hanna into that situation. Nor does it minimize the role of religious identity, age, and gender. But at that very moment, luck and fortuitous circumstance shaped her fate.

PLUMBING THE ROLE of the unpredictable and the irrational spurs intriguing questions that *Saints and Liars* explores. What, for instance, are we to make of the heated personal antipathies and the constant quarreling that emerges from contemporary documents? Laura Margolis reported on the dysfunctional relationships among Jews in Shanghai and her own fraught interactions with many. Burritt Hiatt, of the American Friends Service Committee, analyzed the tensions between the central office in Marseille and the branch offices in Toulouse and Perpignan. Unitarian Charles Joy quarreled so heatedly with Elisabeth and Robert Dexter that the Dexters ultimately resigned from the Unitarian Service Committee (USC). What do these tensions reveal about relief and rescue efforts? Are they evidence of overwhelming uncertainty, anxiety, and pressure? Or of fractious personalities? The ubiquitous discord prompts us to map the relief and rescue efforts as they unfolded—to appreciate anew that while the operatives' choices, the courses they pursued, seem straightforward in retrospect, no such clarity existed at the time. And perhaps it suggests something about the people who undertook this work. Perhaps placid people stayed home.

The operatives did not reflect upon their quarreling. Rather, they concentrated on how to determine whom to help. Offering advice to their colleagues, delegates pointed to the temptation of choices governed by the irrational triggers of sympathy and antipathy. "You have to ask yourself continuously am I giving too much time to X because he happens to have an attractive personality and is neatly dressed?" AFSC worker Dorothy Bonnell counseled her fellow delegates, drawing on her experience in 1941 Marseille. "Is Y getting too much attention simply because he has plenty of money?" she continued. "Do I tend to give Mrs. Z anything she asks for just because she brings her baby and it cries all the time till no one in the office can do any work until I get rid of her? (answer: Yes, I do!)"[8] Unitarian Elisabeth Dexter's experience in Lisbon yielded similar advice three years later: "Each client should have the time which his problems require, but don't let a pushing or talkative client upset your schedule and interfere with other work." She cautioned to guard against the pull of sympathy; battle the temptation to give more than the standard allowance "because he is such a nice man." And "be doubly cautious about giving aid 'personally' . . . by taking money from your own pocket."[9] The advice gives us a window onto the role of emotional response by relief and rescue workers to their clients and how those visceral, irrational reactions shaped their actions and decisions.

If both ethical precepts and emotional responses influenced operatives' work with the people they sought to assist, both ethics and emotions spurred some relief and rescue workers to serve as secret agents for the US government. How and why did they join the intelligence service ranks? Political principles and wartime patriotism certainly played a part. As Elisabeth Dexter put it, "The Unitarian Service Committee was founded from humanitarian motives, but not from these alone. We try particularly to help the victims of tyranny and to strengthen the forces of Democracy. . . . We have never been neutral."[10] At the same time, covert activities also offered excitement and appealed to a sense of adventure as well as duty.

Women figured prominently in the relief efforts. Philanthropy and service have long been women's work. But *this* philanthropy and *this* service offered unimagined avenues for independent action. And the women loved it. They were committed to their missions, and they relished the independence and the freedom from social norms that their overseas assignments offered. As we shall see, their experiences changed them. Their work proved transformative—transformative for those they managed to help and for them, too.

Europe, 16 March 1939
Greater Germany

Finland

Norway

Sweden

Estonia

Soviet
Union

Latvia

Lithuania

Denmark

GDYNIA

Netherlands

Poland

VLISSINGEN

Sudetenland

Germany

Belgium

PRAGUE

Bohemia
and Moravia

Luxembourg

Slovakia

France

Switzerland

Austria

Hungary

Romania

Yugoslavia

Bulg

Italy

Albania

Greece

0   250   500 miles

• ONE •

PRAGUE, 1939

Martha and Waitstill Sharp

ARTHA AND WAITSTILL SHARP stepped off a train into Prague's Wilson Station on a cold February day in 1939. Selected by the Unitarian leadership in Boston to travel to Czechoslovakia, they were charged with aiding the 250,000 refugees who had fled from the Czech border district of Sudetenland into the Czech heartland of Bohemia and Moravia as a result of the Munich agreement.[1] That pact, signed by Germany, France, Britain, and Italy on 30 September 1938, gave Sudetenland to Germany without a shot fired. But it galvanized the American Unitarian Association (AUA) four thousand miles away. When the Germans had marched into Austria half a year earlier, no one had jumped into action; the assault on Czechoslovakia, by contrast, seared the Unitarian leadership's political imagination and emotional core.

In 1938, Czechoslovakia was home to thirty-five hundred Unitarians, a community founded in 1921 by Norbert Čapek, with the main church, Unitaria, in Prague. Ties of kinship and friendship abounded between Unitarians in the United States and Czechoslovakia,[2] and these bonds added weight and gravity to the AUA assessment of the situation. "I have just listened to the news broadcast from Prague in regard to the Czech crisis," a Howard Matson wrote to AUA president Frederick Eliot. "We Unitarians have so many connections with our fellows in Czechoslovakia [that] we have a special obligation for action."[3] If personal relations triggered response, so did denominational rivalry. The Quakers had a service committee; the Unitarians could, too. As Robert Dexter, director of the AUA Department of Foreign Relations, pointed out to the board of directors at a meeting on 5 October, the Unitarians counted more members than the Quakers and were at least as wealthy. Yet the Quakers had taken the lead in the social service field for the past twenty-five years. Furthermore, he argued, "I venture to say what they have done has done more to create respect and admiration for [that] particular religious body and [their] particular religious point of view than any publications they have ever printed, than any buildings they have ever built."[4]

The AUA board agreed and dispatched Dexter to Europe. He was joined by Robert Wood, a Philadelphia Quaker; together they formed the Commission for Service in Czechoslovakia. Refugees crowded into Prague. Many of them needed to emigrate immediately.[5] To the best Dexter and Wood could ascertain, by November, "92,000 refugees have registered from the Sudetenland and Silesia, and the estimates are that there are over 150,000 more scattered in private homes and small villages who have not registered." Jews in particular sought to make themselves invisible, afraid they would be deported. Maintenance, providing food and shelter, was one problem. Moving people elsewhere was another. Dexter and Wood noted that the "Old Reich" refugees, coming from Germany and Austria, many of whom were thrice displaced, were especially vulnerable. These counted some five thousand, half of whom were Jews and half gentile. All were at risk; none could remain in Czechoslovakia much longer. "The dangers of anti-Semitism are real," they warned. "There is also a fear that if the Republic harbors anti-Nazi Germans it will get into serious trouble with its now all-powerful neighbor."[6]

Faced with this assessment, the Unitarian leadership did not dither: they looked for a minister and his wife to serve as field representatives of the now established Commission for Service in Czechoslovakia. Although only the minister's salary would be covered, the AUA board sought a couple of the "type who would make a good impression on people there, government and otherwise. One or other of the two must have social service experience—case work or administrative—or both. . . . Must be well enough known here to have their reports accepted. [And] preferably with Anglo-Saxon name."[7] The Reverend Waitstill Sharp, age thirty-seven and minister at the Unitarian Church in Wellesley Hills, Massachusetts, and his wife Martha, thirty-three, a trained social worker, met the criteria. Educated in elite institutions, they were articulate, personable, and handsome. Still, according to Waitstill, seventeen men and their wives were approached. All declined.[8] He and Martha were the eighteenth, and they accepted.[9] The opportunity to be of service resonated with them. And the challenges they would face appealed to their sense of adventure. Martha and Waitstill sailed for Europe two weeks later. They took $41,000 (about $907,500 in 2024) in relief funds to disburse. And they left their two-year-old daughter Martha Content and their seven-year-old son Hastings with close family friends. The Unitarian leadership had sought a couple for the posting, Waitstill wanted Martha as his partner in this endeavor, and she wished to undertake the work. Nevertheless, parting with her young children stood contrary to gender role norms and hinted at an ambition to make her mark beyond the home.

Grave problems loomed ahead. Reports from Prague had alerted the Sharps to the increasingly grim situation of hundreds of thousands of unemployed and homeless refugees pouring into the city and, more ominously, of Gestapo infiltration and unexplained disappearances of individuals. Disembarking at Southampton, they stopped off in London and then Paris to meet with international aid organization workers in order to develop their relief network. They also gained practical advice as to how to keep innocuous-looking notes, how to destroy incriminating papers, and how to elude tails when shadowed.[10] None had been trained in clandestine actions. The relief workers passed on what they had learned from experience.

Martha and Waitstill Sharp depart New York City for Europe,
February 1939. *(Martha and Waitstill Sharp collection. Brown Digital Repository. Brown University Library. https://repository.library.brown.edu/studio/
item/bdr:404316/.)*

Arriving in Prague, Martha and Waitstill turned to forging
relations with others involved in similar activities. They called on
Wilbur Carr, head of the US Legation,[11] America's diplomatic rep-
resentative office in prewar Prague. And they met with Dr. Antonin
Sum, chair of the Czech government's Emergency Committee for
Refugees. Sum invited them to become regular members of the
Czechoslovak government's Coordinating Committee, which was
run by Dr. Josef Kotek, head of emigration at the Ministry of Social
Welfare. Welcoming them to Prague and to the refugee relief effort,
Dr. Kotek offered the Sharps two spacious rooms for their operation
at the Central Institute for Refugees. Located at 16 Vyšehradská in
the southern part of the city, this nineteenth-century baroque pal-
ace housed all of the government refugee activities, as well as some
of the foreign agencies to centralize aid for and resettlement of the
quarter of a million people who needed help.[12]

Martha and Waitstill soon began to evaluate which projects to support. The Unitarians had established a working relationship with the American Committee for Relief in Czechoslovakia, or AmRelCzech, a new initiative chaired by Nicholas Murray Butler, then president of Columbia University. The Sharps represented AmRelCzech as well. AUA funds supported individual casework, while Martha and Waitstill were to decide which large-scale (Czech) government-planned or -approved resettlement projects to underwrite with AmRelCzech donations.[13] Thus, for example, they toured an initiative presented by Ruzena Palantova, deputy mayor of Prague, who sought to convert an abandoned castle in Lysá nad Labem, about forty miles outside of the city, into a hostel for two hundred refugee families. She counted on the refugees to provide the labor for the conversion. They would also serve as medical staff, teachers, cooks, and gardeners. Still, the project required funds for building supplies, beds and bedding, and other basic furnishings. The Sharps found it worthy of AmRelCzech support. "The wonderful inventiveness" of this initiative "filled me with admiration," Martha recalled years later. "I realized how important it was to be able to harness experience and imagination with money."[14]

Castle used as a refugee hostel in Lysá nad Labem. *(United States Holocaust Memorial Museum.)*

At that point, the Sharps' primary goal was to offer relief. As they decided upon investment in big projects, they worked with organizations already on the ground, helping to feed and clothe thousands of destitute people. Emigration of people at risk was a priority, too. With the help of trilingual Czech students, Martha processed dossiers of people needing to escape, particularly German Social Democrats and Jews, who were most threatened by Germany's policies. The Sharps' work brought unwelcome Nazi attention, and they were shadowed as they moved around the city. Agents hovered in their hotel lobby to spy on their visitors and, growing bolder, entered their hotel room while they were out under the pretext of painting it.

Loss of Sudetenland had destabilized the young multinational republic. In October 1938, soon after the Munich Pact, the Slovaks moved away from the union to establish an independent state, and the Ruthenians joined Hungary. Seizing this unhappy internal situation as an opportunity for Nazi Germany, Hitler mobilized his forces and ordered Czech president Emil Hácha to Berlin on 14 March 1939. Invasion was imminent, he barked, and Hácha signed a German-drafted declaration stating that "the Czechoslovak President . . . confidently placed the fate of the Czech people and country in the hands of the Führer of the German Reich."[15] The German army rolled in the next day, imposing a "protectorate" upon the remaining Czech lands of Bohemia and Moravia.

This protectorate was like none other. Normally, protectorates do just that: "protect" a weak but sovereign state. Instead, Germany brought on the Protectorate of Bohemia and Moravia as part of the Greater German Reich. Broken in spirit, the Czechs adjusted to the ever-deteriorating situation. Germany wanted goods as well as territory. Depredation ensued. By the end of March, 35 billion Czech crowns of merchandise had been shipped to the Reich. The Germans sought to hide their theft by ordering a 9:00 p.m. curfew to empty the streets. "Then the trucks which . . . were massed in great fleets in the less travelled squares and about the public parks, were backed up before the stores of meat, sugar, flour," an AUA *Report on Prague* observed. "The looting went forward from nine until midnight, and then the long haul toward the impoverished lands of the conqueror."[16]

Worse: the Germans summarily snatched up people they identified as anti-Nazis. Swooping down on Social Democratic party headquarters, they grabbed the passports of hundreds of people who were to leave for England and then picked up the passport owners and jailed them. Marie Schmolka, director of the Prague Committee for Jewish Refugees, was taken into custody, too. The British government moved quickly to bring several anti-Nazis whose leadership they prized to their Prague embassy. Understanding the urgency of convoying these people to sanctuary, Martha jumped into action. Every step was fraught with danger. "I found a taxi in the early darkness, and noting that the driver had a companion on the front seat, gave an address which was near but not actually the one which was my destination. The 'extra cargo' tried to engage me in conversation, but I parried his questions," she recalled. Upon arrival, she "hastily paid the driver and hurried around the corner hiding in the first doorway to watch and see whether I was being followed. The 'companion' came around the same corner, looked up the street, down an alley or two and then walked along the street. The driver honked. My heart skipped a beat. I realized that the driver's associate must be a Gestapo agent. I flattened myself against the entrance and, in the darkness, he walked right by." This was merely the first step of her mission. She went to fetch "M. X.," as she called her mark, from a fifth-floor apartment. Martha explained to him that he was to proceed to the British embassy for safety until he could be transported out, and she told him about the agent in the taxi. They then set out on foot rather than drive, although the snow and wind would have suggested a cab. Stopped twice by German soldiers who demanded to see their identity cards, Martha took charge; she showed her passport and said they were on their way to the American legation. Her ruse worked. And she delivered M. X. into the hands of the British.[17]

———

THE *EINMARSCH* (invasion) was a turning point. German officers crowded into the city's hotels, including the Hotel Atlantic, where the Sharps roomed. Germany jammed BBC transmissions. There were no newspapers. The Sharps, like many others, were subject to constant surveillance on the street and elsewhere. "I changed from a rather naive, friendly, and outgoing person who trusted everyone, to a self-contained, reserved and increasingly wary individual who began to weigh every word and to watch where it was spoken and to whom," Martha reflected.[18]

The couple's focus shifted. "With the German occupation our entire project had to be changed with the main emphasis on emigration, and the difficulties of working became constantly more acute," they reported. In their view, the regulations and restrictions to which they had agreed before they set sail no longer applied. Their brief had been relief, not rescue. The sole principle that prevailed now was to act responsibly.[19] Two lines of work emerged: urgent emigration casework and, to help those who remained, emergency mass relief measures.

Whom to help? This question plagued relief and rescue workers throughout the Nazi era. Robert Dexter emphasized that "our major aim from the very beginning [has been] the salvaging of worthwhile people who are in danger in Europe because of their democratic attitudes."[20] Or, as Waitstill itemized, "These, then, were to be snatched from the burning: intellectuals—editors, social workers, professors, clergymen, research specialists, lawyers, physicians—whose political records made it necessary for them to flee."[21] The Unitarians' mission was clear in principle: save leaders with liberal values who would return to their countries of origin to rebuild democratic states when the Third Reich fell. They were the "worthwhile people." Mostly male, universally well educated, and predominantly middle class. But life on the ground widened the Sharps' scope. And when an opportunity opened not ten days after the *Einmarsch* to lead a convoy of thirty-five desperate people to safety in London, Martha took ownership instantly.

Friday, 24 March 1939. Waitstill was in Brussels when Tessa Rowntree, an English Quaker in Prague representing the British Committee for Refugees from Czechoslovakia (BCRC), tapped Martha to conduct a group of refugees to England. Their papers were in order: the adults had British visas identifying them as domestic workers and they had German exit permits. Rowntree would accompany some fifty on a train departing at 4:00 that afternoon. Would Martha take the rest on the 4:30 train?

Martha was an American and a minister's wife. Those were factors in her favor. She did not have an exit permit but, as she had arrived before 15 March, she could get one locally; she did not need to apply to Berlin. Martha understood that the mission was fraught with danger and risk. "I knew that the 'household workers' included some of the most wanted 'politicals,' ardent and well-known anti-Nazis. If the Gestapo should charge us with assisting the enemies of the state to escape, prison would be a light sentence; torture and death were the usual punishment." But, she calculated, "saving endangered people seemed worth the risk."

Rescue initiatives turned on many factors: luck, chance, fortuitous circumstances, trustworthy persons, timing. Once she decided, Martha raced against the clock to get the papers she needed. She turned to the US legation, which phoned the Gestapo on her behalf to ask for exit and reentry visas. The officer agreed to issue them—in ten days. Martha hurried to the Gestapo office to press the process forward in person. It was closed for lunch. The doors opened again at 2:00, but she had to wait for a superior officer. Martha finally got the documents signed at 3:30. "I had just time to get back to the office, pick up some papers and to leave a note for Waitstill explaining that I was going to London with Tessa's refugees." A Czech colleague caught her at the door and, learning she was about to leave for England, asked her to take on another clandestine task: the colleague's mother needed an operation and the sale of her gems abroad would cover the costs.

Suitcase in tow and jewelry in her traveling case, Martha arrived at the station where she found Miss Bull, the BCRC secretary, compiling a list of the convoy participants as they appeared; she used a fountain pen filled with green ink borrowed from a man, a physician, standing near her. Often, refugees came out of hiding just in time to board a moving train, and indeed two, newsmen from the United Press and the Associated Press, jumped on at the last minute. Not all of the thirty-five participants were immediate prey, but all were in peril or had suffered tragedy: two children whose parents had committed suicide were among the group.

Martha's charges occupied one train car. The journey proceeded fitfully, with their wagon unhitched and shunted to the side for hours at a time. Finally nearing the Dutch border, the convoy was ordered to disembark for customs inspection. Martha's effects were given only a cursory glance; the jewels went undetected. But the Germans robbed the refugees of all their valuables, "even their wedding rings off their fingers," Martha fumed, before allowing them to return to their carriage. Waiting to ensure everyone got back on the train, she heard a cry from the rear of the customs shed. "I ran back and opened the door before the guards could stop me." There were the newspaper men stripped to their waists, bags torn apart. Asking if anyone spoke English, and learning that no one did, she picked up a letter with a United States seal, hoping it would serve. "This letter puts this man under my protection as an American citizen," she asserted. "You see the seal of the United States? He and the others are members of my group going to London and I will not leave without them." Waving Miss Bull's notes in the air, she declared, "They are all on the list." Against all odds, she prevailed.[22]

The train soon reached the border, and Martha surrendered Miss Bull's list to the Dutch officials to check against the refugees' visas and passports. But having jumped on the train at the last minute, the newsmen had not been registered by the BCRC secretary. The Dutch authorities barred their entry. Martha reached for a solution. "I ran along the car looking for the doctor with the pen filled with green ink before the train should start," she recalled. "With the pen, I wrote the names of the men on the reverse side of 'the list' and just before the train was to pull out I found the passport officer." He quizzed her: "I am sure the names were not there before," he argued. But she insisted, and they were allowed to board. It was the "second near miss," Martha reflected. "Such a thin line between life and death!"[23]

Nazi Germany's aggression and the AUA and BCRC determination to aid victims of the regime framed the event. Were it not for policy, ideology, and actions on the ground, there would not have been a convoy. And social class, gender, age, religion, and profession were key factors in determining who was in the group that sought to leave that day. Still, training a close lens on this rescue initiative as it unfolded yields additional information. It makes visible what is hidden in a larger picture: the role of the unpredictable. The fortuitous circumstance of that unusual green ink—and Martha's quick action—saved those newsmen from detention and interrogation (at the least) and enabled them to proceed. The chance factor of green ink, in short, afforded the margin of credibility the situation required.

Martha's anxiety as all of this transpired did not prevent her from noting a gap in refugee aid right there at the border that she could tackle. Refugees seeking to join relatives in England crowded the station; they had been allowed out of Germany but denied permission to enter the Netherlands. "There they sat at the frontier, afraid to go back, unable to go forward." Martha recorded their names and passport information and promised to contact their families when she got to England. She did not disappoint. When the night boat from Vlissingen docked, she found people waiting for the relatives held at the border station. Learning of their predicament, and obtaining their passport details from Martha, the families in England phoned the Dutch border station and managed to get their kin released.[24]

The convoy had left Prague on Friday, 24 March 1939. The thirty-five people under Martha's charge, who all arrived safely in London on Sunday, 26 March, understood the significance of her help. "Dear Mrs. Sharp," a group note read. "We shall never forget what you have done for us and wish to thank you from the depth of our hearts. Yours ever gratefully."[25]

———

IF RESCUE INITIATIVES turned on unpredictable factors such as
fortuitous circumstances and timing, they also turned on irrational
impulses. It had taken less than a fortnight for Martha to choose to
put herself in danger in order to save lives. She knew what she was
risking and the possible consequences. It was a principled decision.
And it was an impulsive decision, spurred by loathing for the Nazi
regime and appreciation for bold action. Now committed to effecting the rescue of as many people who were Nazi targets as possible,
she took advantage of being in London to write frankly to Brackett Lewis, AmRelCzech executive secretary in New York, about the
situation in Prague and the obstacles faced by would-be emigrants,
many of whom were Jews. "We know that there are between six hundred and one thousand people moving around Prague who are starv-
ing and who dare not sleep in the same place twice," she reported.
They needed to be fed, and no entity offered that aid. The Jewish
philanthropic organization HICEM, dedicated to helping European Jews find their way to the New World, "is closed and Madam
Schmolka is in jail." In any case, meals, while necessary, would not
solve the core problem. "All of the Jewish professors and outspoken
Liberals from the University of Prague must leave as soon as possible," she emphasized.[26]

Martha was acutely aware of the Germans' surveillance. "We cannot write you much from Prague," she warned Lewis, "and I beg you
to be most careful in your letters and telegrams to us." Yet she and
Waitstill remained determined. "We would like to stay as long as we
think there is any real possibility we can be of help."[27] She conveyed
the same message to the home office in Boston. "Important we stay
Prague unless war," she telegrammed AUA treasurer Seth Gano.[28]

Brackett Lewis took Martha's advice and communicated with the
Sharps through Malcolm Davis, director of the European Center of
the Carnegie Endowment for International Peace in Paris. Emigration cases claimed their attention. With no mass-scale solution in
sight, the American rescuers sought individual placements, match-
ing skills and competencies with specific openings. These favored
educated middle-aged men whose reputations accorded them value

and whose experience had proved their professional worth. Personal investment counted for a lot, too. In a letter of 31 March to Waitstill, Lewis specified that he took a special interest in Jan Blahoslav Kozak, professor of philosophy at Charles University in Prague, as well as three others.[29] He elaborated in his accompanying note to Davis that Stephen Duggan, director of the Institute for International Education in New York and founder (1933) of the Emergency Committee in Aid of Displaced Foreign Scholars, had secured a position for Kozak at Oberlin College. Lewis had pressed Kozak's case, and his file had risen to the top of Duggan's list. "We read of his [Kozak's] arrest among the first on March 15," Lewis explained to Davis. "Kozak was a Member of Parliament, a leading member of President Benes's Party, the Czech Socialists up to Munich, and since then he has taken a leading part in the organization of the National Labor Party of whose educational department he was head."[30] Kozak ran into difficulties even with Lewis's support and Duggan's efforts. Typically, a job offer such as the Oberlin post was sufficient for an exit visa, but not in Kozak's case. Additional personal investment was needed. Martha stepped in and, drawing on the rapport she and Waitstill had developed with US consul general Irving Linnell, appealed to him for help. He obliged and ran interference with the German authorities. "The consul general felt that he was doing something for America," Martha reported to Davis.[31]

The American operatives understood the importance of personal connections to effect their goals in general and for successful placements in particular. Rational appreciation of the hopeful emigrants' peril and sympathy for their plight were insufficient spurs for committed action. Friendship, personal investment, proved much more potent drivers. Seeking to find places for author and journalist Oskar Butter (1886–1943), linguist Paul Eisner (1889–1958), literary scholar Otakar Vočadlo (1895–1974), and poet Otto Pick (1887–1940), Lewis had sent their dossiers "to some 25 friends in various universities." His connections were to no avail. It was the scholars who needed to have the contacts; the support of their colleagues, faculty on staff, would counter the prevailing hostility against refugee employment, especially for the German Jews.[32] Butter, Eisner, Vočadlo, and Pick did not have such friends. Butter was deported and murdered in Auschwitz. Eisner survived the occupation protected by his marriage to a gentile woman who withstood pressure to divorce him. Vočadlo endured Terezin, Auschwitz, and Buchenwald. And Pick escaped via Poland to London, where he died of a heart attack.

No one predicted these fates at the time. The Germans had not yet launched the war, and neither Auschwitz concentration camp nor Terezin transit camp existed. But the Sharps witnessed the violence, arrests, and incarceration. They were determined to help, and they railed against others' more tepid efforts. They believed that the Gestapo had identified "2,000 leaders in Prague alone," Waitstill told Lewis. Is there "one central organization in the USA which will take the curriculum vitae of a Czech refugee scholar and try like the devil to get that man a job in an American college—NOT JUST FILE IT AND WAIT FOR SOMEONE LIKE YOU OR ME TO SELL THE MAN'S SERVICES?" Martha and Waitstill worked with Marie Ginsberg, chief of the Comité Pour le Placement des Intellectuels Refugiés in Geneva and, as Waitstill reported to Lewis, she was "of the opinion that Duggan's outfit will not take any initiative with the colleges, that a friend or some other organization must do that."[33] "Miss Ginsberg is right," Lewis replied. The Emergency Committee for Displaced Scholars "files information but does not undertake to place men."[34]

If few intellectuals had the advocates abroad they needed to secure emigration opportunities, young people had virtually none. With so many needing help, operatives privileged youngsters in their social and professional circles. Thus, although Waitstill knew that Harvard University's scholarships had already been assigned, he approached the associate dean on behalf of Anthony Francis Sum, son of Antonin Sum, the chair of the Czech government's Emergency Committee for Refugees, who had welcomed the Sharps when they first arrived in Prague. Grounding his argument in the young man's pedigree, Waitstill championed Anthony. "He comes from the very finest Bohemian lineage," Waitstill averred. "His father, Dr. Antonin

Sum, is one of the most distinguished citizens and public servants of the Czech nation. The whole family is marked by its intelligence and broad outlook. Young Sum is already showing the effects of his life spent in these surroundings." Nor did he lack personal charm. "He is handsome and attractive, well set up and prepossessing."[35]

Emotional ties inspired operative engagement and action. Other considerations counted, too, as the Sharps' dossiers reflect. In April, soon after Martha returned from London, the Germans summarily evicted the Unitarian Commission for Service and their Czech colleagues in the Institute for Refugees. Undaunted by the sight of their office furnishings on the ground, Martha (Waitstill was in Paris) found new quarters in the rather shabby *studentský domov* (student house) on Albertov and resumed operations.[36] The student staff she had hired to help process the masses of refugees anxious to leave after the *Einmarsch* continued to work with her. Comprising four young Jewish couples, the trilingual (Czech, German, and English) staff interviewed clients and, by the time of the transfer to the *studentský domov*, had begun to identify people with a special claim to Unitarian Commission support. Investigating the university students who applied, they selected thought leaders who would be able to serve as conduits of cultural learning to the next generation. They included young physicians, lawyers, clergy. In Waitstill's estimation, "this may have been the most valuable single thing they [the staff] did before their martyrdom at the hands of the Nazis." No one saved them and they could not save themselves; the Jewish staff "all went to the gas chambers, every one of them." One couple, the Wellers, had passports, but Mr. Weller's middle initial D had been incorrectly recorded as O, and that discrepancy prompted the British government to deny him entry.[37]

In the spring and summer of 1939, however, the staff investigated applicants and identified those likely to make a cultural contribution. To that end, Waitstill granted 10,000 crowns to each student or young professional to help them escape. "Some of them are the finest people of Checho—fleeing now simply because the Germans consider Checho a vast concentration camp," Waitstill wrote to Robert Dexter.[38] Their clandestine route took them to the coal fields of Moravska Ostrava, where they sought out tipples, great steel structures with wheels atop; these signaled the entrance to a mine. The young people descended and there, below ground, met with Polish student resistors. The Czechs doffed their clothes and donned a Polish railway or postal worker uniform. They then walked through the underground mine galleries until they passed the Polish border. Exiting into Poland, they were taken to the seaport of Gdynia and spirited onto British submarines. Landing in England, they were greeted by British army, navy, and air force recruiting officers.[39]

FINANCES WERE KEY to clandestine escape or lawful flight, whether a 10,000-crown grant or funds for a train or ship ticket, and currency regulations stymied rescue efforts. Neither the US government nor philanthropic contributors wanted dollars to flow into a German-controlled banking system, and the Nazi regime prohibited refugees from taking their resources with them. In a traditionally gendered division of labor, Martha took primary responsibility for open and clandestine rescue while Waitstill developed an extensive system of illegal currency exchange to underwrite the costs. She took care of people; he bargained with them. Waitstill's financial transactions were, he declared years later, "the most risky and perhaps most dramatic aspect of the operation in Czechoslovakia." Writing (from Paris) to Robert Dexter, he cautioned, "I trust you to tell no one." Knowing the Friends' aversion to breaking local laws, he insisted, "I don't want the Quakers to know of it at all." And in case Dexter did not realize what was at stake, he clarified, "what we have been doing is a capital offense under German financial law."[40]

Waitstill developed his monetary exchange in response to the plight of Jews and gentiles who hoped to find their way out of the country. They had Czech crowns to convert and needed to access American dollars, British pounds, or French or Swiss francs once they escaped. "These people began very cautiously to visit me in various secretively chosen places," Waitstill recalled. Compromising his safety, these meetings nevertheless assured the hard-pressed refugees that they would have money to live on if they managed to flee. And they yielded significant sums for Waitstill and Martha to use for relief and rescue projects. "My business was to negotiate, even mercilessly, as high a rate of exchange for dollars as I could drive," Waitstill explained.[41] The Germans had tied the Bohemia and Moravia crown to the reichsmark, setting the exchange rate at 10 crowns to 1 reichsmark. Thus, the official rate stood at 2½ cents ($.025) per crown, or 40 crowns to the dollar. Waitstill set the figure according to what he surmised his interlocutor could afford; the hardest bargain he negotiated settled at 160 crowns to the dollar. Using his business cards as chits, he tore a card in half, jotted the dollar amount due as a result of the transaction on the half he gave to the hopeful emigrant, and kept the other half as a record of the deal.

It was one thing to set the exchange rate and to promise funds abroad and another to ensure that the refugees got the sum owed when they safely landed in a host country. Taking advantage of his ability to travel in and out of occupied Czechoslovakia, Waitstill deposited dollars given as philanthropic donations to the Unitarians' relief and rescue initiative in banks in London, Paris, and Geneva. He told bank officials to expect refugees with half his business card; they were entitled to the sum handwritten on it, to be drawn against the monies he had paid in.[42]

Waitstill's system was both irregular and illegal, as he emphasized to Parker Marean, the AUA accountant in Boston. "All the ordinary rules of bank procedure and accounting must be suspended during such times as the Czech people are passing through." His currency manipulations "carry a sentence of twenty-five years imprisonment." Distrusting the ability of someone sitting in peaceful Boston to grasp the peril he faced, Waitstill declared, "Absolutely no word of this arrangement should ever come into the Protectorate. It would certainly mean my surrender to the Gestapo, and in all likelihood my imprisonment." In closing he warned, "P.S. All the foregoing is of life and death significance. . . . If you want to see us back in America please keep this letter in your confidential files, and make no reply to me."[43]

Slightly concerned about the optics of the matter, Waitstill hastened to alert Robert Dexter that he could not keep financial records, and he asked Dexter to so advise AUA treasurer Seth Gano and the auditors. "It would imperil the life and liberty of myself and every Czech with whom we do business if the Germans came across either receipts for money paid over, the notes of financial transactions . . . or account books showing how we were spending our money." By "our money" he meant the thick bundles of Czech cash he got. Those funds defrayed the cost of flight out of the country and supported relief programs in Prague. By the end of April, he had pledged $21,000 to those intending to emigrate in exchange for nearly two million crowns, which, with Czech social service agencies, was used to lay in a secret supply of food for the winter, to cover dentistry costs, and to support antituberculosis summer camps for poor children.

Waitstill undertook these illegal and clandestine transactions thoughtfully, with deliberation and consideration. He acted on principle and had rational reasons for the decisions he took and the choices he made. But irrational motives swayed him, too; he enjoyed a rebellious streak. "It has been dangerous, but Yankees like to run on thin ice," he confessed. "I am terribly thrilled by the secrecy, the wisdom of distribution, the care in anticipating social needs which my advisers have shown as they have taken charge of Kč [crowns] 1,805,000 so far."[44]

He and Martha knew the potential danger. Every time they left occupied Czechoslovakia, they faced the choice of whether to return. Neither hesitated. As the weeks passed, the position of foreign nationals deteriorated. By mid-June, few Americans or Britons remained in Prague. But the Sharps evinced a certain imperviousness, confident that Americans held a privileged position. Indeed, Waitstill warned Dexter, "If it should happen that we are immobilized by the Gestapo, please do not worry unduly." Even if "we have been arrested, just keep your shirts on." To which Dexter replied,

"Don't stick your neck out any more than you have to and we will try not to worry, no matter what happens."[45]

IF THE POSITION of foreign nationals was becoming more precarious, the situation for Jews grew dire. After the *Einmarsch*, the Nazi regime relied on emigration to solve what it saw as "the Jewish Problem." But Jews were not leaving sufficiently rapidly to satisfy Berlin. To increase pressure on them and to grasp as much of their wealth as possible for the Reich, Konstantin von Neurath, the so-called Reichsprotektor and imposed Nazi German ruler of Bohemia and Moravia, proclaimed his own laws on 21 June 1939, defining who was to be considered a Jew and stripping such persons of their property, businesses, stocks, bonds, and valuables. Reinhard Heydrich, chief of the Reich Security Main Office, sent his second-in-command, Adolf Eichmann, to Prague the following month. Eichmann had headed the Central Office of Jewish Emigration in post-Anschluss Vienna, where he oversaw the forced departure of 150,000 Austrian Jews in one year. According to a Unitarian report on "The Jewish Question," likely written by Waitstill, the German government "wants to secure an emigration of 250, and later 300 Jews per day. Those who do not succeed in emigrating go to jail." The figures spoke for the misery thousands endured. "There are at least 120000 Jews in the Protectorate. Of these 40000 live in Prague, and the other 80000 have to move there before they can emigrate." There was no housing for these people, but that was of no consequence to the authorities: "Eichmann says it is not his business. Every effort to negotiate is in vain. The law is what Mr. Eichmann orders."

The author of the report had no illusions about the Jews' impossible position. "Whereas Jews in Germany and Austria could escape to Czechoslovakia, Jews in the Protectorate now have no place to go, save concentration camps from which only foreign aid can liberate them." As release depended on proof of emigration, inmates hoped ardently for help as they suffered mightily. Enduring the harsh working conditions, near starvation diet, ferocious corporal punishment for everything and nothing, and draconian disciplinary regimen that characterized concentration camp life, prisoners perished as they waited for immigration papers. The report pleaded the victims' case. "The Jew in the Protectorate more than elsewhere needs somewhere where he may go and earn his living." Make no mistake about it, the author concluded, "The Jewish question has become a moral problem for the whole of Europe."[46]

More immediately, however, it became a flashpoint between the Unitarians and the Quakers. As the stakes mounted, so did rivalries. The possibility glimmered that the United States would accept ten thousand children in 1939 and another ten thousand in 1940, thanks to the introduction of two identical bills by Democratic senator Robert Wagner (New York) and Republican representative Edith Rogers (Massachusetts). This bipartisan initiative was initially applauded widely, and many thought the Wagner–Rogers Bill (also called the Children's Bill) would become law. The Sharps wanted primary responsibility for selection of the children. The problem was that "the Quakers seem to think that they are going to do all of this," Waitstill bristled in a letter to Robert Dexter. He was particularly irked because the Quakers had delegated operations on the ground in Czechoslovakia to the Unitarians, claiming they were strapped financially and did not have the necessary funds. But "now that Prague has become very interesting, some of the Quakers dash in here," conveniently forgetting the original agreement.[47] As frankly as Waitstill and Martha wrote to Dexter, they spoke more bluntly with each other. "I am sick of all conferences with the conceited Quakers," Waitstill blazed to Martha after a meeting in Paris with Quaker representatives and Morris Troper, European director of the American Jewish Joint Distribution Committee (JDC).[48] Many people objected to the Quakers, Martha reported to Waitstill. She had discussed the possibility of American successors in Prague with the Sharps' Czech colleagues. A number were "sure that Quakers ought not be sent 'because they are so simple minded and difficult to get along with' I quote—feelingly!"[49]

United in their commitment to provide relief, the Unitarians and the Quakers nevertheless differed with regard to philosophy and ideology. As we have seen, the Unitarians sought to save politically liberal leaders as well as the intellectual and artistic elite. The Quakers claimed not to discriminate. The Unitarians pursued a militantly prodemocratic political program, proved willing to engage in illegal transactions, and did not blink at covert operations. The Quakers, by contrast, pursued a militantly humanitarian project, embraced pacifist neutrality, and were punctiliously law-abiding. Then, too, organizational reputations and prestige were at stake, and each wanted the public acclaim that would accompany success.

Inevitable, indeed as logical, as clashes may have been, these tensions offer a lens on relief and rescue efforts. They betray the operatives' overwhelming uncertainty and anxiety, and the pressure that they felt. The discord encourages us to map the relief and rescue efforts as they unfolded—to appreciate anew that while the operatives' choices, the courses they pursued, seem straightforward in retrospect, no such clarity existed at the time. Confusion reigned. Grappling with an ever-changing situation with which they had no prior experience, no one knew the best way forward. And tempers flared. Then, too, perhaps these antagonisms suggest something about the people who undertook this work. Perhaps unflappable people were not inspired to work abroad. Or perhaps people who held strong convictions and were willing to do battle for them accepted the challenge of the job. In any case, the Sharps could have saved themselves the irritation. The Wagner–Rogers Bill died in committee in summer 1939.

As they awaited action in Washington, the visible violence against Jews in Prague spurred the Sharps' efforts. Martha recalled years later that "armed soldiers beat them [Jews] up when they walked on the sidewalk or attacked them in cafes." Little time remained for the Sharps' mission; Waitstill's leave of absence from his Wellesley Hills pulpit would end in September, and they were due to return to the United States in August. And as Martha noted, the other foreign refugee organizations had received official termination notices, effective 25 July.[50]

Waitstill had committed to speaking at a religious youth conference in Switzerland on 10 August. Leaving the Protectorate two days earlier, he was stripped of his return visa by the German frontier guards. Martha remained in Prague winding up her emigration cases until a friend sent her a frightening message: "I have heard that you are to be arrested on Wednesday." Martha left for Paris on Tuesday, 15 August; she learned later that the Gestapo came to arrest her the following day.[51] Martha and Waitstill traveled to England and embarked for home on the *Queen Mary* on 30 August. The Germans invaded Poland while they were at sea.

MARTHA AND WAITSTILL'S EFFORTS proved transformative. They fed 350 refugees two meals a day for half a year and contributed significantly to a housing project for 30 refugee families, thus keeping hunger at bay and offering shelter to unmoored people who needed support as they figured out their next steps.[52] And they had handled the emigration of 3,500 families,[53] saving lives through their legal and clandestine rescue efforts. But we will never know the precise number or what percentage managed to escape and then to survive the war.

Martha and Waitstill were changed, too. Waitstill's engagement with relief and rescue operations reenforced his Unitarian convictions, both spiritual and with regard to service. "In no place have we ever expressed to you our sense of the privilege which it was to serve as the representatives of the American Unitarian Association over seas," he acknowledged to AUA president Frederick Eliot. "It was the experience of a life-time, something which can never be repeated as to intensity or breadth of contacts."[54]

Martha's tenure in Prague, by contrast, was but the beginning of a previously unimagined professional trajectory. They had arrived in February, and by June Waitstill had taken note of Martha's skills and abilities, now in evidence as never before. Looking ahead, he broached the prospect of possible future opportunities with her. "You will be returning from this experience abroad with, I believe, a good deal of prestige and some rather steady glances fixed your way," he predicted. "Those glances in the church and in Wellesley and in Boston and now perhaps among liberals in the country at large will be asking whether you can lead and interpret as well as administer and manage." Yet Waitstill undermined the affirmation he offered. At the same time, he asked her to take a short break from the work that earned her this esteem in order to go on holiday with him in Switzerland when he spoke at the youth conference in Arcegno. After all, he argued, "The refugees, like the poor, will always be with you. Just look ahead in your calendar and write them notes of self-excuse and say that you will be back within a week or ten days."[55]

But Martha was utterly committed to her work. Indeed, her emotional center rested on rescue activities. Writing from Prague to Waitstill in Paris, she admitted, "Somehow I seem to have dried up emotionally spiritually—and every other good way—But I send you my best—such as it is." And she added, without pause or segue, "P.S.: No scholarship for Sum at Harvard." Finding a route out for her clients and friends claimed her attention, not her inner self.[56]

Waitstill held little hope that Martha would agree to join him, but he pressed her again. "Now the time has come to decide finally whether or not you are going to Arcegno. Shall I go through with the registration or not? WILL YOU PLEASE MAKE A MEMO OF THIS AND WRITE ME SOON? There is no use making a reservation if you are intending to stay by your beloved cases."[57] "My darling Waitstill," she replied. "I am terribly lonely without you. . . . I think that the experience here has made me realize how much I love you. . . . We need more quiet times together when we aren't really rushed to death by the clock. Somehow, we've got to begin to tell the world where it gets off."[58]

She didn't. Nor did he.

The war in Europe spurred the AUA to formally establish (15 November 1939) the Unitarian Service Committee (USC) and once again Martha and Waitstill were asked to undertake its programs on the Continent, although—once again—only he would be paid to do so.[59] They planned to set up an office in Paris, but the Germans occupied the city the day before they were to fly there. The geographic possibilities for an operations hub narrowed: The Germans had invaded Denmark and Norway in April, and the Netherlands, Luxembourg, Belgium, and France in May. All had fallen. In France, Prime Minister Paul Reynaud resigned on 16 June and the eighty-four-year-old hero of World War I, Field Marshal Philippe Pétain, succeeded him. The armistice Pétain negotiated with Berlin recognized him as premier of the French State. Headquartered in the resort town of Vichy, Pétain's government controlled an unoccupied "free zone" in the south of France.

With little space in which to maneuver, the Sharps traveled to Lisbon, where Waitstill initiated USC rescue and relief activities. For Martha, Lisbon served as a jumping off point for work in unoccupied France. What that work would be soon emerged. The German invasion of France had sent millions of people on the road from the north to the south, where the food supply buckled under the pressure of the rapidly multiplying population. With the roads choked with refugees and the railways disrupted, distribution broke down. Most urgently, there was no milk for babies, as Martha heard from a number of people informed of the situation.[60]

Madame Amé-Leroy, wife of the French ambassador to Portugal, helped the Sharps negotiate a good price for their purchase of powdered and condensed milk from the Swiss Nestlé company, and the Portuguese and Spanish railway companies offered free transportation of the milk to France. Clayton Williams, minister of the American Church in Paris, gave them his car, which they loaded with milk, sugar, and soap to take with them. Crossing Spain, the Sharps met Donald Lowrie of the International YMCA at the French border, and the three traveled together to Marseille where they conferred with Richard Allen, then the American Red Cross delegate in Europe. He explained that Berlin's recalcitrance in negotiating with the Red Cross meant that the organization would not distribute goods in any district that was partly occupied or that even touched on an occupied region, and he suggested that they operate in an area the Red Cross could not enter.[61]

Lowrie and his International YMCA staff had fled from Paris to the Basses Pyrénées and, as it was a region in dire need of milk, the Sharps chose it for their operation. Martha joined Donald and his wife Helen in Pau, the district capital, and Waitstill returned to Lisbon. With Helen offering Martha her help as a volunteer, the two took off by car to visit village midwives and child health nurses and to assess needs on the ground.

Their tour also offered Martha an opportunity to pursue a children's emigration project she held dear. Prior to her departure from the United States, Percival Brundage, a member of the AUA board and of the United States Committee for the Care of European Children (USCOM), had bruited the possibility of receiving children "who need to come to America, either because they are in danger of bombing or starvation, or for any other reasons." USCOM had grown out of earlier efforts to bring children endangered by war to the United States. Formally incorporated in July 1940, it boasted Eleanor Roosevelt as its honorary president, while Marshall Field III, heir to the Chicago department store, took the helm. Key to its strategy was a streamlined immigration track; the State Department granted USCOM a corporate affidavit that covered selected at-risk children up to the age of sixteen as a group, rather than individually. During Martha's August visits with midwives and nurses, she asked if they knew of children who should be sent to the United States. She asked Protestant pastors, too. The response was overwhelming.[62]

The railway car arrived in Pau on August 20; the milk it carried fed eight hundred children through October. A great success locally, the program roiled the leadership in Boston and triggered mutual frustration. As we have seen, relief and rescue work was marked by quarrels, and this was no exception. "I have received a very strong rebuke this morning from Bob Dexter," Waitstill raged to Martha. Ernest J. Swift, vice president of the American Red Cross, had objected to Dexter about what he saw as interference with his organization's relief mandate. "I have seldom been so burned up as now," Waitstill continued. "Bob's subservience to the censorious Swift of the Red Cross makes me sick," he blazed. The conflict was sparked,

Martha Sharp's milk distribution project, August 1940. *(Unitarian Service Committee, bMS 16135/3, Harvard Divinity School Library, Harvard Divinity School, Cambridge, Massachusetts.*

in part, by the vagaries of the post and lack of communication. "How would you like to be here day after day getting not an answer to any wires or letters sent to the sphere of operations?" Waitstill demanded of Dexter. But it also highlighted the differing perspectives of operatives on the ground and the home offices a continent away.

Dexter supported the British blockade of goods and food needed by Germany. Failing to differentiate between German-occupied and Vichy France, he adamantly opposed sending food to Vichy. The Sharps, acutely aware of the demarcation line, were equally adamant that their milk program did not undermine the blockade and met an urgent need. Similarly, Swift, sitting in the United States, challenged the Sharps' project, while Allen, in Marseille, approved wholeheartedly. And Waitstill, in Europe, was aggrieved by the distant Dexter's lack of confidence in their judgment. "Over and over it was said, 'We will back you in whatever you decide the best course of action on the spot.'" Yet, Dexter reproved them for doing precisely that, and

Waitstill was having none of it. If the AUA was "interested in the success of a distinctive Unitarian record," its commissioners needed the freedom to act and home office support.[63] Disrupted communication and proximity versus distance surely weighed in the discord, but the most significant factors were stress, tension, and uncertainty about a successful outcome. These emotional responses framed the interaction. The successful relief and rescue story we read about today was not a foregone conclusion at the time.

HAVING BROUGHT the milk project to fruition, Martha turned her attention to actualizing a children's convoy. She wired the AUA (5 September) for permission to proceed, having "already found intelligent middle class protestant french children,"[64] and was authorized to do so ten days later. While the Boston office and USCOM petitioned the State Department for the necessary immigration authorizations,[65] Martha tackled the required European documentation. Marseille, home to consulates and foreign aid organizations, served as her operational base. Calling on Monsieur Surleau, prefect of the Bouches-du-Rhône district, Martha secured his promise of an exit visa for all the children selected in his prefecture. With this assurance, she visited the Portuguese and Spanish consulates, both of which granted visas locally. Portugal required proof of passage from Lisbon to the United States and an American visa. Spain required US and Portuguese visas.[66]

The way forward seemed clear, and Martha opened an office on 17 September in collaboration with the International YMCA. Helen once again volunteered to help. The question of whom to choose loomed as large as always. Both the USC and USCOM charged Martha with that decision; indeed, "U.S. Comm. does not wish to specify proportions as to religions, etc., except that some Catholics should be included. You are to use your best judgment and select on the basis of need."[67] However rational that calculus was meant to be, personal factors entered. Reviewing the matter with Waitstill, Martha noted that one Madam Sachar, who had been suggested to her as a secretary for the Marseille office, had two sons: Christian, aged ten, and Bernard, seven. "Her boys are marvelous," she enthused. "I wonder if you would like the 10 yr old to come to us to be a playmate for Hastings? He is worth the effort."[68] In any event, both boys were included among those chosen and for whom application for documents was made.[69]

Neither personal predilection, nor social class, nor family status offered perfect protection against policy changes. Stumbling blocks to the whole project soon emerged. "We had just completed the registration forms and picked out fifty children from some of the most distinguished families in France who were now either refugees or in great distress, when we received word that the visas de sortie [exit visas] could no longer be given by M. Surleau," Martha reported. She went to Vichy to obtain a block exit visa to cover fifty children and ran into a bureaucratic and political thicket. The Ministry of the Family and the Ministry of the Interior agreed, but the Ministry of Foreign Affairs refused to allow French children to go to America. Persuading a number of "influential people" to argue the case, Martha prevailed to a point: French children with relatives in America and foreign refugee children would be permitted to leave the country.[70] She shifted her sights from a convoy of French youngsters to "gathering a group of children whose immigration plans were fairly in order," she explained. "The group now has French, German, Austrian, Czech, Hungarian, and Russian children in it."[71]

Obtaining the required permissions and papers for the children and adult chaperones proved an obstacle course. Uncertainty, instability, and constant changes shaped the process. American visas granted on the strength of philanthropist and department store magnate Marshall Field III's personal guarantee were issued in early November. In the meantime, Portugal imposed new visa regulations. As the rules kept shifting ground, Martha would meet one requirement only for another to pop up. She appealed to Lisbon through the Portuguese consul in Marseille, who instructed her to apply for blanket permission for thirty-five children and ten adults. Spain then changed its rules, demanding Portuguese and American visas in each person's passport before application could even be made to Madrid. But since Martha had selected some stateless people, she needed ambassadorial intervention to get Spanish visas for them. Just when everything seemed set, Portugal decided upon yet another process. Martha had aimed for the group to sail on 30 October and they had missed that opportunity. Now she had to cancel a second booking on 22 November. Undaunted, or perhaps daunted but undeterred, she pressed forward. With interventions from others, including a Bank of Portugal officer, she managed to secure the needed documents. The final group of twenty-seven children and ten adults, all wearing an identifying beige beret, pulled out of the blackened Marseille train station on Tuesday 26 November at 5:30 in the morning. Their grueling four-day journey brought them to Lisbon at 4:30 in the afternoon on 29 November, only to learn that their berths on the ship to sail that evening had not been held for them. It would take another few weeks before the first four adults

Child refugees shortly before their departure for the United States in 1940, thanks to USCOM and the USC's children's emigration project organized by Martha Sharp (standing, fifth from left). *(Martha and Waitstill Sharp collection. Brown Digital Repository. Brown University Library. https://repository.library.brown.edu/studio/item/bdr:420329/.)*

and two children, followed a week later by the remaining chaperones and youngsters, left for New York. Martha, in the first group,
docked on 23 December. The Sachar brothers were not in the convoy from Marseille.[72] Two other boys, Josef (seven) and Alexander
(nine), handwritten into the "Complete List of Children for Mrs.
Sharp's Group," seem to have taken their places.[73]

So far as Martha was concerned, "The most important thing
about the whole experience was the fact that it proved it could be
done." Then, too, she had seen the transit camps of Gurs in the
Basses Pyrénées and Saint Nicolas near Nîmes and she had determined that, however terrible the conditions for refugees were, the
worst were in "the concentration camps for foreigners." Indeed,
she reported, more than four hundred inmates had died in Gurs in
November 1940 alone: "There are thousands of refugees of Austrian,
Czech, German and Polish background who will starve to death or
be permanently disabled by malnutrition. Thousands of these children could come to America and be placed in homes for the duration of the war, and be saved in body and spirit, even if their parents
can never be rescued from the same state."[74]

THIS TIME when Martha chaperoned the refugees to the United
States, she remained there for a few years, until 1945. She returned
to Wellesley Hills and her children, but not to her previous life. She
had found a place in the larger world. A persuasive speaker, she was
soon on the road to raise awareness of the USC and its mission and
to raise funds to support rescue initiatives. By February 1941, she
was so busy that Seth Gano suggested that she receive "an appropri-
ation" to "provide competent help in her home, inasmuch as she is
away from the family so much of the time on behalf of the Service
Committee."[75] No salary, but a housekeeping subvention. Inspired
by the Jewish women's charitable organization Hadassah and its
Youth Aliyah program, which sent endangered Jewish adolescents
from Europe to Palestine, Martha began to speak on behalf of that
endeavor as well. A new initiative took root in her imagination, and

she founded (1943) Children to Palestine. She envisioned it as a multidenominational Christian organization to support Youth Aliyah. That, too, took her out on the road.

Spooling ahead through the war and Martha's lecture tours throughout the country for weeks on end, followed by her return to Lisbon in January 1945 to serve as the now salaried director of the USC's operations in Spain and Portugal (while Waitstill was appointed head of the United Nations Relief and Rehabilitation Administration in Cairo), December 1945 found her back in the United States accepting a position with AmRelCzech and well remunerated as a key fundraising speaker. "I have at least $350 in fees for speaking <u>extra</u> coming in this month," she informed Waitstill. Relying on her earning capacity, she leased an apartment on Beacon Hill: "It will give me a place to take the children for Christmas holidays where we can be alone and it gives me a hotel room when I am in Boston."[76] Unlike the various rooms and flats she had rented in Europe to have a place to live while engaged in USC work, she leased this apartment solely because she wished to do so. It was a physical and emotional move away from Wellesley Hills.

Martha's wartime work had captured media interest, and her public speaking ability earned her broad visibility. Political groups took notice. "<u>Now here is a bombshell</u>," she wrote to Waitstill, whose relief work had taken him to Prague. "I was visited by the Independent Voters League of Mass—and the Citizens P.A.C. and asked to run for Congress" as a Democrat against the powerful Republican incumbent, Joe Martin. "They have decided out of the <u>blue</u> that I am the only person from the area who can beat him." She had the support of the Democratic party as well. "I think it is my duty to do it. . . . It is a great honor and a great responsibility," she concluded.[77]

Waitstill sent a bleak response. He readily acknowledged her abilities, and his admiration and love for her warmed his words. Yet, he feared the deleterious effect of this opportunity on the children and urged her to step away from it. "I can't see much prospect of rootage with the family in the mad glare and dash of public life," he worried. "Perhaps none of the rest of you three want any rootage, but I suspect that two out of the three of you <u>do</u>—and want it with thoughts too deep for tears." Shifting topic abruptly, he reflected, "Seven years ago at this hour you and I were getting off the train here in [Prague's] Wilson Station, and all our world has been different ever since."[78]

Waitstill recalled how inaccessible Martha had been in spring 1944, when all of them were in Wellesley Hills, but Martha was often away on speaking tours. "Of course you were making money. You were making a lot of it for us; I don't deny it." But, he charged, her choices had consequences that Martha failed to acknowledge. "I don't believe that you have ever taken in the continuous sinking feeling that beset the parsonage when you were headed outward. It was so real you could have weighed it. . . . We finally could not count

Campaign photo: Martha Sharp's run for Congress in 1946. (*Martha and Waitstill Sharp collection. Brown University Library.*)

on any time you wouldn't be off to a talk or a tea or a committee meeting or across the Continent (twice in one Springtime)."[79]

Waitstill then turned to himself. "There have been times out here when I have been almost desperate between the amount of work to do . . . and the loneliness," he confessed. "I can't touch a woman; I see nothing but men's things in my wardrobe. I smell no perfumes. I see in my mind's eye that hotel room in Lisbon and all your beauty junk on the shelf; it was in the way then, but I wish it were in the way now!" And again he recalled what he seems to have seen as the start to the chain of events that had led them to this pass. "Seven years ago tonight we stepped off the train into Wilson Station—and into a new world."[80]

Martha, however, did not heed his worries. She won the Democratic primary election and went on to stump the district. Writing to Waitstill in June 1946, by which point he had been gone a year, she beamed, "I spoke 14 times the last Sunday." And, she exulted, "love all of it."[81] Which she did. Even though, in the end, she lost the general election. She had discovered her voice.

Martha and Waitstill's marriage limped on for another eight years. They divorced in 1954. Martha's experiences had changed her. She had outgrown her role as The Minister's Wife.

Europe, 1 January 1940

  - German-controlled territory
  - USSR-controlled territory
  - Former Poland border

Finland

Sweden

Norway

STOCKHOLM

TALLINN

Estonia

Soviet Union

RIGA · Latvia

Denmark

Lithuania

KAUNAS · VILNA

Netherlands

SWINEMÜNDE

Suwalki Dist

WARSAW

Greater Germany

General Government

Belgium

Luxembourg

Bohemia and Moravia

Slovakia

France

Switzerland

Hungary

Romania

Yugoslavia

Italy

Bulg

Albania

Greece

0 250 500 miles

◆ TWO ◆

VILNA, 1940

Moses Beckelman

"**A**MERICAN JEWISH JOINT DISTRIBUTION COMMITTEE
which for many years has conducted philanthropic activities in Lithuania with the fullest cooperation of Lithuanian government, is most anxious tender its assistance this time
to Jewish communities Vilna and districts," the New York office
cabled (26 October 1939) Tovilas Zadeikis, head of the Lithuanian
legation in Washington. "We would therefore be very grateful if
through your channels permission will be accorded one of our representatives, Moses Beckelman, American citizen now in Kaunas,
to enter Vilna," the communication continued.[1] Established in 1914
to rebuild Jewish communities in Europe and Palestine devastated
by World War I, the American Jewish Joint Distribution Committee
(JDC, or "Joint") had grown into a robust philanthropic organization by the time Germany invaded Poland from the west on 1 September 1939 and the USSR attacked from the east on 17 September.[2]
And, as the cable claimed, it had a history of relief work in Lithuania,
now a neutral country bordering both German- and Soviet-occupied
Poland. Moses Beckelman had recently joined the JDC staff and had
been sent to Kaunas. A trained social worker with an accountancy

49

degree, Beckelman was born and educated in New York City.[3] He had held a number of jobs before the JDC hired him—City College of New York faculty; New York City civil service examiner; managing editor of *Jewish Social Service Quarterly*—and he had developed a critical, if not cynical, perspective on the world around him.

Beckelman needed every skill and competency he had accrued to manage the tasks he now faced. No sooner had he arrived in Kaunas than his remit expanded: Russian-occupied Poland included the Vilna region, which the USSR subsequently ceded to Lithuania. A 10 October bilateral agreement between the Soviet Union and Lithuania announcing this development turned what had been a stream of Jewish refugees from Poland since mid-September into a wave; the migrants saw Vilna as a way station to Palestine or the West. Rumor had it that the Soviet Army would withdraw from Vilna at the end of the month, and the JDC was eager to get Beckelman into the city to organize relief for the resident and newly arrived Jews.

Zadeikis did not disappoint, and Sunday 29 October found

JDC field representative Moses Beckelman. (*NY_16202, Courtesy of JDC Archives, New York.*)

Beckelman in a second-class compartment on a train from Kaunas to Vilna. The Red Army had left the previous day. Beckelman had heard that the Russians cleaned the city out of everything that they might find useful, from consumer goods to industrial equipment. He foresaw shortages of everything and alerted his boss, the JDC's European director, Morris Troper, that Lithuanian supply stocks would not suffice to meet burgeoning needs.[4] Traditionally one of the poorest districts in Poland, Vilna was now utterly impoverished.

Beckelman was an astute observer who scanned the world around him for information about the situation in which he operated and the hardships the JDC aimed to alleviate. At the same time, an ambitious man, he cast a critical eye on his colleagues. Isaac Giterman, director of JDC operations in Poland and a known anti-Nazi activist, had fled from Warsaw to Vilna at the outbreak of war. If in retrospect it would appear that the two worked harmoniously for the communal good, Beckelman's diary entries tell another story. Competition was at work here, not leveraged strengths. Beckelman saw Giterman as a rival and looked at him with suspicion, often assessing Giterman's motives, assuming ungenerous intent, and validating his analyses by adducing the corroboration of others. Beckelman devoted diary page upon page to parsing information gleaned from others about Giterman and to analyzing and castigating his actions.[5] He constantly disparaged what Giterman said and what he did, chastising him even for his choice of hotel for Beckelman in Vilna.[6]

Moving back and forth between reports on his coworkers and events unfolding on the ground, between (irrational) professional animosities and (irrational) popular animosities between Lithuanians, Poles, and Jews, Beckelman turned to the situation in Vilna. Not only was the city stripped bare, it was also rife with tension. The temporary vacuum left by the transfer of authority from the Soviets to the Lithuanians had been marked by "the beginning of a pogrom," Beckelman learned upon his arrival. Some "500 Poles assembled in the main square and began shouting 'Down with the Lithuanians, Down with the Jews.' Some shouted 'Up Stalin,' some 'Down Stalin.'" According to the accounts Beckelman heard, Poles "had said that all they wanted was half an hour interval between the Russian evacuation and Lithuanian occupation to settle accounts with the Jews." Threats soon turned into violence. Poles thrashed Jews on the street, smashed Jews' shop and house windows, and tried to force their way in to plunder what they could carry. The marauders miscalculated; the Soviets were still in town and they took action, closing off the square with tanks and arresting rioters.[7]

Harassment on Saturday spun into butchery on Tuesday (31 October). With a view out of his hotel window onto the square below and city hall opposite, Beckelman watched the carnage unfold under Lithuanian protection. "In addition to [Lithuanian] police and soldiers I now saw a number of men accompanying them, wearing civilian clothes and white armbands. These pointed out various people walking along the street. A policeman and a soldier would then run up to the person pointed out and club him down with the butt end of the gun and the policeman's club." The victims were Jews, as Beckelman learned from colleagues who had made their way to his hotel room. They reported that these assaults befell anyone thought to be Jewish throughout the city.

Emboldened by the support from the new state authorities, the white-armbanded civilians took to carrying sticks and stones to club and bash Jews. If the victim resisted, a soldier joined in the beating. And the police arrested the beaten and clubbed. Vicious attacks occurred across Vilna. When, depleted of Jews, one area grew quiet, attacks erupted in fresh quarters. By midday mobs began to break into stores and homes. Beckelman "saw windows broken as high up as the second and third stories; streets littered with merchandise from stores; Sadowa Street was white with feathers from ripped up pillows."[8]

However shocking the pogrom, it was but one of Beckelman's concerns. The violence aimed at Jews was a matter to record and analyze; his professional future, a goal to pursue. And Giterman stood as a major factor in that endeavor. Beckelman moved without pause from a discussion about the carnage to career machinations. Giterman had suggested that Troper meet with the two of them either in Lithuania or somewhere else in Europe to discuss the JDC's plans for operations in Germany and the USSR. Beckelman approved wholeheartedly, hoping the conversation would clarify his relationship to Giterman. As he confided to his diary on 1 November, the day after the riot, "If the possibility of working in Russia opens up he [Giterman] would like to take charge of that (so would I!) but if it doesn't he would like to go to the United States."⁹ Much was in play. Vilna was hardly Beckelman's dream assignment. What that might be, he did not specify. But perhaps he had his eye on somewhere more visible, like Russia, somewhere he deemed more important. "Troper called from Geneva," he wrote. "He may come to Kaunas at the end of next week and I have a notion that I'm going to be pulled out of here. I'm keeping my fingers crossed hoping."¹⁰

THE POGROM was an inauspicious start to Beckelman's mission, and the following days brought new crises. Thousands of Jewish refugees from German-occupied Poland had crossed the border into Soviet territory every day with relative ease since 18 September. This ended with the Red Army's withdrawal from the Vilna district. As the demarcation lines of Lithuania, German-occupied Poland, and Soviet-occupied territory stabilized, Berlin saw an opportunity. Germany expelled Jews from the land it occupied and forbade them to take any belongings with them. They fled into Russian territory, where "aid at present limited one meal daily which not all able get regularly," Beckelman cabled the JDC office. "Half million people without winter clothing and impossible obtain Russia." The Soviet attitude shifted. They were overwhelmed by refugees. "Formerly received hospitably now encountering difficulty," Beckelman emphasized.¹¹

The Germans pushed Jews over the Lithuanian border, too. Jewish refugees had fled into the frontier district of Suwalki, initially held by the Soviets, in an effort to escape the German advance and in the hope of reaching Lithuania, with its connections to the out-

side world.[12] Returning to Kaunas from Vilna on 2 November, Beckelman learned that as the Soviets ceded Suwalki to the Germans,
the Reich annexed the district and the situation had grown acute.
Announcing that the fifteen thousand Jews in Suwalki were to go to
Lithuania and that Germans in Lithuania were to come to Suwalki,
Nazi authorities ordered Jews to pack up and leave, giving them
twenty minutes to two hours to do so. The Germans marched them
to the frontier, but the Lithuanian border guards refused to admit
them. Warning the Jews not to return to German-occupied Poland
under penalty of death, the Germans seized their papers and passports and pushed them over the border. Lithuania was in a bind. In
a report to the JDC, Beckelman quoted Vice Premier Bizauskas's
observation that "while Lithuania could perfectly well admit 500 or
even 1000 such refugees this would simply constitute an invitation
to the Germans to send in thousands more which would swamp the
country." Still, several hundred made their way into Lithuania, and
about a thousand were stuck in no-man's-land. Asked to send aid,

This rare photograph of historical importance shows Jewish refugees after four days in an open field on the Lithuanian-Polish
border. In hats: members of the JDC delegation visiting the scene
on 15 December 1939. *(NY_01895, Courtesy of JDC Archives, New York.)*

the Lithuanian Red Cross declined, arguing that these Jews were not Lithuanian citizens and they were not on Lithuanian territory. At the same time, Lithuanian frontier guards refused to allow local Jews to cross into the exclusion zone to bring food, clothes, and blankets to their stranded coreligionists.[13]

Hearing conflicting reports, Beckelman concluded that no one had accurate information about the situation. An official delegation was to visit the frontier two days later, and he secured permission from the Ministry of the Interior to join them. What he saw beggared the accounts. "Touring Suwalki frontier zone," he cabled Troper (4 November). "Impossible adequately describe brutality barbarism German treatment expulsion our people aged infants paralytics."[14]

Jewish communities in the border towns scrambled to help. A meeting of the Kalvarija (Lithuania) Jewish Committee that Beckelman attended "revealed the existence of an underground railway for the smuggling of refugees as complete as anything I had read of in Civil War days." It was a busy operation. "The house we were in was obviously the center of the frontier running activity. Messages kept coming in all the time we were there and one man or another would get up, take a flashlight from the wall and go out to guide a party in from some house out of town where the refugees had been brought."[15]

Previously, Polish and Lithuanian peasants had smuggled the refugees across the border, but they had begun to demand more money en route, which the Jews did not have, since they had been stripped of all their possessions and cash by the Germans. A few days before Beckelman's visit, local young Jewish men took on that clandestine operation. They made their way to the frontier in search of refugees to escort over the border. Organizing themselves into shifts, the young men went out night after night. Determined to leave no one behind, they carried the elderly and infirm on their backs for several miles until they reached a safe destination. "Refugees wept telling me of the kindness that had been shown them," Beckelman reported. This was a community effort, he explained. "In a town of fifty Jewish families every home has seven or eight refugees who were being housed and fed." The "railway" continued in Lithuania. "Elaborate patrol systems were worked out for meeting refugees along various roads and guiding them to prearranged houses where they would be sheltered until morning and then passed on."[16]

Beckelman admired the participants' dedication. Yet he had reservations on behalf of the JDC about the illicit nature of the initiative. Asked by the local Jews for JDC financial support, Beckelman demurred, but said he would speak on their behalf with the Ezra Committee, which comprised all the Jewish aid organizations, local and foreign, dealing with refugees in Lithuania. Upon reflection, however, he wondered "how far I'm within my rights in discussing this activity with them in view of the JDC's well known desire to be like Caesar's wife."[17] The JDC had long held the position that its effectiveness, its ability to provide relief, rested on its strict observance of the laws in the lands in which it operated. To what degree could he support, or be seen to support, urgent, lifesaving, but clandestine operations? He soon decided that he and the JDC could play no role. He could not even "officially attend a meeting where methods of effecting illegal entry would constitute the agenda," he concluded.[18]

Beckelman's decision may have been prompted by punctilious adherence to the JDC's rules and culture, but it may have flowed from his own lack of compassion for the victims. Granted permission to go to no-man's-land, he saw distraught, unkempt people standing in a field, the women "wailing and screaming," the men "grim looking, dirty, unshaven." Yet "these people struck me as inhabitants of another world, and aroused practically no feeling in me whatever."[19]

Beckelman's emotional distance from the people he was deployed to help and his yearning to be posted elsewhere emerge repeatedly in his journal. Quarrels and questions about his career claim his attention. "Katz [a Vilna colleague] and I had supper together and Katz pumped me for all he was worth on my relations with Giterman," Beckelman reported on 8 November, shortly after his return from the frontier. At issue was a rumor that Giterman was vying for the position of JDC representative for eastern Europe. "Katz thinks that's doing me dirt but I'm not so sure. I'd be just as well satisfied to be shifted elsewhere. I've about had my bellyful of this part of the world except that I would like to look at Moscow before I pull out. And I'm beginning to feel more and more that this will turn out to have been the junior prom for which I was waiting and that when I get back to the States I'll be ready for a cushy administrative berth, a house in the country, and a wife. Kids I'm still not sure about."[20]

IN THE MEANTIME, Jewish refugees continued to arrive, winter approached, and conditions grew dire for many. The Jewish population of Vilna stood at sixty thousand before the war, ten thousand of whom, mostly young people, had left with the Soviets when they ceded the district to Lithuania. By late 1939, some fourteen thousand Jewish refugees had made their way from Poland to Vilna. This included at least twenty-five hundred young Polish Jews, *halutzim* (pioneers), who dreamed of going to Palestine and had trained on farms and in workshops to develop the skills needed to contribute to the creation of a Jewish homeland. An organized cohort, they fled to

Refugees study at the Lubavitcher Yeshiva in Vilna, 1940. (*NY_00237, Courtesy of JDC Archives, New York.*)

Vilna as a first step toward further emigration. A second group was composed of more than two thousand yeshiva (religious school) students, their teachers, and their school heads. Their institutions belonged to the Vaad Hayeshivot (Council of Yeshivas) network. Founded in 1924 and headquartered in Vilna, the Vaad Hayeshivot was authorized by the Polish government to provide spiritual and financial support to Orthodox yeshivas. At war's start, the council supported a network of about seventy schools, some of which moved in their entirety from Soviet-occupied Poland to Vilna. In addition to these two groups, a number of leaders of Jewish political parties as well as thousands of Jews from all walks of life who could not remain in Soviet territory slipped across the border and made their way to Vilna and, to a lesser extent, Kaunas."[21]

No definitive count of refugees obtained. The authorities instituted a registration system for newcomers, but many avoided it because they feared political reprisals by the Soviets when they were in power or expulsion from the city by the Lithuanians when the latter took control. Typically without financial resources, the refugees' weak economic position was exacerbated by currency exchange speculation. They had zloty, which officially exchanged at two to one lit, while street trade stood at thirty zloty for a lit. The refugees' funds were thus devalued and exhausted; even people who expected to be self-supporting soon needed to be fed. They needed clothing, too. As Beckelman noted, most of the refugees left with nothing more than what they wore. Then, too, they fled during a warm spell that fall and took only raincoats, if they took a coat at all. Outerwear became a marker, Beckelman observed. "One can practically identify the refugees in Vilna by the fact that they wear raincoats."[22]

While the need for clothing remained urgent, it was but one of the pressing problems Beckelman requested funds to alleviate. "First clothing," he telegraphed to the JDC's office in Paris. "Second problem housing. Impossible to convey adequately crowded unsanitary living conditions especially yeshivahs." And third, "nutrition problem acute."[23] A number of extant and newly established organizations claimed authority for relief of these problems, each seeking to privilege a single sector of the population. Mayhem ensued, as a contemporary report on the Vilna refugee aid budget for November and December 1939 suggested. The key problem was that the Jewish leadership "intended to concentrate all activities at the community which was the only legal institution accepted by the Russians." And indeed, the Vilna kehillah (Jewish community administrative body) established the Refugee Relief Committee shortly after the Soviets took the district. But the committee "was unable to do the work. It has even proved that it was an essential mistake to establish the committee together with the community. All partisan fights and frictions were carried onto the work of the committee."[24]

Beckelman agreed that the persistence of long-standing rifts affected the Refugee Relief Committee adversely. Then, too, he felt that the lack of clarity and logic from which the JDC directives suffered exacerbated the situation. "New York has sent a telegram saying that the cultural committee has allocated $5,000 for Yeshivoth and $2,000 for school organizations but why or on what basis the distribution was made or what especially the money is for God only knows," he fumed. Beckelman and Giterman visited the chief rabbi of Vilna, Hayim Oyzer Grodzienski, "and tried to make a deal about the $5000. With him was the Krinkso Rabbi [rabbi of Krink]. They're crazy as hell." The rabbis argued that the yeshiva students should be considered as a separate unit and, to Beckelman's disgust, they pushed for what they considered to be that unit's fair share of the JDC relief funds. Irritated as he was by the rabbis' naked money grab on behalf of those of interest to them and at the expense of other Jewish refugees, he acknowledged that they had identified a structural weakness of the relief system. As the situation stood, the kehillah was in charge of the Refugee Relief Committee, which did not work. In Beckelman's view, this state of affairs called for radical changes; the question was "How and When."[25]

Beckelman insisted on a rational calculus of decision-making. The infighting frustrated him, and the Jewish leaders' doggedness, both in Lithuania and the United States, in protecting individual groups rather than tackling the tragedy that gripped the whole community baffled him. "The more I see of these disgusting political squabbles in the face of the existing emergency," he wrote, "the more I am convinced that if the JDC is to do a worthwhile job it must stop blowing hot and cold, and being influenced in its decisions with respect to relief programs by the logically irrelevant consideration of repercussions in America resulting from squawks raised by groups who think they have been wronged." The JDC should determine what it believed to be the correct course and follow that path without wavering. The problem was that if every organization or institution, "Yeshivah [religious study], Poale Zion [Marxist-Zionist workers' organization], Bund [Jewish socialist political party], Chalutz [agricultural training for Palestine] etc can go crying to its friends in the States that it ain't being done right by and force the JDC to tell us to give them their candy we're licked." No special pleading; no separate deals. He sought "a logical relief policy." In his view, if the home office backed the field operatives in Vilna, "we can stick to our guns over here and hammer out a unified organization."[26]

Tapping power centers in the United States was only one manifestation of interorganizational strife. Relations in Vilna were so fractured that Beckelman wondered about his mission. At one meeting of TOZ (a Jewish philanthropic organization dedicated to providing health care) and kehillah leaders, for example, Beckelman noted that "everybody had an ax—not only to grind but to bury in somebody else's neck." Seeing no leadership emerging from the kehillah or anywhere else, he concluded that the JDC "may need to take over the administration of relief under our own auspices." He went on to note, "and I doubt very much whether Giterman is the man for it."[27]

Clear-eyed about the deleterious effects of interorganizational rivalries, Beckelman nevertheless continued his critique of Giterman and remained suspicious of his colleague's motives about nearly everything, including prioritizing aid into Russia over Germany. Beckelman queried whether this was a legitimate position, shaped by the needs of Jews in the Soviet Union, or whether Giterman was simply providing himself with a job while avoiding the dangers he would face in Germany. Beckelman did not entertain the possibility that, even if true, trepidations about safety in the Reich would be a legitimate consideration. Nor did he note that his perspective as a citizen of a neutral nation (the United States) differed from that of Giterman, whose country was occupied. He did remark upon his own skepticism, however: "Interesting. I never would have reacted this way six months ago . . . but listening to the plotting and counter-plotting that goes on around here, one gets the fever."[28]

BECKELMAN, it turns out, was suspicious of many people, including a certain Miss Lerner, a JDC secretary whom he saw as a potential marriage partner. Yet he took umbrage at the note he detected "of taking our eventual marriage for granted in her letters." And then there was the question of where he would be, and what his options were in each location. "If I'm going to stay here for several years I might as well get married," he argued to himself. Even as he debated whether marrying her or anyone made sense at that time, he evinced some paranoia. "I definitely feel that [a number of people] have put one over on me," he admitted to his diary. Ultimately, Beckelman chose to defer making a decision about his private life until he had met with Troper. Then he would see "what the prospects are for avoiding coming back here and of finding a plausible excuse for a furlough in Paris."[29] In which case, there would be no reason to marry Miss Lerner.

Looking to improve his situation ("I'd much sooner keep a roving commission . . . that's the angle to watch for"), Beckelman continuously expressed his discomfort with the work he had been dispatched to do ("I've got no stomach for the job") and lack of engagement with his colleagues and clients. Even when he sought to save them, individually or as a group. Thus, for example, when his colleague, the Bund activist and journalist Maurycy Orzech, a refugee from Warsaw, was picked up by the Lithuanian police, Beckelman bestirred himself grudgingly. Orzech's papers were not in order, so the police sent him to a small frontier town. Alerted to his presence, the local bank director phoned Beckelman's colleague Katz. The call got through by pure chance: one of a group of four who had left Katz's house worried that they'd left a light burning and returned to switch it off when the phone rang. Orzech was to be turned over to the Germans at 9:00 that night. Beckelman did not feel he had a role to play, and it was with some reluctance that he called on Owen J. C. Norem, the American envoy extraordinary, who was out, and Thomas Hildebrand Preston, the English chargé d'affaires, who promised to phone the Lithuanian authorities. Preston's efforts met with short-term success: Orzech's deportation was stayed overnight. Despite his aversion to getting involved in the case, Beckelman went to the Ministry of the Interior the next day to appeal further on Orzech's behalf. "I got a cold reception," he complained. Still, he persevered, arguing that giving Orzech into German hands meant his death. Beckelman suggested that Orzech be returned, under arrest, to Kaunas for a few days while his friends sought visas for him to exit the country legally.[30]

Orzech had to leave Lithuania or face deportation; Beckelman and Giterman had to leave to meet with Troper, whose plans to come to Kaunas had been vetoed by the New York office. Orzech departed first. Beckelman and Giterman met him at the railway station in Riga on 8 December, where the three boarded a train to Tallinn. There they were to catch an Estonian ship to Stockholm. Somehow, the steamship company had lost their reservations, but space was found for the three. "Giterman and I shared the cabin of the second engineer, hot, stuffy," Beckelman grumbled. "Orzech had no bunk at all but was scheduled to sleep in the smoking room. We really had no beds either."[31]

It would have been better had they never boarded. Beckelman awoke early on 10 December to learn that, against international protocol, the neutral ship had been stopped by an armed German merchantman serving as an auxiliary cruiser and forced to detour to the then German port of Swinemünde. The occupying crew assured the passengers that they would be allowed to proceed as they wished from there. They were not under suspicion; it was the cargo that needed to be checked against the ship papers. Nevertheless, Beckelman noted, unease grew "as the belief spread that the Poles and English would be taken off the boat and interned." Anxious about the files they had brought, Beckelman, Giterman, and Orzech "spent the morning [of Monday 11 December] going through our papers carefully sorting out any references to German affairs, particularly atrocities in Poland, sewed it up in a towel and dumped it overboard. We all felt much relieved when that was out of the way," Beckelman confided to his diary.[32] He did not say where he hid his journal.

Beckelman slept poorly that night. He began, he said, to worry about Giterman, but not about his colleague's safety. Rather, Beckelman fretted that if Giterman were imprisoned, he (Beckelman) would have to remain in post in Vilna, which he did not want to do. And he worried that if the Germans delved into the JDC's activities, he himself might be interned. His trepidations were well founded. The Germans began to interrogate the Polish passengers the following morning. "Giterman disappeared about noon; Orzech at nine," Beckelman reported. "I saw Giterman for a brief word and handshake" before the Polish men were escorted off the ship. "I must say both he and Orzech who will be up against it even more than the rest, once their identity and previous activities become known, have taken it more bravely than I think I should be able to do in a similar case."[33]

It was the last time Beckelman saw either man. Despite American diplomatic efforts to secure Giterman's release, he was imprisoned in Germany until March 1940, and then was returned to Warsaw, where he resumed his role of attending to the needs of the Jewish population.[34] The Germans shot him dead during the first phase of the Warsaw ghetto uprising in January 1943. Orzech, too, was imprisoned and sent back to Warsaw, where he served as deputy chairman of the Bund Central Committee.[35] He managed to slip out of the ghetto in 1942 and hid on the so-called Aryan side while he sought a route to Palestine. Caught trying to get to Romania, he was incarcerated in Pawiak prison. The Germans murdered him a few months later. Beckelman, protected by his American passport, was permitted to disembark. There was no customs inspection. He could have taken a whole archive with him. He proceeded to Amsterdam, where he met with Troper. The end of December 1939 found him with his boss in Brussels; Troper had closed the premises in the Netherlands and opened a new office in Belgium, in a building that, conveniently, housed another Jewish organization, HICEM, which had been founded in 1927 to help European Jews emigrate.[36]

BECKELMAN RETURNED to Vilna in January 1940, where the JDC program continued under his sole direction.[37] There was much to do. Perhaps he found his experience of German aggression against a neutral ship sobering, prompting him to reorder his priorities. Then, too, Giterman's incarceration and forced removal to Warsaw meant that he was no longer in Beckelman's daily life. Perhaps Giterman's absence released Beckelman from the competitiveness that had narrowed his perspective, freeing him to engage more fully in relief work. Possibly his singular leadership role buoyed him. Fretting less about his career, he seems to have focused his energy and attention on his mandate. According to Wayne C. Taylor, of the American Red Cross, who called on Troper after a site visit to Vilna, "The work of the J.D.C. in Vilna and Lithuania is excellent . . . it is by far the best organized relief work now being done in that section."[38]

Whatever the reason, Beckelman addressed the problems of Vilna's Jewish rooted residents and recently arrived refugees with great dedication. Their situation had deteriorated since the Soviets had ceded the district to Lithuania. Now half of the local Jewish population (thirty thousand people) needed support, and new groups of refugees were flowing into the city from the Soviet Union. Taylor claimed that they were smuggled into Vilna at the rate of three hundred a day. This signaled trouble: Lithuanian officials insisted that their small and poor country could not absorb more people and had not been able to restore or replace the goods the Russians had stolen, nor set up the industries they had hijacked.[39] The diminished employment options increased the poverty of an already indigent population. Joining with representatives of the Lithuanian Red Cross, American Red Cross, and another American philanthropic organization, the Commission for Polish Relief, the JDC supported feeding stations, kitchens, and medical care, and sought to fill warehouses with fabric and food, secure housing, develop workshops, and provide clothing, sheets, and towels.[40]

The structure through which aid was provided flowed from the demographics of the refugee population. Of the 9,824 Jewish refugees in Vilna who complied with the Lithuanian compulsory registration order (and a significant number continued to avoid doing so), 7,415 were men, 1,926 were women, and 483 were children. As these figures show, individuals, mostly male, had fled; families had not. Without families as the dominant social unit, refugees self-segregated by profession, occupation, or political affiliation, choosing to take the three meals offered daily in one of the fifty-two dining rooms established throughout the city frequented by a like clientele. Thus, Beckelman reported, there were dining rooms for a range of

Jewish refugees dine in their Vilna canteen in 1939. *(Photo by Boleslawa and Edmund Zdanowscy [Lithuanian: Boleslava and Edmundas Zdanauskai], 1939; M. K. Čiurlionis National Museum of Art, ČDM Ta 4690/82.)*

groups, including journalists, Zionists, halutzim, and labor unionists. These canteens became distribution sites for clothing and other necessities, and they served as cultural and social centers.[41]

Beckelman calculated that at least half of the Jewish refugees to Vilna were educated, previously prosperous, belonged to a yeshiva, or sought to be a pioneer in Palestine. These attributes, he concluded, pointed to emigration. It made no sense to create employment opportunities in Vilna itself or to invest in the establishment of additional dining rooms, both of which required substantial capital outlays for equipment. Instead, Beckelman favored training courses in various trades and language classes to support their success as emigrants. An estimated two thousand refugees attended language classes, most learning English or Hebrew.[42] Beckelman also favored the more temporary solution of refugees taking meals with and housed by Vilna families. His consistent message to the home office: JDC programs should aid emigration.[43]

The Lithuanian attitude toward the refugees pointed to emigration, too. Only people who resided in Vilna prior to the absorption

Jewish refugees learn tailoring skills in the Kibbutz Shahriah workshop, Vilna, 1940. (NY_00259, Courtesy of JDC Archives, New York.)

of the district into Poland in 1920 were eligible for Lithuanian citizenship. That excluded some 90 percent of the resident Jewish community. They had dim long-term prospects. And seeking to delimit the number of refugees, the Lithuanians deemed legal entrants only those who could prove that they had come to Soviet-occupied Vilna before 28 October 1939 (that is, before the Lithuanian army entered the city). Their prospects were even murkier than those of the resident Jews: they were threatened with deportation from the country. Furthermore, as Beckelman noted (9 May 1940), the Lithuanians were eager to convert Vilna "into their capital city as quickly as possible" and claimed the buildings and rooms the refugees occupied for government use.[44]

Russian tanks rolled in on 15 June 1940, before that transformation was actualized. Reporting to Troper shortly thereafter, Beckelman referenced the Soviet policy of objecting to private philanthropy—only the state provided welfare—and predicted that the JDC would need to close its operations within a month or two.[45] Until that time came, however, he urged the JDC to continue to fund relief activities; he would remain at his post in Vilna. The Soviets installed a communist government in June and formally annexed Lithuania on 3 August. Still, they did not shutter the JDC. Beckelman's requests for funds to support relief programs and emigration options grew increasingly adamant. "Remaining till further notice," he cabled New York on 8 August. He assumed, he said, "continuance adequate funds as long activity continues." Ten days later, after the Soviets announced that all foreign consulates would be closed on 25 August, he emphasized that a solution to the problem of transmitting funds needed to be found, "otherwise position untenable." Dealing with a desperate situation, he railed against the JDC's refusal to circumvent US Treasury Department regulations blocking Lithuanian accounts by transmitting funds through neutral Switzerland, as the Commission for Polish Relief was doing. Initiated by former president Herbert Hoover and established in late 1939 following the German and Soviet invasion of Poland, the commission (usually referred to as the Pate Commission, as it was led by Maurice Pate)

provided humanitarian relief to people in Nazi-occupied Poland
and to Polish refugees throughout Europe, including in Lithuania. "Pate Commission transmission coming Switzerland uninter-
ruptedly," Beckelman cabled on 18 August, while JDC funds had
stopped completely on 9 July. Why couldn't the JDC "transmit via
Switzerland exactly as Pate Commission doing past month"? he
hammered two days later. But New York would not budge. "After
thorough discussion, it was decided to inform Mr. Beckelman that
in view of all the factors in the situation, the J.D.C. was unable to
remit funds to him and unwilling to evade governmental regulations in that regard." Holding fast to the JDC policy of strict adherence to legal directives, the administration committee promptly
dispatched a cable: "Irrespective methods used other organizations
we cannot evade regulations."[46]

Beckelman continued relentlessly. Although he was "convinced
pointless reopen argument," he cabled, he proceeded to do just that.
"Dutybound enquire whether you considered possibility making
contribution Pate Commission New York" requesting that they ear-
mark the funds for Jewish refugees and transmit the sum to Lithuania with their funds for Polish gentiles? A circuitous but serviceable
route. And he concluded, "Wish record categorically your unwilling-
ness continue same basis Pate renders my remaining impossible."[47]

Yet there were people to help and, notwithstanding the New York
office's refusal to transmit funds, Beckelman did not leave. Fearing
religious repression by the Soviets, yeshiva communities of students
and rabbis in Russian-occupied eastern Poland had fled to Vilna in
1939. Now that the USSR had annexed Lithuania, the Polish refugee
and resident Lithuanian yeshivas found themselves in the same precarious situation. Representatives of major American Jewish organizations met in New York to consider the political and financial
viability of bringing 2,800 rabbis and students to the United States.
The idea met with little enthusiasm. "It was the consensus of opinion
that so large a number of yeshivoth and rabbis could not possibly be
successfully absorbed in this country."[48] If not to the United States,
where were they to go?

Among the yeshiva students seeking somewhere to settle were a few Dutch nationals. Determined to find an exit route, they approached Jan Zwartendijk, the honorary Dutch consul in Kaunas. The Netherlands was occupied by that time, but perhaps he could help them get to the Dutch colony of Curaçao, in the Caribbean, or Surinam (also called Dutch Guiana), in South America. Zwartendijk checked with the Dutch ambassador in Riga, L. P. J. de Decker. No visa was required to enter either.

The Orthodox comprised but one segment of the Jewish community that welcomed this news. The Soviet announcement that all consulates were finally to close by 4 September—a delay to their original date—had prompted a stampede for papers, and the news about Curaçao and Surinam swept through the refugee community. With an official final destination, Jews could obtain exit visas from Russian-occupied Lithuania, transit visas across the Soviet Union, ferry tickets from Vladivostok to Tsuruga, in Japan, and, with Japanese transit visas, move on to Kobe, Tokyo, or Yokohama.

The travel permit process flowed in reverse, starting with the end point. With de Decker's approval from Riga, Zwartendijk went to work issuing official signed-and-sealed statements to the effect that no visa was required for Curaçao or for Surinam. Now, would the Japanese consul issue transit visas? Japan had signed the Anti-Comintern Pact with Germany in 1936 and afterward drew ever closer to the Axis. There was no reason for the consulate to help Jews and every reason to avoid involvement.

Against all odds, Japan's consul in Kaunas, Chiune Sugihara, thought differently. An earlier history of diplomatic intrigue in Manchuria had led to his status as persona non grata in the Soviet Union. And he knew about the gulag. He also knew what was happening to Jews in German-occupied Poland. Hundreds of desperate, distraught people gathered outside his office every day, pleading for help. According to his wife, he cabled Tokyo three times asking permission to grant them transit visas. His requests were denied. Realizing that he might well suffer consequences, he nevertheless decided to issue visas—thousands of visas, each good for a whole family.[49] Like so many rescuer decisions, this was both a principled action and an emotional response.

With a final destination and a Japanese transit visa in hand, the refugees obtained exit visas from Lithuania and transit visas through the Soviet Union. Curaçao and Surinam were just smoke and mirrors. No one went there. But they served as legitimate destinations for the purpose of obtaining permissions to cross borders and travel through one country to the next. Sugihara saw other sites on refugee documents: Shanghai, the United States, Palestine, Latin America. Some were authentic, others forgeries. But as the days passed and the Soviet-imposed deadline for closing the consulate drew nearer, he didn't even look at that part of the application. He simply signed and stamped Japanese transit visas steadily until the moment of his departure. And then, people say, he threw blank stamped forms from his train window. According to Beckelman, who was not involved in this initiative and seems not to have known him, Sugihara issued some thirty-five hundred transit visas "on bases which I am convinced must have been known to the Japanese Consul . . . to be invalid and insufficient bases for the issuance of transit visas, but they were issued."[50] Sugihara suffered severe consequences after the war for his insubordination in Kaunas. He was dismissed from the Japanese Foreign Service and made a living doing odd jobs. But he had signed those visas; he had saved thousands of lives.

IF THE SOVIET CLOSING DATE for the Japanese consulate loomed large in August 1940, another Russian deadline soon loomed, too. Moscow offered citizenship to all Polish refugees in Lithuania residing there as of 1 September 1940; those who declined had to emigrate or face deportation to Siberia. The Soviets set a deadline of 25 January 1941 (later extended to 10 February) for Vilna district. Throughout December, Beckelman continued to ask the home office to find a way to send funds to support rescue efforts, or to move him elsewhere. But New York was loath to pull him out. Beckelman's Vilna associate, a Mr. Bider, reported that he had been told by "important officials of the Russian Government" before his departure from Lithuania that so long as a JDC operative remained, Jewish refugees would be afforded some measure of protection. Physical presence was key.[51] The Commission for Polish Relief shared that view. It planned to keep its representative in place as long as possible. Beckelman disagreed and revisited the matter regularly. If he was to receive no funds, nothing was to be gained by his remaining in Lithuania, he argued.[52] Frustrated as he may have been, he did not give in or give up.

Pressure mounted both in New York and in Vilna as the citizenship deadline neared. The Soviets were prepared to allow the refugees to emigrate, and thousands sought to do so. Meeting in New York on 15 January, the JDC executive committee took stock. At least three thousand persons were poised to depart if the JDC funded their transport. The committee understood that this was an emergency situation and the window of opportunity was closing. But the JDC faced many emergencies every day. With limited funds to defray travel costs, the core question that haunted all rescuers now arose for the home office: Whom to help? Who claimed priority? "The J.D.C. offices here [New York] and in Lithuania were besieged by individuals and representatives of the rabbinical groups, labor leaders, etc., urging that transportation be arranged for their adherents," Moses Leavitt, JDC secretary, informed the executive committee. In response, committee member Harry Fischel opened the discussion: "I'd like to know who is going to make the selection of people—whom to take out of Lithuania." Beckelman had already weighed in on the matter, and Leavitt drew on his telegram texts. "The only one who can make the selection is Mr. Beckelman," he declared. "We don't know and can't give him any instruction to favor one group as against another, because he has already cabled us that it is impossible for him to pick out one person as against another. . . . He does not want any earmarking."[53]

Having said that, Leavitt promptly pivoted to the economics of the situation and argued in favor of those with financially solvent relatives who can help fund them: "those people will have to receive preference." Fischel disagreed vehemently, championing yeshiva students and rabbis, as the Soviet system held them in suspicion. "The danger to life of rabbis and students is much greater than to anyone else. Isn't it our duty to try to save these men who are in greater danger, and to give them preference over others?" The way forward was clear: "I believe we ought to give orders to Beckelman to give [them] some sort of preference." Alexander Kahn, another member of the committee, advocated by contrast for "people connected with labor organizations known to be unfriendly to the Soviet Government"; they were at as great a risk. Still, noting that the committee was distant from the situation on the ground, Kahn acknowledged, "It is very difficult from this side to direct Beckelman as to who is to be given preference." He relied on the operative's objectivity. "Mr. Beckelman certainly has no prejudices in the matter. We must leave it to him to use his judgment as to who should be served first as they will be the first victims in case they are not taken out."[54]

Fischel was not persuaded. He tried another tack, arguing that yeshiva students "are of a special type. We need them in America today." He sought to save Jewish culture and learning by safeguarding rabbis and yeshiva students, who would revive Jewish life in the United States. Indeed, "we may leave a man interested in labor or businessman, but if we leave one of those students . . . we can never reproduce them." Fischel did not prevail.[55] Nevertheless, some one thousand of the total number emigrated from Lithuania with JDC aid were rabbis and yeshiva students. The JDC went on to provide maintenance funds for them in Japan. Most subsequently emigrated to Shanghai, where they continued to be helped by the JDC.[56] The trajectory of the Mirrer Yeshiva exemplifies this pattern. Founded in 1815 in the small Polish town of Mir (now in Belarus), the entire yeshiva community fled as a group to Lithuania when the Germans invaded Poland. The Soviet occupation prompted the more than three hundred members of the school to flee again. With Curaçao papers from Jan Zwartendijk and transit visas issued by Chiune Sugihara, they crossed Siberia by train and went on to Kobe and then to Shanghai. JDC financial support proved crucial.

Reporting to the executive committee when he returned to the United States a few months later, Beckelman readily acknowledged that the "problem of selecting the persons who were to leave Lithuania" probably gave New York "as much of a headache and perhaps more" than he had suffered. The difficulty he had faced was balancing the pressure brought to bear by funders against "the logical approach," which suggested "people with valid visas" and "people with probable chances of making an adjustment in the country to which they were going." For his part, he focused on the number rather than on the who. His goal was to get as many refugees out of Lithuania as possible.[57] With Soviet-Lithuanian exit visas and Soviet as well as Japanese transit visas, they proceeded to Japan where, Beckelman and the New York office assumed, they would wait; some would receive US visas, while many would go on to Shanghai until other destinations were secured.

For Beckelman, immediate departure was key; further emigration would be tackled later. And, he noted, "we did get well over 2,000 people out" before the Japanese authorities refused to admit more. Arguing that Japan was a small country that could not accommodate a large foreign population, Tokyo indicated that if some moved on, others might enter.[58] Beckelman pressed for the removal of the refugees to Shanghai to open space for more people to leave from Lithuania. While the Soviets remained prepared to issue exit visas to Polish Jews who had fled into Lithuania and might include Lithuanian citizens as well, the refugees had to wait on others moving on from Japan. Once again, however, rescue depended on the unpredictable factors of others' actions and of timing. Germany invaded the Soviet Union on 22 June, and the exit from Lithuania, reduced to a trickle by then, came to a stop.

WITH VANISHINGLY LITTLE SCOPE for constructive action, Beckelman left Lithuania on 21 February 1941, traveling via Moscow to Japan, then on to Shanghai, and arriving in the United States in April. His mission had been marked by discord: his frustration with Troper in Europe, irritation with the executive committee in New York, and competitiveness with Giterman in Vilna; acrimony between the Jewish communal organizations in Kaunas and Vilna; rivalry between sectors of the Jewish community. The battles and bitterness speak to the anxiety and uncertainty everyone endured. That record stands in contrast to typical relief and rescue accounts that describe valiant efforts. With the known end in view, such narratives strip the unfolding situation of its dominant features: instability, unpredictability, and incomplete and insufficient information.

Spurred by ambition as well as principles and professional ethics, Beckelman achieved a great deal in Lithuania. His stewardship of JDC funding benefited thousands of refugees to Vilna as well as residents of that city. Beyond the major relief initiatives of food programs, housing, medical care, clothing distribution, and educational and cultural activities, perhaps most important was Beckelman's insight that the refugees' occupations would not translate into long-term financial prospects. They needed to emigrate. Relief aid transformed into rescue services. Thanks in no small measure to his efforts, thousands managed to flee.

RESTORING THE IRRATIONAL DIMENSION of Moses Beckelman's character—its weaknesses and its strengths—and the unpredictable factors of chance and timing to the history of his activities in Lithuania on behalf of the JDC enriches our understanding nearly a century later of what such operations entailed and augments our appreciation of his success. Beckelman went on to a JDC assignment in South America (1941–42). He left that post for the Office of Strategic Services (OSS), the predecessor to the CIA, when appointed to head the OSS's Foreign Nationalities Branch (FNB) in June 1942, half a year after the United States had entered the war. His main task was to oversee an operation spying on Jews in America. It ended abruptly in July 1943 after an internal investigation by the OSS security department. Oddly, neither he nor any of the Jews who worked for the FNB suffered any negative consequences in the Jewish community; their work was seen as a patriotic mission.[59]

Indeed, Beckelman sailed into an outstanding career, holding several powerful and highly sensitive positions. He directed the United Nations Relief and Rehabilitation Agency's (UNRRA) first refugee camp in Morocco, opened in mid-1944 to house refugees from the Nazi regime. A relief agency, UNRRA was founded by the Allies to aid and repatriate victims of World War II. The camp closed in November 1944, and Beckelman went on to serve as the assistant director of the Inter-governmental Committee on Refugees (appointed February 1945) before rejoining the JDC in 1946, the same year he married. He became the second-in-command at the JDC's European headquarters in Paris, then was promoted to the position of JDC director-general for overseas operations in 1951. Beckelman had achieved his professional ambitions.

But as we have seen, chance and happenstance shape life. Moses Beckelman died suddenly of a heart attack in 1955. He was forty-nine years old.

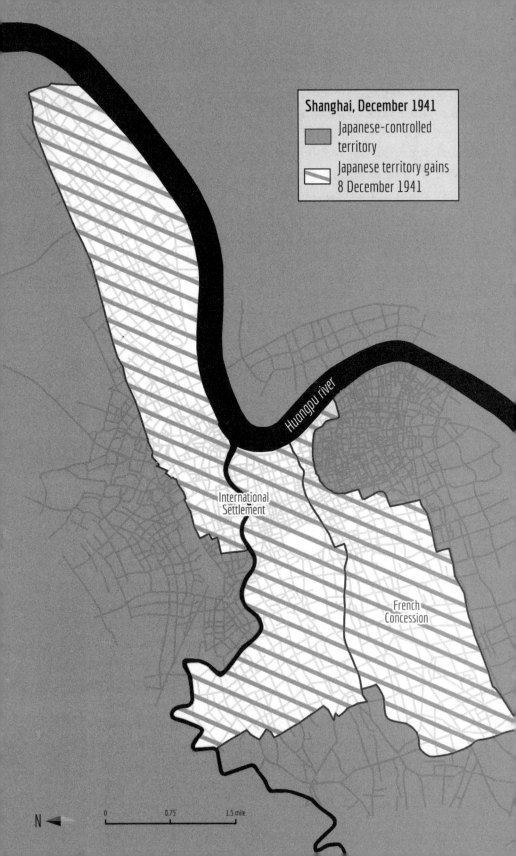

Shanghai, December 1941

Japanese-controlled territory

Japanese territory gains 8 December 1941

Huangpu river

International Settlement

French Concession

N

0   0.75   1.5 mile

THREE

SHANGHAI, 1941

Laura Margolis

"**M**UST SECURE HAVEN SHANGHAI" JDC'S NEW
York office cabled the Committee for the Assistance
of European Jewish Refugees (CFA) in that Chinese
city. Worried about conflict with the Japanese government, the
JDC was also under pressure from the Jewish community of Kobe
(called JEWCOM, its telegraph address), which was responsible for
the welfare of the Polish and Lithuanian Jews who had found refuge
there.[1] Japan objected to so many foreigners failing to move on, as
they were meant to do by the terms of their transit visas, and JEW-
COM objected to the cost of refugee support. "Critical situation
here," Kobe cabled. JEWCOM was "bitterly disappointed" by the
Joint Distribution Committee. With no funds to disburse, the community was forced to cease refugee support as of the following day.
"Fates 1700 refugees on your conscience," JEWCOM warned.[2] The
JDC, for its part, was sensitive to the politics and the economics of
the situation. It sought to send the eastern European refugees from
Kobe to Shanghai and leaned on the CFA to accommodate them.
But the Shanghai committee wanted money too, as Moses Beckel-

man reported, pressing the home office to approve an increased budget for Shanghai to receive the newcomers.[3]

One thousand to fifteen hundred eastern European refugee Jews migrated from Kobe to Shanghai in the seven months between April and November 1941, initially in small groups of ten to fifteen persons and increasing later to fifty and more.[4] These Polish and Lithuanian refugees joined their coreligionists who had fled to Shanghai from Greater Germany in the late 1930s. For German, Austrian, and Czech Jews with no prospect of immigration visas to anywhere, Shanghai beckoned as a destination. One of five Chinese cities opened to foreign residence and trade as a result of the "Opium War" (1840–43), Shanghai had allowed Europeans and Americans to establish extraterritorial "concession areas"—settlements—each governed by its own consul.[5] Efficiently run and lightly taxed, the concessions became an economic engine attracting nearly all the foreign investment in China. By the 1930s, the so-called International Settlement measured 5,583 acres and the French Concession 2,525 acres, with a combined population of 1.5 million people, of whom sixty thousand were foreigners who enjoyed extraterritorial status. These two areas were embedded in a great metropolis under full Chinese jurisdiction of another 1.5 million people, which made Shanghai the fifth largest city in the world.

According to the nineteenth-century agreements, Chinese officials had no right to refuse a visa for Shanghai to Americans and Europeans so long as they paid a set fee. In the twentieth century, the city known as "the Paris of the Orient" thus became "the Home of the Homeless" and "the Haven of Undesirables."[6] More than twenty-five thousand Russians found refuge there after the final defeat of the czar's forces by the Bolsheviks in 1923.[7] Some got jobs as policemen, watchmen, doormen, barmaids, masseuses, or rickshaw drivers, but most fell into destitution.

The Japanese occupation of Manchuria in 1931 brought horrendous destruction to Shanghai, as anti-Japanese riots by the Chinese spurred the Japanese to attack the city. Still, the International Settlement remained intact and open for business. When Japan occupied most of northeast China in 1937, including greater Shanghai, it, too, respected the extraterritorial integrity of the International Settlement and the French Concession. But the economy plummeted, and the situation in the two concessions deteriorated further with the arrival of one million Chinese refugees. Isolated in an area under harsh occupation, Shanghai began to unravel. Thousands of foreigners left for their home countries, and well-to-do Chinese moved to Hong Kong.

It was at this moment that Jews in Greater Germany grew desperate. The allure of Shanghai, a destination for those who had nowhere else to go, grew ever greater. As a contemporary account reported, "Everywhere the same answer is given: No . . . nein . . . non . . . impossible . . . lo siento mucho . . . I am sorry. . . . All these negative answers prevail in every country in the world . . . except in the city of Shanghai." And the author went on to explain: "Here there is no one to say NO. No one exercises any right to refuse you a visa, if you are prepared to pay the Chinese Consul his fee of three dollars. . . . No necessary papers, no references. If you have a passport . . . that's all right. If you have no passport . . . don't let that worry you . . . you can still get into Shanghai."[8]

Frank Foley, the British passport officer in Berlin, knew all too well that many Jews had no prospect of visas. Desperate applicants denied British visas had raised the idea of Shanghai with him and, as he reported to the Home Office in London, he and his colleagues had warned them not to go there. "They refuse to listen to us and say that Shanghai under any conditions is infinitely better than a Concentration Camp in Germany. One can perhaps understand their point of view." Foley framed their choice in stark terms. "They would rather die as free men in Shanghai than as slaves in Dachau. The people who sail for Shanghai have usually been warned to leave Germany within a few weeks or enter or return to a Concentration Camp. They know the horrors of a Concentration Camp, but remain hopeful about Shanghai in spite of warnings."[9]

Panic-stricken German and Austrian Jews bought ship tickets knowing that upon arrival they would face an utterly strange metrop-

Jewish refugees enjoy an outdoor coffeehouse in Shanghai. *(Courtesy of the Leo Baeck Institute, New York.)*

olis that promised nothing but the most destitute and temporary refuge from persecution—a squalid waiting room for better times. Still, they clutched at hope and set sail.[10] According to Beckelman, there were about twenty thousand refugees from Greater Germany in Shanghai by early 1941; the Polish and Lithuanian Jews increased that figure to twenty-one thousand.[11] No one expected that the refugees would remain. They had landed in "a city occupied by a foreign enemy, parts of it in ruins, with foreign trade on the decline and foreign capital pulling out."[12] Few would be able to gain a toehold in that environment. The sole solution lay in emigration elsewhere, and the JDC leadership tapped social worker Laura Margolis to go to Shanghai to expedite the process.

"IF I'D BEEN A MAN I would have joined the Navy and seen the world but, since I was a woman, I joined the JDC," Laura Margolis

reflected nearly forty years after her first Joint assignment.[13] Margolis's professional trajectory was marked repeatedly by the unpredictable and the irrational. Born in Constantinople in 1903, she and her
family immigrated to the United States in 1908 and settled in Cleveland, Ohio. At five years old, she spoke French, German, Greek,
Turkish, and Spanish, which proved useful decades later in her chosen field of social work. Earning her degree at the School of Applied
Social Sciences, Western Reserve University, in 1928, Margolis joined
Cleveland's Jewish Social Services Bureau the next year. By 1933, she
had achieved her goals in that position and, as she explained, "I felt
I could move on." Bored by routine, she sought fresh opportunities.
"This has been a pattern of mine," she observed. "Once I meet the
challenge of a new situation and overcome it so it's functioning, I
want to go on." Against her colleagues' advice, Margolis accepted
the job of director of the Jewish Welfare Society of Buffalo. She had
been told that the Buffalo community "was under the dictatorship
of a few men who were big givers, with no professional standards,
no professional practices, and no agency structure." All of which she
found to be true. And all of which she rectified in just four years. It
was, she said, "a revolution . . . meaning that people in power began
to lose power." She left behind an efficient operation that employed
professional staff. And she had found a way to manage her relationships with the power brokers. "I was friendly with all those people;
[I] had become one of the group I'd been fighting. I was at home
there." Her work was done. "In accordance with my natural pattern,
I became restless and wanted a new challenge."[14]

   That new opportunity came in the form of an international posting. The National Refugee Service (NRS) had recently become the
successor agency to the National Coordinating Committee, which
was founded in 1934 as an umbrella organization to coordinate the
activities of affiliated agencies engaged in immigrant relief work.
Now the NRS needed a social worker who spoke Spanish and German to go to Cuba. The five thousand refugees who had fled to that
island from Nazi Germany required help. While the NRS employed
Margolis, the JDC paid her salary. And her remit brought her into

Laura Margolis. *(Photo by Anna Riwkin-Brick. Jewish Museum of Stockholm.)*

close contact with the US consulate and thus to the attention of Avra Warren, of the visa division in the State Department. "We became a functional arm of the U.S. Consulate" in Havana, Margolis recalled. She and her staff filled out forms for the refugees and translated documents and letters. Perhaps most important, the consulate asked her to evaluate the cases she helped to process. She and her staff were effective; the queue began to move and the refugees to depart for the United States.[15]

Warren, who had come to Havana a number of times and saw how efficiently she functioned, took note. And when twenty thousand refugees foundered in Shanghai, he asked the JDC, "Would you send Laura Margolis over? She did the job in Havana."[16] The New York office welcomed the State Department's willingness to allocate quota numbers to refugees in Shanghai and readily agreed to appoint Margolis.[17]

Margolis's brief was clear: emigration, not refugee relief. Arriving in Shanghai, however, she was appalled by what she found and soon chafed against the constraints of her charge. "I have been here just two weeks and I feel that a preliminary report is in order," she wrote (28 May 1941) to JDC executive officer Robert Pilpel. "First—

the relief program." The CFA, the local organization responsible for providing aid, was run by a martinet, housed refugees in squalid group shelters known as *heims* (homes) or camps, and offered only one meal totaling fourteen hundred calories a day. "The so-called 'Heims' were a terrific shock," she said bluntly. "In some of them the refugees are so crowded; the atmosphere so depressing; and the people look so completely hopeless and lost that one visit is enough to know that ultimately this condition must be alleviated." It went without saying that the feeding program was insufficient. Yet, Margolis held, the solution to these problems was "not more money; at least not from us." The whole system needed to be overhauled, starting with a fresh look at the CFA director, Captain Herzberg.[18]

Margolis labored to offer a balanced portrait and analysis of Herzberg, who came from a German Jewish family and had lived in Shanghai since birth. His employment experience at the Hapag shipping company had honed his skills at creating procedures large and small, including wholesale purchasing and overall planning, as well as investigating, filing, and cross-indexing processes. And she noted that graft, all too common before he took charge, had diminished with his appointment. With that, she ran out of points to applaud and turned to the effect of his leadership: "constant friction and tension and a terrific hatred of the Committee" that prevailed across the entire community, not refugees alone. The core problem was that "the Captain has no understanding of handling people. . . . His whole manner is one which leads to heel clicking and obedience and fear of authority. One has the constant feeling of being in the German army." However sober her assessment, Margolis's antipathy shines bright. It was an immediate, visceral reaction. Less than a fortnight on the ground, and Margolis found Herzberg irksome, if not insufferable.[19]

Margolis was besieged by people who wished to register their complaints. She listened but, in accordance with her mandate, took no action. Speaking with Herzberg, she learned that he operated on the premise "that they're all a bunch of crooks and thieves" who sought to game the relief system. For her part, she was persuaded

The main kitchen facilities at the Ward Road *Heim* for Jewish refugees. Residents wait in line outside for food distribution. *(United States Holocaust Memorial Museum, courtesy of American Jewish Joint Distribution Committee.)*

that only indigent circumstances would induce a person to endure such fetid housing as the *heims* offered.

Margolis did not act. But she argued. Looking critically at the eight thousand refugees who lived independently and received one meal a day from the CFA, she opened her campaign for an expansion of her responsibility. These clients were assessed according to a graded financial scale, which spurred resentment and did not serve its intended purpose. She wished she could interview them all, believing she could whittle the eight thousand down to two thousand who would receive the two meals a day they desperately needed.[20] This was Margolis's opening salvo. As we shall see, control over relief systems was a point to which she returned with increasing determination.

If Herzberg's dictatorial attitude impeded effective relief work, so did the fraught relations between sectors of the Jewish community and the aid organizations each supported. Initially, Sir Victor Sassoon, a Baghdadi Jew who had moved the headquarters of his family's business empire to Shanghai in the mid-1920s, had led the communal response to the influx of refugees. He had founded (August 1938) the International Committee for European Immigrants (IC), headed by a Hungarian-born Shanghailander, Paul Komor. Factional quarrels finally forced Komor and his supporters to resign in January 1940. Sir Victor then created a new IC, which Komor led. The remnants of the original IC became the CFA. In Margolis's view, the IC attended productively to refugee needs beyond feeding and housing, such as hospital care and occupational skills training.[21] Both the IC and the CFA focused on the central European Jewish refugees who had flooded into Shanghai in the late 1930s. The Committee for the Assistance of East European Refugees (EastJewCom, or EJC), by contrast, was established in March 1941 to raise and dispense funds to support Polish and Lithuanian Jews,

International Committee for European Immigrants staff at work, Cathay Hotel, Shanghai, February 1940. Seated at desks in the back: Paul Komor, his brother-in-law Jack Rogalsky (right, wearing glasses), and Eric Goldstaub (seated in the center). (*United States Holocaust Memorial Museum, courtesy of Eric Goldstaub.*)

especially the Orthodox among them. The IC and CFA were funded primarily by members of the Sephardic Jewish community, whose families had emigrated in the 1840s from India and Iraq to Shanghai when that city first opened to foreign settlement. The EJC was supported by Ashkenazi Jews, Russians who had fled the pogroms under the czar in the late nineteenth and early twentieth centuries and in the wake of the Russian Revolution.[22] While all three organizations stood prepared to work with Margolis, they would not cooperate with each other. "Local feuds existing long before my time will make any real integration impossible," Margolis predicted.[23]

She was correct: the feuds had existed long before she arrived. And the chasm this created in relief efforts on behalf of the central European refugees and the eastern European refugees predated her arrival, too. Authority was at issue; the CFA leadership was adamant in its desire to claim control. The per capita sum for needy refugees was at issue, too, with the eastern European Jews demanding a higher figure than that allocated to the Jews from Greater Germany, and the CFA arguing for equal support for all.[24] The EJC promptly protested to the JDC. If their proposed minimum sum of six dollars a head per month was unacceptable to the JDC, the EJC threatened to dissolve itself.[25] Moses Beckelman, then in Kobe overseeing the migration of Polish and Lithuanian refugees to Shanghai, soon weighed in. He contended that the higher maintenance cost requested for the eastern European Jews was objectively justified because the Japanese authorities in Shanghai insisted that the newly arrived refugees live in the French Concession, which was more expensive than Hongkew, where the German Jews were housed, and also because many of the latter were at least partially employed, while few of the eastern Europeans would be able to find work.[26] Beckelman did not take a position as to whether the CFA or the EJC should be charged with the responsibility for delivering relief, but the Jewish Community of Kobe (JEWCOM) did not hesitate to appeal to the JDC to subsidize the EastJewCom efforts. They urged accommodation of the eastern Europeans' Orthodox practice to prevent a great disruption to the foundations of their entire lives.[27]

These competing claims challenged the JDC policy of supporting only one local committee. But as the New York office held firm, the CFA and EJC reached a compromise. EastJewCom took responsibility for the Polish refugees and submitted bills to the JDC-subsidized CFA at the same per capita rate as was allocated for German Jews. And the Russian Jews raised money independently to increase the funding for the eastern Europeans in their charge.

While Margolis devoted much of her preliminary report to the problematic relief program in general and the specific issue of support for the Polish Jews who were slowly making their way from Kobe, she did not lose sight of emigration.[28] In this arena, too, the Shanghai community came up short in her estimation. Refugees pooled in the city, yet for reasons Margolis could not fathom, no organization or individual had developed a channel to the US consulate to help them immigrate to the United States. Contacting Consul General Frank Lockhart directly, she learned of his problems with lack of staff and competing demands on consular officials' time. That was a dynamic she could influence. A Mr. Smith had recently been put in charge of the visa division, with another officer to share the load. Margolis was encouraged by Mr. Smith's interest. Key to her goals, he stood ready to develop a work plan with her to deal with the eight thousand people currently registered for emigration. Looking ahead to all available options, Margolis bruited the possibility of a corporate affidavit for those who did not have sponsors but would prove model citizens if afforded the opportunity. Heartened by Mr. Smith's engagement, Margolis asked Pilpel for permission to open an office. "This will be absolutely necessary," she predicted, "for when we get going I shall be doing much more of the technical work than I did in Havana, and of course seeing people." She saw a plan taking shape with a six-month timeline. "International conditions allowing, I feel satisfied that the main purpose for which I came to Shanghai will be attained."[29]

New York's consent was one issue, finding premises another. Local feuds narrowed Margolis's options for office space; she could not work on the premises of one of the organizations without alienating the others. Nor could she locate suitable space in real-estate-poor Shanghai. Her room at the famed Cathay Hotel (built by Victor Sassoon and opened in 1929) became her work quarters where she reviewed documents and interviewed candidates for immigration. It was not the best situation: "I'm living on the job twenty four hours a day and I don't like it."[30] She made do, and within a fortnight had identified the key weakness of many of the visa applications and had devised a remedy. Reviewing a number of dossiers, Margolis noted that the problem rested with the affidavits of support. From conversations with the applicants, she realized that most had only a dim idea of what constituted persuasive documentation and thus could not properly instruct friends and relations who sought to help with these affidavits. Deploying the insights she had gained from the files, Margolis developed ten suggestions on how to compose a robust affidavit. "This list must not be circulated," she emphasized. Essentially telling sponsors what to say and how to state it, Margolis's "cheat sheet" was to go to a single National Refugee Service caseworker assigned to Shanghai immigration, whom affiants could contact directly.[31]

If, on behalf of her clients, Margolis back-channeled information she had gained through her access to consular files, she also attended to her connection with the American officials. "The relationship with the Consulate couldn't be any nicer than it is," she confided. They shared a goal and looked forward to moving refugees out of Shanghai in short order.[32]

Margolis's hopes were soon dashed. The work with the consulate was running smoothly, she reported (18 June), "but we're getting nowhere fast." Both officers assigned to the visa section were inexperienced, and "being new and insecure they're bending backwards on technicalities." They lacked perspective and were flummoxed by legal details that a more seasoned person would ignore. Time might have changed that, but time was not on their side. Margolis had heard that Washington was poised to announce new impeding instructions.[33]

The rumors proved correct. Fearing that the Nazi regime might coerce Jewish refugees into spying by threatening their families who had remained behind, the State Department instructed consuls as of 1 July to deny visas to applicants who had close relatives living in German-occupied countries. Parallel reasoning led to a ban on applicants with relatives in the Soviet Union or Italy. These new rules had a devastating impact, since nearly all refugees had family members who had not been able to leave their home countries.

Margolis had spent her time in Shanghai developing a constructive relationship with the consulate and instituting a new system to work through the bottleneck of visa applications. But the "close relative clause" brought her efforts to nought. As she put it, "What I supposedly came out to 'put over' is 'put over'; but what's the use of it all?"[34]

THE MOMENT Margolis learned her work would be stymied by the State Department's policy, she pivoted from the project she had been brought in to do to what had been her central concern since she arrived: relief and her role in its delivery. She loathed the CFA leadership's values and the way it did business. "All the local Committee cares about is to make sure the money comes from N.Y. every month; and that they be left in peace," she observed in a letter to Pilpel on 2 July. She named Herzberg "Dictator #1; and Mr. Ellis Hayim, Chairman of Housing and Disbursement . . . Dictator #2." Far from deploying their social status and communal authority on behalf of the refugees' welfare, they used their power punitively. "The result is that any refugee dependent on the Committee who has the starch to talk back gets his relief suspended." Fear forced thousands of people into passivity. "Now I understand the look of absolute hopelessness on the faces of the people in the Camps [group shelters]," Margolis observed.[35]

None of this was new information. A fortnight earlier (18 June) she had sent Pilpel a handwritten private note as well as a report for the file. The CFA's treatment of the refugees in its care "is much worse than I want to put into an official report," she confided. And

she could do nothing about it. Margolis's career had been defined
by her successful resolution of challenging situations. In Shanghai,
she saw the structural problems that hampered relief efforts, but
the JDC leadership had not granted her the authority to address
them. "Never ever will I say 'yes' again [to a JDC assignment] in
such a hurry," she warned. Her personal life was equally trying. A
thirty-eight-year-old single woman without friends or congenial colleagues, her daily life was as "lonesome as can be." In closing, she
confessed, "I hate Shanghai. But I'll see it through."[36]

Margolis's analysis and the arguments she adduced to Pilpel
remained consistent. Relief efforts in Shanghai were a "mess." Using
the then-common but derogatory term for an unskilled Chinese
laborer, she complained that Herzberg's "approach to the refugees is
a combination of coolie and German dictatorship." She understood
that the picture she presented wasn't a "very pleasant one." But it was
not her problem to solve. As often as Margolis reminded Pilpel of
the JDC leadership's responsibility and her own role as a dutiful field
agent who respected the boundaries of her mandate, she expressed
her frustration just as frequently. One sentiment followed the other.
"My own conscience is beginning to bother. . . . Here I am, obviously sent out to handle just the Shanghai situation and to stay here
for the purpose of working it out; and I refuse to do anything about
it. It's a little ridiculous."[37]

Neither Margolis nor the JDC executive addressed why her
scope was confined to emigration. Looking at assignments and gender, however, points to a ceiling for her as a woman. Beckelman, for
example, was not so constrained in his operation in Vilna. Then, too,
Margolis referenced him to verify her assessment of the CFA, opening with "Beckelman can bear me out," as if his (male) agreement
provided needed validation.[38] Evidently, the New York leadership
was not prepared to empower a woman to take over the totally male
realm of Shanghai relief. But clearly, Margolis was not prepared to
accept the limitations they imposed. And every time she expressed
such a willingness, she promptly undermined her own obeisance,
calling it "embarrassing" or "ridiculous."

As the weeks passed, she grew increasingly vexed. Relief was "given on an entirely personal and unintelligent and inefficient basis," she wrote in exasperation (17 July 1941). Holding that the CFA leadership needed to be discharged or reshuffled, she knew that if allowed to take over, the reorganization and education process would claim her time and energy. Isolated and feeling "stuck out here," she was prepared to return to the United States. She had been pushed to the limit of what she would tolerate as a professional.[39] Not taking chances on mail delivery, Margolis sent a cable the following day: "Please believe my reluctance step in but situation makes total passivity impossible," she declared. "Must have your backing and support."[40]

Every letter reiterated her assessments and each adduced additional problems. Margolis had long argued that their clients were fed poorly and housed worse; they got little clothing and nearly no medical care. Finances were not the issue. The problem was that the JDC funds were not used effectively on behalf of the refugees. The core obstacle was the CFA's attitude: "The refugees were all no good; they had to be treated with an iron hand." The situation on the ground cratered. Antagonism ruled. Margolis sought to convey the dysfunction to Pilpel; passion, not reason, shaped decisions, even by groups as fed up with the CFA as she was. "As far as the IC [International Committee] is concerned, it's just enough for the CFA to turn a person down for them to automatically accept him." Margolis found herself responding just as irrationally. "I can hardly blame [IC chairman] Komor, because, with all this so called objectivity, I feel the same way. It's just enough for Herzberg to say a fellow is a scoundrel for me to be sure he's pretty decent."

Offering a slew of examples to add weight to her charges, Margolis turned to actions taken by Ellis Hayim, chairman of the CFA's Housing and Disbursements division, who wielded his power arbitrarily, leaving visas to languish because he found the applicant unworthy of the immigration transportation cost. "He decided any way he likes, depending on any number of unpredictable factors," she fumed.[41] She adduced a specific instance a few days later. A young couple, the Wolfskehls, had fled Wiesbaden (Germany) for Shanghai in April 1939. Within half a year, he had found work as a salesman and she as a waitress. Eager to immigrate to the United States, Frau Wolfskehl secured an affidavit of support from a cousin in San Francisco. The couple was interviewed by consular officials in Shanghai, and they and their application were found acceptable. They were to return in two days with the eighteen-dollar visa fee, which, the cousin assured them, was on the way. But Hayim did not believe them and refused to release CFA funds to front the sum due. They offered their possessions as security, but he spurned the gesture. Desperate, they turned to Komor, who gave them the visa fee. Furious that the Wolfskehls had found a solution, Hayim called the consulate to cast suspicion on them. They were reinterviewed and their visa application was denied. Struck by the impact of this arbitrary, irrational action, Margolis cautioned, "Many a refugee's destiny is dependent on such a person."[42] Whim trumped reason, with Hayim exerting his power merely because he was in a position to do so.

Margolis was in an impossible situation. She realized that the New York office might have valid reasons for its reluctance to empower her. At the same time, however, she believed that the JDC executive minimized her concerns. "I have the feeling from the last few cables that you probably think I'm unduly excited about something which really isn't so serious," she remarked. Gendered interpretation being as it was, Margolis undoubtedly was correct. Demanding that her reports (and she) be taken seriously, she declared, "I'm truly not excited." She was an experienced professional, she reminded Pilpel, and in her best professional opinion, the relief situation in Shanghai was dysfunctional.[43]

Margolis had little scope for productive activity. By the end of July, the close relative clause that had taken effect at the start of the month had cut emigration to a trickle. "Am really not very useful," she admitted.[44] She continued to hope that working with the consulate, she would be able to effect the departure of a small number of refugees. But the whole operation was not what she, the JDC, or the visa division had envisioned. Their timing was wrong. As Margolis lamented, "It's just a shame that I am a year too late."[45] Perhaps she should return to the United States, she wondered in a cable to Pilpel. What did he advise?[46]

USEFULNESS WAS ONE CONSIDERATION in the decision to leave Shanghai. Risk to life and limb was another. Germany had invaded the Soviet Union on 22 June 1941, and many worried that war would come to Shanghai. Joe Hyman, executive vice-chairman of the JDC, raised the possibility with Avra Warren. Most particularly, he was concerned that as a woman Margolis was especially at risk. Warren agreed, noting that a man would be able to attach himself to the US consular staff and leave with them; a woman could not. Why the consulate could not absorb a woman was not clarified. But everyone seemed to accept this as fact, and Warren and the JDC decided that Margolis should proceed to Manila at the earliest date possible. If the situation quietened, she could return to Shanghai to reactivate emigration efforts.[47]

By the time of this interchange, it was nearly impossible to secure a spot on a ship to Manila. Margolis packed and waited until she finally got a reservation (15 August) on the *President Harrison*. Laid up with an infected toe, she wrote a detailed report to Robert Pilpel that summarized her observations and reiterated her chief requests. Her diagnosis: the CFA saw the refugees as a most unwelcome burden. The leadership, she asserted, "probably wouldn't care too much if several thousand were bayoneted into the Whangpoo. So much less for them to worry about." She decried Ellis Hayim's imperious stance and irrational decisions. The Wolfskehl case was just one example of a larger pattern of behavior, she declared. Refugees who did not need financial support were allocated transportation funds, while others who were indigent were denied help. Hayim's decisions depended on his mood, she declared. And if Hayim proceeded erratically, Herzberg was an autocrat who "beat the coolies" when he worked for Hapag and now treated refugees similarly: just "substitute the word refugee for coolie," she advised, using the pejorative term for emphasis. Margolis could not tolerate either the CFA's attitude toward the refugees or the way its relief programs were run. The refugees looked to her for help she could not give. "It's like being a soldier in a front line trench without a gun." With no way at that point to help the refugees, she was going to Manila "to await further instructions about the work in Shanghai." If New York agreed to the reorganization of the relief work and wanted her to take charge of that project, she would need full support: a detailed cable to the CFA advising them of this decision; written instructions to her; and another person to help with the task. She did not wish to return to Shanghai without explicit authority to implement change.[48]

Her arguments prevailed. Previously deaf to her analyses, or simply not finding them compelling enough to warrant a change in policy, the home office was sufficiently startled by her rationale for departure to review the situation anew. The JDC leadership had assumed she left because she felt vulnerable. They now realized that frustration spurred her departure. Should she be asked to return? The executive board easily reached a consensus to urge her to take up her position in Shanghai again. Acknowledging her skills, experience, and insight, the leadership would not presume to give her directions. They relied on her to effect a new mandate: to work with local individuals and committees to reorganize refugee aid activities until the Shanghailanders were competent to run the new systems. The New York office estimated that the training and transfer process would take three to twelve months.[49] And with that, the discussion pivoted to the persistent problem of the Polish refugees arriving from Japan who were championed by the Vaad Hatzalah. Established in November 1939 by the Union of Orthodox Rabbis of the United States and Canada to rescue Polish rabbis and yeshiva students who had fled to Lithuania, the Vaad Hatzalah brought great pressure to bear on the JDC for preferential treatment of this sector of the Jewish community.[50]

Having gained her point, Margolis hastened to tell the JDC what the project entailed: The committee needed fresh leadership and personnel, and the operating procedures as well as the day-to-day systems, including distribution of food and medical care, had to be dismantled completely and constructed anew. The changes she envisioned required a trained professional (or two) who could direct the whole enterprise and develop local talent to be able to take over. She suggested her colleague Manny Siegel, with whom she had worked in Buffalo and Cuba. With one other person trained in relief and community organization, she predicted, she could develop a functional system in six to eight months.[51] Poised to leave Manila, Margolis pressed the New York office to advise CFA chairman Michel Speelman of her new remit to ensure she had the power to effect change without opposition.[52]

In addition to drafting these plans, Margolis turned her attention to the immediate issue raised by the New York office: the Polish refugees. Addressing their needs was now her problem to solve. The original arrangement between the CFA and EastJewCom had held for some months, during which only 100 to 150 Polish Jews had transmigrated from Japan to Shanghai, and many did not need financial assistance. Still, the CFA and EJC remained at odds. The CFA, for instance, demanded that the Polish Jews accept quarters in CFA camps. The refugees, backed by the EJC, refused. If they could manage independently at the same cost, EJC argued, they were entitled to do so. Margolis agreed. "The CFA had no logical objection," she pointed out, "except that they can't stand anyone refusing to take their orders."[53]

Animosities between the two committees ballooned in August 1941 when they learned that hundreds of refugees were due to arrive. Forbidden by the Shanghai Japanese authorities from housing them in Hongkew, a district in the International Settlement where many refugee Jews had located in the 1930s, the CFA scoffed at the order.[54] The EJC pointed out that they, Russians and Poles, were immigrants themselves with no extraterritorial rights in Shanghai. They could not risk defying the Japanese. Unable to help their coreligionists, they informed the CFA that the refugees were entirely in that committee's care.[55]

Margolis faced both the Polish Jews' needs and the discord between the CFA and the EJC immediately upon her return from Manila in October. CFA's Herzberg was waiting at the jetty as she left the ship, ostensibly to report on his discussions with the EJC, but in fact to pan them. He "spent fully three hours telling me what an unco-operative, unreliable bunch the EJC were and that the CFA has concerned itself with the whole problem of the influx. This is absolutely untrue." The CFA had done nothing to prepare for the Polish Jews, except print cards that were handed to the refugees as they disembarked, instructing them to register at the EJC office.[56]

About half of the one thousand Polish Jewish arrivals were rabbis; the other half were yeshiva students and their teachers, including the entire Mirrer Yeshiva, which had remained an intact

Students and teachers of the Mirrer Yeshiva study in the sanctuary of the Beth Aharon Synagogue on Museum Road in Shanghai. (*United States Holocaust Memorial Museum, courtesy of Rabbi Jacob Ederman.*)

community throughout the war. The CFA quartered the rabbis in an old synagogue with dirty mattresses on the floor. Thanks to the unflagging efforts of Meir Ashkenazi, chief rabbi of Shanghai's Ashkenazi community, additional housing was identified. And arguing that maintaining Orthodox observance cost more than secular life, Rabbi Ashkenazi bargained with the CFA for a direct allowance of five US dollars per person per month.

Now empowered by the JDC to rationalize relief and to coordinate efforts, Margolis began a series of meetings with the CFA, the EJC, Rabbi Ashkenazi, and representatives of the Mirrer Yeshiva, because that community would not accept Ashkenazi as a spokesperson for them. Her efforts yielded some success: Ashkenazi agreed to work through the EJC, and the EJC agreed to serve as a subcommittee of the CFA, responsible for the eastern European refugees. It fell to the EJC to investigate the cases of these Polish Jews and to offer basic relief to the extent of a five-US-dollar monthly subvention, which the CFA would reimburse with JDC funds. With the CFA responsible for housing and food, the EJC once again began to raise money to cover the Polish refugees' other costs. Still, they continued to refuse to pool resources. "It is useless to ask the EJC to contribute their monies to the CFA," Margolis remarked. And she added parenthetically, "(I can't ask them to do it, because I can't blame them for not trusting the CFA in their management.)" Margolis herself took on the supervision of both committees and served as liaison between them.[57]

Captain Herzberg may have waited for her at the dock, eager to present his case against the EJC, but he was equally eager to challenge her authority. Within a week of Margolis's return, he sent an opening salvo to her, complaining that her secretary, Mr. Glueckmann, had ordered a full accounting of all CFA medical personnel, noting position and salary. Mr. Glueckmann, Herzberg argued, had no right to tell them what to do.[58] If Herzberg thought he could intimidate Margolis, she quickly disabused him of that notion. "The time had come to make an issue of it and I did," she explained later to Pilpel.[59] To Herzberg, she replied, "Please remember hereafter that I am not one of the 'refugees' dependent on the 'Committee', and therefore do not have 'to take it' without a reply. I don't believe I need to point out that the relationship between the 'Committee' and myself as representative of the 'Joint' is quite the reverse." She did not need to explain or even respond, she observed. She was now charged with a new task, the situation had changed, and the dynamic of their interaction had shifted. Her role with the JDC gave her every right to any information from any source she deemed necessary.[60]

Margolis had copied in Michel Speelman, who, as the CFA chairman, tried to defend Herzberg by gaslighting her and resorting to gender stereotypes. "I think you are over-sensitive," he suggested, "because on reading Mr Herzberg's letter, I do not find anything offensive in it."[61] Margolis replied immediately, setting boundaries and insisting upon her authority. She was to have joined a committee meeting at noon that day to discuss the Shanghai relief budget, and she hastened to say she would not, since Herzberg would be present. "I'm truly sorry that you can find an excuse for his letter to me. Were I 'over-sensitive' as you put it: I couldn't have stood by these past months and watched his treatment of the refugees."[62]

Vested with JDC authority, Margolis spoke frankly to Speelman, telling him that Herzberg "is totally incompetent and limited. . . . His idea of 'co-operation' is to give orders for the other fellow to follow." Failure to do so is "labeled as 'unco-operative'." The result: a refugee staff "who 'yes' the Captain to keep their jobs." Perhaps worst of all, "the only people who get relief are those who haven't enough 'guts' left in their beings to contradict [him]." Her learning period was over, she told Speelman. It was time to correct the problematic areas in the relief system: the camps, the refugee investigation department, and the hospitals.[63] Yet, as she explained to Pilpel, she had to proceed carefully. While she appreciated that the incident "brought things to a head finally," she was reluctant to step in too authoritatively because doing so would offer the local people an exit ramp. "They feel absolutely no responsibility themselves," she reminded him. Neither she nor Manny Siegel (when he arrived) would take over "the executive's chair."[64]

Margolis continued to address the needs of the nearly fourteen thousand Jewish refugees who required assistance, to negotiate between the CFA and the EJC, and to encourage efforts to raise funds in Shanghai rather than look to New York. And the process continued to be fraught. Her perspective on the problem and her commitment to finding solutions differed radically from that of the CFA leadership. Planning the December 1941 budget, for example, Herzberg noted a projected shortfall of 270,000 Shanghai dollars ($13,500 USD at the time; $276,282 USD in 2024) for the month. How was the committee to address this difficulty? He suggested that they kick people off the aid program. Herzberg readily acknowledged that well over five thousand refugees would suffer grievously from this harsh step. But, he argued, the CFA had supported them for three years and more and no longer had the funds to do so. There was, he asserted, no alternative. Margolis was aghast at his proposal. Rather than deprive helpless people of food, more money had to be raised. Meeting that need, she told the CFA executive board, was the "normal responsibility of any Committee into whose custody 13,000 human beings have placed their welfare."[65]

This constituted progress: Margolis had opened discussion about communal obligation. And the EJC, which had begun to function as a subcommittee of the CFA, had tackled fundraising energetically, asking individuals for donations and hosting a socially and financially successful ball. Still regretting her lack of authority upon her original arrival in Shanghai, she was nevertheless on the path to fulfilling her mandate.[66]

WITH THE JAPANESE ATTACK on Pearl Harbor and, on the other side of the Pacific, their occupation of the whole of Shanghai, her plans evaporated. How was she to help the refugees in a city under siege? Unlike other American operatives, whose relief efforts morphed into urgent emigration initiatives from Europe, Laura Margolis's work arced in the opposite direction. She had been sent to Shanghai to help with the immigration to the United States of Jew-

Japanese naval forces parade along Nanjing Road in Shanghai, 8 December 1941. *(Courtesy of the Leo Baeck Institute, New York.)*

ish refugees who had found their way to that port city. The close relative clause had slowed that work to a trickle. The Japanese bombing and America's entry into the war brought it to a stop. The refugees were trapped in the city under Axis control, and so were she and the recently arrived Manny Siegel. Charged with the relief operation less than two months earlier, Margolis's mission changed again and appeared even more impossible. The refugees faced critically important immediate needs of food, housing, medical care, and education that stretched into an uncertain future.

Planning for wartime disruptions, the JDC leadership had authorized Margolis to borrow up to two months of allocations. Communicating through Moses Beckelman in neutral Paraguay now that war had cut direct contact, the New York office extended the emergency funding to six months.[67] The Japanese, perhaps to avoid disorder and unrest, allowed enemy nationals to continue to live and work in Shanghai. Still, while permitted to raise money using the JDC name, Margolis did not have the funds in hand. And while permitted to carry on operations, the CFA lacked the money to do so. At Margolis's suggestion, Michel Speelman, Ellis Hayim, and D. E. J. (David Ezekiel Joshua) Abraham, a leading member of the Sephardic community, called upon Captain Koreshige Inuzuka, the Japanese official charged with Jewish affairs, to apprise him of the refugee situation. "He listened to their story, but his only response was that he would have no dealings with any of these three men, who prior to Pearl Harbor had constantly defied him," Margolis recalled in a confidential report to the JDC leadership, written from memory upon her return to the United States at the end of 1943. "Capt. Inuzuka virtually threw the men out of his office."[68]

Responsibility for securing Inuzuka's interest in the refugees' predicament fell to Margolis and Siegel, and Margolis drew on the goodwill of her relationship with the Japanese official to engage his cooperation. The agreement she and Inuzuka reached may have been a logical conclusion to the situation in which they found themselves, but achieving that end rested on a track record of amicable social encounters. "My luck was that having met Inuzuka on several occasions socially before the war, I was not snubbing him," she reflected.

Inuzuka lived in the penthouse of the Cathay Hotel, where she and Siegel also had rooms. "So I simply phoned upstairs and asked him if I could see him, and he very cordially invited me to tea." Margolis recalled speaking very frankly with him. "You and I now represent two nations fighting each other, but we have a job to do." Inuzuka had to maintain calm; he could not afford hunger riots. Margolis undertook to prevent disturbances if he permitted her to borrow money legally on the JDC's guarantee of repayment after the war.[69] Inuzuka agreed, on condition "that Mr. Siegel and I take over the entire administration of the refugee program." Inuzuka also stipulated that Margolis report the lenders' names to him. Finally, he charged Margolis and Siegel with dissolving the CFA, and he insisted that they fire Herzberg, "with whom he had had many previous clashes." Ellis Hayim, she noted parenthetically, had already been arrested.[70]

Funding was key. Accepting Inuzuka's conditions, Margolis sought loans from neutral nationals against the total $180,000 USD guaranteed by the JDC. No one stood ready to help. Abraham's position, for example, was that "since the Japanese took Shanghai, they could also worry about the refugees." Margolis continued operations day by day, but by mid-January she had reached a dead end. Help came from an unexpected source. "It was just at 6 P.M., January 15th that a reporter from the Shanghai Times came to see us." If Margolis's professional path in Shanghai before Pearl Harbor was shaped by the irrational (intra-communal feuds, sectarian loyalties, personal antipathies), it was shaped by the unpredictable as well thereafter. In this case, knowing that the Japanese did not want publicity, she had not sought news coverage and would not have approached a journalist of her own volition. But she grasped the opportunity when it fortuitously came her way. "Hungry, Starving Refugees in Hongkew" read the Shanghai Times headline the following morning.[71] Other news outlets picked up the story. Loan offers from Shanghai residents soon followed, including one for $10,000 USD from a Mr. Kaufman, a German Jew, and another for the far greater sum of $138,500 USD from Jacob Shriro, a Russian Jew.[72]

While these transactions ensured some months of stability, Margolis aimed to reduce costs as well. She learned from Abraham Levenspiel, a Polish Jew and engineer long resident in Shanghai and deeply concerned about the refugees' welfare, that the CFA's kitchen boilers were highly inefficient. According to his calculations, of the 60 Chinese cents each meal cost, 50 cents went to coal consumption and 10 cents to food. A new steam kitchen—structure, pipes, and fittings—with the capacity to feed ten thousand people at one sitting would cost 100,000 Chinese dollars ($5,000 USD at the time; $102,327 in 2024). But the technology depended on a type of boiler that was impossible to purchase in China. By chance, Victor Sassoon's Cathay Land Company had two such steam boilers, and Margolis asked to borrow them. Her request was declined, possibly because Sassoon, a British citizen and thus an enemy national, no longer had the right to dispose of his property without permission from the Japanese authorities. And it was they whom Margolis approached next, tapping her social network to do so. Levenspiel was acquainted with Carl Brahn, a prominent German Jew whose good friend, Mrs. Nogami, worked in the Gendarmerie, the Japanese army's military police. Mrs. Nogami was able to obtain the requisite removal permit. With the boilers in her possession, Margolis constructed a new, much more economical kitchen. Contacts and a fair bit of luck had made the project possible.[73]

Margolis moved forward on several fronts simultaneously. While raising money on JDC credit and building the steam kitchen, she also continued to reorganize the CFA and relief administrative systems and to shift the community culture toward accepting greater responsibility for the refugees. The CFA with which Margolis had contended prior to Pearl Harbor no longer existed; a new committee was needed. To bring in all who would want a say, Margolis contacted the leaders of the Sephardic community, the Ashkenazi community, and the *Jüdische Gemeinde*, which represented the German Jews. Forging a single committee forced unwelcome compromises. The Ashkenazi leadership insisted on the higher standard of relief for the Polish refugees that had obtained prior to Pearl Harbor. Margolis had agreed to that earlier, believing that they were simply in transit. Once they moved on, the discrepancy in their treatment would disappear. But that was no longer the case, and she now held that relief should be administered on the same per capita basis. The EJC remained adamant about the better provisions, and the EJC was key to local fundraising. Despite numerous meetings, they would not compromise at all and Margolis acquiesced, "even though we felt that this was wrong."[74]

Margolis faced myriad problems in a persistently unstable situation. Still, she had the support of the JDC, with which she continued to communicate through Moses Beckelman in South America. That ended on 21 May 1942 when she received a last cable "asking that we discontinue all contact." The US government forbade communication with Americans in enemy territory, which included Japanese-occupied China. The directive came as a shock. "Shanghai Jewry was entirely on its own and would from this point on have to survive on its own resources."[75]

Those resources had never been secure, and funding remained a problem. Margolis had asked the New York office for permission to raise another $180,000 through local loans but had not yet received a response when communication ceased. In the ensuing silence, she lit upon the idea of a conditional contract: she believed, but could not guarantee, that the JDC had the funds to meet loan obligations and would do so after the war. All but pledging the JDC to cover the money she raised was a difficult decision to make. But, she reasoned, if she "came out of this alive, fine. If the JDC is then displeased, they can fire me. But in the meantime, we have money to help the refugees."[76]

Human resources remained a problem, too. Having trained local people to take over the CFA administration, Margolis and Siegel resigned from their positions on that committee in early July 1942. But the CFA itself did not have long to live. The Japanese arrested many of its leaders, and although they were soon released, fear spurred every member of the committee to resign. Margolis and Siegel promptly created a local JDC committee to handle matters pertaining to the Joint and appointed Brahn as chair, even though she considered him "a very unreliable, frustrated, sadistic person with a strong desire to dominate and show his power over those dependent on him." He was selected "simply because of his influential contact with the Japanese." She felt she "had no choice." While they organized a local JDC committee, two of the wealthier refugees, Erhard Pulvermacher and Alfred Silberstein, established what they called a "Kitchen Fund." Margolis had doubts about them, too. Keen, capable, and energetic, Pulvermacher and Silberstein also tended toward an insular leadership style and did not seek help from or share authority with anyone outside their inner circle of friends. By early September, they had taken on the responsibility for the refugee program in Shanghai. "The situation was very tragic," Margolis observed, "but we had no alternative, since no one was ready to step in and take over."[77]

If financial and human resources were not secure, neither was the liberty of stateless persons. The Japanese authorities issued a proclamation (18 February 1943) ordering all stateless persons who had come to Shanghai after 1 January 1937 to move to a designated area in Hongkew by 18 May. This forced transfer affected about fifteen thousand refugees, increased crowding, and robbed many who had established businesses of their livelihoods. Enemy nationals—any member of the Allies—had lost their freedom of movement even earlier. The Japanese began to intern them in November 1942. Siegel was picked up on 31 January 1943 and sent to Pootung, an all-men's camp. Margolis's turn came on 25 February; she was detailed to the Chapei camp, a school campus outside of Shanghai that had been damaged during the Sino-Japanese War. Some fifteen hundred people from all the allied nations were quartered there. Margolis shared a room with forty women. She volunteered for farmwork and kitchen duty and, as mail was permitted, she kept in touch with Siegel and abreast of the situation in Shanghai through a prearranged code. Still, the lack of privacy wore on her. Determined to find an exit route, she stopped eating and, weak and pale, was transferred to Shanghai General Hospital in July.

Once again Margolis's social life and personal relations stood her in good stead. The medical director was an Italian physician, Dr. Vio, whom she had met on a number of occasions. He proved willing to follow her lead and claimed that she was so ill she could not remain on the general ward. Speaking with her quietly, he explained that she could have a private room, for which he needed permission from Tokyo, or she could choose the semi-private option, which he was authorized to allocate. Opting for the latter, Margolis joined a young Russian patient, a woman whose lover happened to be a German Nazi employee of the German Bank of Shanghai. It was Margolis's good luck that, due to his status, the hospital administration allowed the young woman to receive visitors at any time. Margolis was not permitted any. It was also Margolis's good luck that the woman proved generous. "So what happened was that with the help of a German Nazi and a White Russian girl friend I was able to have all the visitors I wanted." Margolis's guests simply said they wished to see her roommate. They kept her apprised of the refugee situation.[78]

The news "was not very encouraging." Some months prior, the Japanese authorities had decided that they would communicate exclusively with Russian Jews. This triggered the establishment of SACRA, the Shanghai Ashkenazi Communal Relief Association. The Japanese dealt with SACRA, and SACRA dealt with the Kitchen Fund and the Shanghai JDC. In hospital, Margolis learned that the divisive "politics, personalities, and power drives" that obtained among the refugee relief leaders were exacerbated by feuds among the Japanese. Indeed, SACRA and the Shanghai JDC served as pawns in what Margolis called a "deep-seated political quarrel between two factions of the Japanese government," with the Office for Stateless Refugee Affairs under the Japanese Consulate backing SACRA, and the Gendarmerie backing the local JDC committee.[79]

Rumors that Italy would capitulate ended Margolis's hospital stay. Dr. Vio realized that if he became an enemy national, he, too, would be interned. Anticipating that he would no longer be in a position to cover for Margolis at the hospital, and learning that she was on the list to be repatriated in a citizen exchange between the United States and Japan, Vio urged her to return to Chapei. She met a final time with a few trusted community leaders to get "an absolutely last-minute up-to-date picture" with regard to finances, mortality figures, and the refugees' current conditions, and then went back to the internment camp. She did not wait long. With departure imminent, she sought a way to circumvent the authorities' prohibition against carrying out written materials. Margolis took "toilet paper and I wrote down all the facts and figures I had." She rolled up the contraband text "like cigarette paper" and, tucking it into the rubber waistband of her underpants, passed inspection before boarding the Japanese ship that transported the passengers to the exchange point in Goa.[80]

Margolis drew upon these notes as well as her memory to write an extensive report detailing Shanghai refugee relief efforts under Japanese occupation as of the day Pearl Harbor was bombed (8 December 1941, local time) until her departure in September 1943. "I sincerely believe that everything that could possibly have been done was done in order to save as many of the refugee population as possible," she concluded. "The handicaps were numerous and least of all these handicaps were the Japanese." Rather, the problem rested with the Jews, especially the pre–Nazi era residents. "We have in Shanghai . . . a group of Jews who have no social consciousness and no feeling of responsibility towards the community. Shanghai itself is not a̲ community." Then, too, as she had emphasized repeatedly in her letters and cables, she was a social work professional while the men charged with refugee relief did not qualify even as amateurs. "At no time did we have a real choice when it became necessary to appoint leaders and committees. We had to accept the best Shanghai had to offer. The best . . . were either men who accepted responsibility because they were forced to by the Japanese . . . or men or groups with strong power drives."[81] Margolis despised them.

She was a determined, single woman endowed with power as a JDC representative; they were men with traditional ideas about women's roles and their own importance. Yet she persevered. She figured out ways to raise the funds needed to maintain basic services for the refugees. In the midst of the occupation, she tackled the problem of modernizing the soup kitchen that served thousands of meals every day. And she found resourceful people to help her actualize her programs. "The group there should be able to hold out (on a very minimum scale of course) at least until the end of 1944," she wrote to JDC secretary Moses Leavitt from the *Gripsholm*, the

2

Swedish ship to which the repatriates had been transferred in Goa. "But all of that will wait for the telling. It is an epic story."[82]

IT WAS A STORY many were eager to hear. Margolis arrived in New York on 1 December 1943, right in time for the JDC annual meeting. She presented at the board of directors dinner on 4 December and delivered remarks at the Sunday afternoon mass meeting on 5 December.[83] The State Department, Treasury Department, and former New York governor Herbert Lehman, now secretary-general of the newly established United Nations Relief and Rehabilitation Agency (UNRRA), wanted to meet with her, too. "So we all went down on the train to Washington." And that "was when I got the story of what was happening in Europe—Auschwitz and the camps. I'd been so completely cut off, I knew nothing."[84]

The JDC leadership urged her to take a quiet assignment. It would have been contrary to her personality. "I just couldn't," she admitted. "I had to be in Europe." It was an emotional decision, spurred by her dismay and horror. She shipped out to Lisbon in March 1944, moving on to Spain for a short-term assignment to set up a Jewish refugee children's home while she waited for military clearance to travel to Sweden. With the orphanage established and the required papers in hand, she flew to Stockholm to start a parcel service to inmates in Bergen-Belsen and Theresienstadt. It took her four months of intensive effort from September to December 1944 to get that running smoothly.[85] January 1945 found her in London, again awaiting clearance, this time to go to France, which came through in March. The JDC had established an office in Paris by then, and Margolis was detailed to work in Belgium, the Netherlands, and Luxembourg. Her mandate was to help returning concentration camp survivors and to support the reestablishment of a Jewish community. "By January-February 1946 I was tired," she recalled. "I hadn't stopped going for years. I was so physically tired that at one point I had a breakdown," she confessed. "The emotional impact was terrific for me." The devastation and destruction she saw and sought to combat overwhelmed her. "I just couldn't breathe any more." She "knew the time had come for a long rest."

Margolis had wrought many constructive changes during the past seven years. And she was changed, too. She returned to the United States. From New York she traveled "to Havana and rested there, my first point of work for the JDC, but it was now a different Cuba and a different me."[86]

Europe, 1 January 1942

German-occupied
and German-allied
territory

Norway

Swed

Denmark

Ireland

United Kingdom

Netherlands

Germany

Belgium

Luxembourg

PARIS

Occupied
Zone

Switzerland

VICHY

GENEVA

BORDEAUX

Vichy France

MONTAUBAN

TOULOUSE

Gurs

Pyrenees

MARSEILLE

Italy

Rivesaltes

PERPIGNAN

Portugal

Spain

ROME

LISBON

Morocco

Algeria

Tunisia

0   250   500 miles

◆ FOUR ◆

MARSEILLE, 1942

Marjorie and Ross McClelland

ARJORIE AND ROSWELL (ROSS) MCCLELLAND stum-
bled into refugee relief work. Ross, a doctoral student in
comparative literature at Columbia University, had been
awarded a fellowship run by the American Friends Service Committee (AFSC) to research archival collections in Geneva related to international reconciliation. It was a wonderful opportunity that came at
the wrong time. In late spring 1940, after the German invasion of
Poland (September 1939) and western Europe (May–June 1940), the
US government no longer issued passports to travel to Europe for
academic study, not even to people like Ross, who had attended university in Munich in fall 1936 and the University of Perugia, Italy, in
1937. The AFSC promptly repurposed the fellowship and suggested
that Ross take over their refugee relief office in Rome. Marjorie, a
child psychologist with an undergraduate degree from Stanford University and graduate work in child psychology at the University of
Cincinnati and Yale University, gave up her position as director of the
Manhattanville Day Nursery in Harlem to join her husband. They
were twenty-six years old, married for twenty months, and eager
to undertake meaningful work together. The AFSC fellowship was

awarded to Ross, but both served as AFSC representatives (or "delegates," as they were called). Theirs was a shared commitment.[1]

It was also an adventure. "I am crazy to write because I've never had such a bombardment of new experiences to tell about," Marjorie confided to her family upon arrival by Clipper in Lisbon on 3 August 1940, the first stop on their journey to Rome. She relished the twenty-one-hour trip and the sights and foods and climate that greeted her in Portugal. Her pleasure, which Ross shared, stood her in good stead as the weeks slipped away with seemingly no progress in their quest for the transit and Italian entry visas they needed to travel onward. "Here we still are & when we will be able to leave no one knows," she reported (17 August). They enjoyed their "vacation" and they waited along with "all the other foreigners in Lisbon . . . some for visas & some for boats & planes," as Marjorie observed. Impatient some days, contented others, Marjorie and Ross shared the common experience: they waited. And they "pulled every string there is." Their efforts finally yielded the papers they needed, and they left Lisbon on 22 September. Their route took them through Spain, France, and Switzerland before they crossed into Italy, arriving in Rome on Sunday, 13 October 1940.[2] They had already learned an important lesson about the unpredictability of bureaucratic processes, which would prove useful as they navigated emigration hurdles on behalf of their clients.

The McClellands were charged with running the AFSC's small relief operation to help central European Jewish and political refugees hoping to sail to the Americas from Italian ports. Established in May 1940, the office opened just three weeks before Italy, with its fascist government, entered the war on Germany's side, and civilian shipping ceased. Still, the United States was not a belligerent; Quaker delegates from the United States could continue to operate in Italy, and emigration over land remained possible. There was a lot to do. Ross and Marjorie tackled cases left by the initial director, Howard Comfort, and as word of their arrival traveled through refugee circles, new clients turned to them for help. "So far we haven't had time to see any of the sights," Marjorie explained to her family

Marjorie and Roswell McClelland, Rome, 1940. *(United States Holocaust Memorial Museum, courtesy of Kirk McClelland.)*

(20 October). "In fact we just walk back & forth on the one street that leads between the office and our pensione & have been busy day & night." Most immediately, they needed relief funds to disburse. "I've been lying awake at nights worrying over what to do about this." Unlike the refugees they saw when in Lisbon, "these are people who literally have nothing and no place to turn." Many of the foreign Jewish men had been incarcerated in Italian internment camps, which Marjorie, betraying her ignorance and perhaps her innocence, suggested was not "so bad," as they at least had food and shelter. The women and children, by contrast, were forbidden to work yet unable to leave. The local Jewish community did what it could, but with American Jewish philanthropic funds now slowed if not stopped, it had little to offer. And in any case, relief was not the answer. Emigration was the sole real solution.[3]

Marjorie's analysis bolstered her commitment. "I feel sure there is need for the Quakers' work in Italy," she declared. She understood that entry visas were nigh on impossible to obtain and that in any case there was little transport out of Italy. But, she wrote, "I cling to the thought that any good done, no matter how small an amount, is that much the better." Her conviction grew even though, attending the American Church in Rome, she noted that "everyone is astounded to see two Americans arrive instead of leave & various people advise us not to unpack or settle anywhere except on a temporary basis."[4]

If Marjorie and Ross's move to Europe challenged their compatriots' expectations, Marjorie's dedication to relief work challenged social norms for a woman of her class. "I am not in a position to spend my afternoons going round and leaving cards on the ladies in the social group of American society in Rome," as she felt was expected of her. And so she made up her mind to do without those ladies, to allocate her time in accordance with the demands of her task. Both she and Ross focused their attention on the refugees. The number of clients climbed, as did the roster of countries from whence they came. With the German occupation of half of France in June 1940 and a national policy of collaboration in the other, some Jews and other targets of the Nazi regime who had fled to that country in the 1930s now slipped over the border into Italy and made their way to Rome. Ross, fluent in German, Italian, and French, interviewed the men and women who crowded into the AFSC office, while Marjorie attended to the extensive correspondence each case required. The dossiers mounted as refugees sought a way out: a spot on a plane to Lisbon while it ran; then news of a route opening up by rail from Torino. And always the quest for exit visas, transit visas, entry visas.[5]

Writing to her family, Marjorie expressed her chagrin and near despair and at the same time her appreciation of how their efforts to actualize their goals shaped her. "This work really breaks your heart; it's as though we were a small blotter trying to absorb a large pond of water," she admitted ruefully. Yet she was learning a great deal. "Certainly I have gotten more education in the four months in Europe than I ever got in four years of college." Indeed, their mission shaped them as a couple, too. "This opportunity to work together is a very precious one to me, as I think it is to Ross. Our work, our new experiences shared, and our sense of aloneness in a world somewhat alien, draw us even closer together," she reflected.[6]

As the months passed, visa requirements continued to shift, borders opened and shut, and ultimately emigration possibilities dwindled. In mid-February 1941, the Italian government temporarily closed the border. Spain refused visas to all men aged eighteen to thirty who came from belligerent countries, and all others had to wait at least a month. Foreigners were confined to the city in which they resided. And Portugal began to issue visas only from Lisbon and only with proof of a purchased ship ticket out of the country. Nor was there steady or reliable transport. As Marjorie observed, "the planes no longer go at all, and the train is very irregular." Marjorie and Ross carried on, searching for ways out and disbursing small sums to their neediest clients. "Our work proceeds busily, but the emigration situation gets more complicated daily," she acknowledged.

Their scope to help narrowed, and the home office in Philadelphia considered redeploying the McClellands. Might they be interested in Vienna? Ross saw such a move as another year's postponement of his studies. And Marjorie heard her biological clock ticking: "I would like to have a family before I am too old to have one." Still, they made a counteroffer: France, a useful posting for someone who aimed, as Ross did, for a position in the field of French literature. And "as they are doing a lot of work with children there now," Marjorie assumed (correctly, as it turned out) that her education and experience would stand her in good stead. However logical their reasoning, the driving motivation was emotional. They found refugee relief work riveting, and their former life plan paled in comparison. Indeed, Marjorie admitted, "the thought of the scholastic life really seems rather remote and somewhat uninspiring."[7]

The situation in Rome deteriorated while they waited for a response from Philadelphia. The Treasury Department blocked the transfer of funds from the United States to Italy, which meant they could not continue the operation. Equally ominous was the news that American consuls in Italy were to close their offices by mid-

July. It was thus "with sorrow, but without much surprise" that they received a cable from Philadelphia asking them to liquidate AFSC affairs in Rome and proceed to Marseille. Easier for the AFSC leadership to direct than for Marjorie and Ross to accomplish. There were decisions to think through and dilemmas to resolve. The case files were too heavy to transport; should they be destroyed or stored in case they might be needed in the future? What if they fell into hostile hands? A priest they trusted offered to store the documents in a convent, and Marjorie and Ross accepted gratefully. Then the Italian government refused exit visas to all Americans, and with French consular offices closed, they could not get visas for France either.[8]

Stymied but protected by their American citizenship, the McClellands empathized with their vulnerable clients—some stateless, some enemy alien, nearly all Jews—who asked what they could do now and to whom they should turn. All immigration to the United States stopped on 30 June, which robbed many of hope and was tragic news for those who were due to secure visas when the new quota numbers opened the next day. Other options, such as Brazil, to which more of their clients immigrated than to the United States, closed too. Refugees in Italy were "stuck here with no prospect of emigration anywhere . . . and nothing to live on," Marjorie worried to her family. "It is difficult to keep ourselves from brooding." Personal contact heightened her emotional engagement. It was "very different when you actually know the people involved, than it seems when you just read about the refugee situation." Assessing their efforts, they counted 108 people they had successfully helped to emigrate since they took over the Rome office in October. This was a comfort. But they wished the number were greater.[9]

MARJORIE AND ROSS brought the expertise they had gained in Rome to the AFSC operation in Marseille when they breached the visa logjam that had prevented them from leaving Italy. Arriving in early August 1941, they "plunged into the new work which is incredibly complicated and complex after our modest program in Italy."[10]

The American Friends Service Committee, established in 1917 to address humanitarian need during World War I, had expanded its operations during the following decades with centers scattered across Europe. The AFSC's French initiatives grew rapidly after the collapse of Republican Spain in 1939. Fearing Franco's fascist dictatorship, 465,000 people fled Spain for France in the first two months of 1939. That was almost the same as the 475,000 who had left Germany, Austria, Bohemia, and Moravia for France from 1933 until 1941. The French government responded to the Spanish refugee crisis by erecting camps on the Roussillon beaches, in the foothills of the Pyrenees, and at locations farther from the border.[11] Intended to be temporary, these internment sites soon became fixed, miserable institutions. Argelès, for example, located on the coast fifteen kilometers from Perpignan, housed thousands of refugees in temporary shacks. A contemporary account detailed the grim conditions:

> Later, frame buildings . . . were thrown together with one story and without floors, and in these the people were herded, the number to a shed being governed only by ultimate capacity. A shed . . . being occupied by from seventy to a hundred humans sleeping on the ground or rather on the sand, as no beds were available. . . . No lights or even candles are available, nor are there any windows [which] makes it necessary for the occupants to go to bed before dark. . . . [T]oilet facilities are few and far between.[12]

Inmates in camps such as Argelès needed help, and the AFSC and other philanthropic organizations allocated staff and resources to meet those needs.

The Spanish refugees began to return to their homes at the end of 1939, when the civil war ended and a degree of stability returned, albeit under a fascist dictator. The French government found a new use for the camps: to incarcerate enemy aliens, stateless persons, and people "under suspicion" arrested after the outbreak of war.[13] More refugees arrived when the Germans attacked the Netherlands,

Belgium, Luxembourg, and France.[14] Arrest and internment were
the order of the day. The camps bulged with people who had fled to
France to escape the Nazis. But when France fell, officials did not
open the gates to give them a chance to escape. Worse, according
to the armistice signed on 22 June, the French agreed "to surrender
upon demand all Germans named by the German Government in
France as well as in French territories."[15] It was sheer luck for refugee Jews in France that the Germans did not want them.[16] The Nazi
government had gleefully bid them farewell in the 1930s and did not
request their return in 1940.

The French prime minister, Paul Reynaud, resigned on 16 June,
and the eighty-four-year-old hero of World War I, Field Marshal
Philippe Pétain, succeeded him and sought an armistice. Agreeing
to harsh terms—among them, German occupation of the industrial north and west, including Paris, as well as the hinterland that
produced milk, meat, and grain—Pétain nevertheless was recognized as premier of the French State. Headquartered in the resort
town of Vichy, Pétain's government controlled an unoccupied "free
zone" that covered the grape-growing southern third of the country. So far as the Germans were concerned, now unoccupied France
served as a dumping ground for Jews from Alsace, Bordeaux, and
the Lower Rhineland districts of Baden and Saar-Palatinate,
with the forcibly expelled swept into the refugee camps by Vichy
French officials.

The demarcation line between occupied France and the free zone
divided the AFSC network, too. Previously central, the Bordeaux
office fell in the occupied zone, while operations in Toulouse, Montauban, and Perpignan were in the unoccupied zone, satellites to the
newly established (August 1940) headquarters directed by Howard
Kershner in Marseille. Like relief workers elsewhere, AFSC staff
sought to provide refugees with shoes and warm clothing, vocational
training and employment, and milk for their babies. Money transfers, small sums from relatives and friends to designated recipients,
who often had to be found as they had moved or been forcibly transferred from one place to another, was another key service the AFSC

delegates undertook.[17] Unlike relief workers elsewhere, AFSC (and other relief organization) personnel in the free zone were allowed access to the local internment camps. Indeed, social work teams from various philanthropies, including the French Jewish Oeuvre de Secours aux Enfants (Children's Aid Society, or OSE), the YMCA, Service Sociale d'Aide aux Emigrants (Social Service Assistance for Emigrants), Unitarian Service Committee, and Secours Suisse aux Enfants (Swiss Children's Aid) , were permitted to live in the camps on a voluntary basis. Thus, for example, according to a report Ross compiled, the forty-six hundred inmates in the Gurs camp as of January 1942 profited from seven social workers, while Rivesaltes with a population of fifty-two hundred had four.[18] The philanthropic organizations sought to improve camp life by providing additional food and clothes; offering medical and dental care; organizing kindergartens, schools, and clinics; and ameliorating the physical, structural

The women's section of the Gurs internment camp, December 1941. *(Roswell and Marjorie McClelland papers, United States Holocaust Memorial Museum, gift of Kirk McClelland.)*

conditions under which the inmates lived.[19] The social workers supported these initiatives. And they served a key function simply by being present: they were a link to the outside world, a sign that the inmates were not forgotten.

BY THE TIME Marjorie and Ross joined the Marseille office, it had a staff of forty and was still strapped for personnel. Marjorie was detailed to correspondence with Philadelphia on all the emigration, money transfer, and welfare inquiry cases, and she also became the information liaison between Marseille and the three branch delegations. It fell to her, too, to respond to the myriad requests from refugees' worried friends and relatives for news of their loved ones. Moving from their modest operation in Rome, Marjorie found the work in Marseille "tremendous and complicated, and confusing to the beginner."[20] Thanks to Ross's language facility, he was charged with the internment camp program, which called for communication with inmates, officials, and other philanthropic organization staff. It also called for robust contact with the branch offices. As Marjorie explained to Mary Rogers, associate director of the AFSC's Refugee Services Committee in Philadelphia, each of the satellite delegations was responsible for the camps in its region. "Perpignan handles Rivesaltes, and Toulouse handles Gurs, Recebedou, Noe, Vernet, and Rieucros." Ross supervised the camp program as a whole, in addition to attending to Les Milles, a camp in the Marseille area, and Hotel Bompard, a group home for camp inmates, transferred there shortly before they were due to emigrate.[21]

A report from the Toulouse delegation to the home office sketched AFSC camp work in unoccupied France in July 1941 and suggests the situation Ross found upon his arrival in Marseille. The Toulouse office was headed by Helga Holbeck, whom Burritt Hiatt (Howard Kershner's successor as director of the Marseille office) described as "big, aggressive, and speaks her mind instantly." Holbeck and her staff were committed to camp relief. "We want to impress upon you the necessity to continue our camp program (additional feeding system)," the report to Philadelphia began. Hoping that the AFSC leadership would be persuaded to renew financial support if they appreciated the aid that Toulouse offered, the author of the report depicted the circumstances on the ground. Delegates visited the area camps regularly and provided daily meals to the inmates. The account described the dire conditions inmates endured and the multiorganizational effort to ameliorate the situation. At Récébédou, a hospital camp for fifteen hundred elderly people, "every day at 4:00 an extra meal is given to all the people, except those who already get it from Secours Suisse." Noé, also a hospital camp for fifteen hundred people, benefited from the same feeding program. The report assured Philadelphia that harmonious relations existed between the AFSC delegates and French officials. Toulouse AFSC staff visited several times a week "and work in complete agreement and even at the request of departmental authorities." The Quakers served an afternoon meal to twelve hundred of the six thousand inmates at Gurs; the Secours Suisse, the Protestant Federation, and OSE were also active in that camp. And four thousand children at Rivesaltes, under the charge of the Perpignan office headed by (as Hiatt described her) "thin, quiet, self-effacing" Mary Elmes, were to benefit from an additional bowl of soup scheduled to start a few days hence. "It is of the utmost importance that the camp feeding scheme should be able to continue from September throughout the Winter, in order to prevent starvation and famine," the report emphasized. Tapping into sectarian pride, the author continued, "The Quakers are practically the only Committee that can enter freely all the camps and the stopping of our food would be a catastrophy [sic]."[22]

Philadelphia willingly supported its relief workers' programs in unoccupied France, highlighting them in its 1941 year-end report.[23] The annual statement foregrounded accomplishment, but hardships loomed large for the field workers. By that point, sixteen thousand adults and children filled the internment camps, and as winter took hold, their plight grew more dismal. "The internees are now going through a time of great suffering," Mary Elmes lamented to Philadelphia. The bitter winds of le Midi added to their misery. Focusing on Rivesaltes, now with a population of 1,379 children, 1,968 women, and 1,028 men, she observed, "They are cold during the night, they are cold during the day, and their food is served to them cold. They crouch in unheated barracks and have no extra blankets or clothes to protect them from the searching wind."[24]

With thousands of people requiring their assistance, Ross and Marjorie—like their counterparts elsewhere—paid particular attention to clients they had come to know or who had simply caught their eye. And while neither was antisemitic, if that person conformed to a philosemitic stereotype, all the better. "I had a rather depressing conversation today with a man [Wilhelm Dreyfuss] from the camp of Les MILLES whom I know fairly well in regard to his mother [Karolina] in the camp of RIVESALTES," Ross wrote to Elmes (20 January 1942). Karolina was sixty-eight, quite ill, and grieving the recent death of her husband, Wilhelm's father. Wilhelm, Ross explained, "was particularly concerned about his mother's welfare, displaying one of the more laudable Jewish traits of filial devotion." If Elmes could obtain any information about Karolina's condition, Ross "would personally appreciate" it.[25] And, if Mrs. Dreyfuss needed it, might she get the supplemental ration the AFSC offered? Spurred by an emotional attachment, Ross engaged more deeply with these inmates and their welfare than he did with the many others with whom he had contact. He took the time and energy to write to Elmes about them, which was no small thing. As elsewhere, human relations were sufficiently powerful to shape the aid offered.

IF ALL FORMS OF AID—food, clothes, medical care—helped, selection for immigration was transformative. And sympathies and antipathies colored emigration work in unoccupied France as everywhere else. As we saw in chapter 1, the United States Committee for the Care of European Children (USCOM), formally incorporated in July 1940 with Eleanor Roosevelt as honorary president, had teamed up with the Unitarian Service Committee (USC) to organize convoys of endangered children from Marseille. Martha Sharp had led the first effort, choosing the children and accompanying them from the south of France to Lisbon, whence the youngsters, chaperones, and Martha sailed to New York in December of that year. Martha saw the operation as a proof of concept and hoped to move forward with additional child transports. The USC held other priorities, however, privileging men with the experience and expertise to reestablish postwar democratic states.

USCOM thus turned to the AFSC to develop the initiative, starting (as we saw in the Introduction) with assembling one hundred children chaperoned by OSE employees Isaac and Masha Chomski to immigrate to the United States.[26] As the project took shape, an array of organizations participated, including HICEM (established in 1927 through a merger of the New York–based Hebrew Immigrant Aid Society, the Paris-based Jewish Colonization Society, and the Berlin-based EmigDirect), the Joint Distribution Committee, Secours Suisse, and OSE. Each had its own agenda and selection criteria. For OSE, nationality and age were key risk factors that advanced a case for emigration. Of the sixteen hundred children in their group homes, three hundred were German, Austrian, Czech, or Polish with parents in concentration camps; two hundred were from the Low Countries "who had lost their parents while in flight." As Ernst Papanek, director-general of OSE homes explained, these five hundred children "do not know what will happen to them if the Nazis enter that part of France where they are living." Then, too, "in France they are undesirable foreigners, growing up without any other outlook than that of going to a French concentration camp when they reach sixteen."[27] USCOM, for its part, was "aware of the great need of Jewish children" and wished "to make every effort to rescue these children." Still, the committee cautioned, "the plight of this group might obscure the need of other children." Eliding the targeted violence to which Jewish children were subject, USCOM argued that in "the interest of fairness" and to accommodate the various organizations involved, it would be best "to work out mixed national groups" of children aged five to twelve.[28]

The OSE leadership continued to worry about older children for whom time hovered as a determinative factor. Adolescents deserved special consideration, OSE wrote to their Quaker colleagues. "The child is considered an adult as soon as he or she reaches the age of 15," and worse, "this situation becomes more and more tragical as the child draws near the fatal age of 17—when he may be re-interned in a concentration camp."[29]

Time was a factor in any case, as Howard Kershner pointed out in February 1941 to his colleague John Rich in the Philadelphia office. His staff had composed lists of 308 children, of whom 295 were Jewish. For their survival, they needed to get out of France. And with shifting circumstances, moving them soon was essential.[30]

The Quaker leadership did not question Kershner's risk assessment or his exhortation for speed. They questioned the fact that so few non-Jewish children had been included. Reviewing the decisions made in Marseille, Margaret Frawley brought a Quaker home office perspective to bear. USCOM, she wrote to Kershner, "assume that you have reached the conclusion that Jewish children are most needy." That may be so, she acknowledged, but a "mixed group" would have served another function: it would have elicited "wider public support" and enlisted "more general interest in the plight of European children." The staff on the ground in France missed the larger picture. "The value of this program is not merely in rescuing a few children from the misery of present-day Europe but in centering public attention on the needs of children—and that means all nationalities and races."[31] Proximity to persecution offered a very different lens: for the delegates in the free zone, rescue trumped public relations. They aimed to save individuals, not to play the long game.

The first group of refugee children left France in June 1941. Numbering between 100 and 132, all of whom were Jewish, these youngsters and their chaperones traveled to Lisbon, where they set sail for New York on the SS *Mouzinho*, arriving on 21 June.[32] USCOM, OSE, and AFSC workers pressed forward with additional transports. Bureaucratic difficulties abounded, as did discussion of selection criteria—again religion, but also age and "intelligence and capacity to adjust to American life." Reviewing the composition of the June transport, Margaret Frawley reminded her colleagues in Marseille that "the presence of some non-Jewish children strengthens the United States Committee position as a non-sectarian group," and she suggested that they might not wish to partner solely with "groups caring for Jewish children" (presumably OSE). She noted the preponderance of teenagers in that first contingent, too, and understood the rationale for their inclusion. Still, younger children were preferable as they "have a better opportunity to identify themselves with life here."[33] Reflecting on their experience, and looking to the next transport, Frawley wrote again with additional advice: "If the selection is to be made on a basis which will bring the most able children, then your own responsibilities of selection are extremely

Jewish refugee children wait to board the SS *Mouzinho*, Lisbon, 20 August 1941. *(United States Holocaust Memorial Museum, courtesy of Milton Koch.)*

heavy." In short, "your own scrutiny of the children will need to be more careful."³⁴

Who had the authority to choose? Whose priorities took precedence? As USCOM's partner on the ground in France, the AFSC Marseille office assembled a second transport of forty-five children who sailed (20 August) from Lisbon on the *Mouzinho* and a third group of fifty-one who left on board the *Serpa Pinto* soon after (9 September). Still, in Kershner's view, OSE and the children in their care had an outsized role. His position had shifted over the past half year, and he was no longer persuaded that "we were doing the States a great service by sending over these children." Then, too, "if it was to turn into a 100% Jewish affair . . . it should be handled by the Jewish organizations rather than ourselves." And if it were "turned over to the Jews they will have hundreds of their own children available."³⁵

Kershner was correct on that point; Jews were desperate to emigrate. The German invasion of the Soviet Union on 22 June 1941 had inaugurated the Holocaust in the East. More than 1.3 million Russian Jews were shot that summer. Once Berlin decided that murder was the solution to what they saw as the "Jewish Problem" in the USSR, it loomed as the "Final Solution" to the Jewish Problem in all of Europe. Then America entered the war in December and Hitler passed a death sentence on all Jews. Writing in his diary about his Führer's announcement of "a clean sweep" to solve the Jewish Question, Minister of Propaganda Josef Goebbels remembered that years earlier, Hitler "had warned the Jews that if they again unleashed a world war, they would be destroyed." Now "the world war has arrived, and the destruction of Jewry must follow."³⁶

The AFSC staff in unoccupied France did not know that Berlin had committed to genocide; they were operating in Vichy France, where native Jews suffered political disenfranchisement, social isolation, and economic expropriation, and refugee Jews were subject to internment or forced residency. The Jews did not know either, but the assaults they suffered spurred them to prize a spot on an USCOM convoy. As Max Gossels, father of eleven-year-old Claus and eight-year-old Werner, wrote to the AFSC in Philadelphia once he knew his sons had reached Lisbon, "I hope that they have left Europe." He was clear as to what that meant: "I thank you for your help that my children are saved."[37]

The Gossels brothers were on the third and last USCOM/AFSC transport before America entered the war. Emigration efforts ceased as rumors swirled that Americans in the unoccupied zone would be repatriated. But that fear "has quieted down," Marjorie wrote to her friend and colleague Margaret Jones, "and there seems to be no reason why we can't quietly continue with the work, as long as funds hold out for it." Indeed, Marjorie hardly mentioned America joining the Allies in her letters. Endeavoring to help her loved ones picture her life with Ross in Marseille, she described their poor diet, the arduous process of keeping clean, and their much-mended attire. "Potatoes twice a day, turnips, cabbage, carrots, turnips, cabbage carrots," she reported. "Ross, unfortunately gets thinner and thinner, when he can't afford to at all." At six feet tall, he weighed 145 pounds. "I am losing some, but very slowly, and I could still afford to." Living in one room at the third-class Hotel Lutetia (and glad to have secured the accommodation), she and Ross were entitled to a single bath once a fortnight. Her "three precious pairs of woolen stockings" were "more darn than stocking."[38]

Unfazed by the lean conditions, Marjorie and Ross remained in Marseille. Offered a posting in Switzerland, they indicated their willingness to grow the Geneva-based operation. But not yet. It was "impossible to pull out of the work in Unoccupied France," Marjorie told her father on 15 March 1942. "The need constantly increases." She had "expected our work to become a liquidating program . . . but we still struggle against constantly growing odds."[39] Indeed, a fourth USCOM transport was planned, Marjorie wrote to her stepmother, Catharine Cox Miles, and while the AFSC would have preferred if an USCOM representative came to France to choose the children and get them off, the war scotched that plan. "We got a cable telling us to do another fifty and recommending me 'as trained psychologist' to select the children," she explained. As it transpired, "the other groups weren't really selected at all." Or perhaps they were selected without adhering to established criteria, which ruled out children with health problems, physical or emotional. "It seems that one epileptic and a number of behavior problems and questionable mentalities turned up amongst them," Marjorie clarified. If it occurred to her that a child with epilepsy might have much to offer or that youngsters who had endured life in camps and experienced the further assault of sudden separation from friends and kin might evince "behavior problems," she did not say. The concerns she discussed with Miles, an eminent psychologist herself, centered on formal professional aspects of the selection process. Lacking equipment and common languages, "I obviously will only be able to do a very half-baked attempt," she worried. Then, too, "almost all of the children available are Jewish, because the other parents just won't part with their children," while USCOM, which is nonsectarian, is "terribly anxious to get non-Jewish children too." Even nationality was an issue, with USCOM wanting "French, Spanish, Dutch, Belgian, etc. and what you can get is German, Austrian, Polish, and Czechoslovakian Jewish children." Marjorie did not elaborate as to why those children were "available" and not the others; she did not acknowledge the persecution to which they were subjected and the hopeless future they faced. Rather, she sought to represent her "country's interests"; she aimed to "pick out the most desirable children from the standpoint of mentality and psychological adjustability . . . a bunch that will make future good citizens."[40]

Marjorie embarked on a three-week tour of the internment camps and children's colonies, and what she saw moved her deeply. Relaying her impressions to her friend Margaret Jones in the Philadelphia office, she emphasized the importance of surveilling the situation on the ground. Her imagination fell far short of actual experience, she observed. Describing her visit to Rivesaltes with Mary Elmes, just a quarter of an hour drive from Perpignan, she found another "world in which is to be seen only endless rows of barracks" yielding an impression "of bleakness and bareness." Nothing grew. "There is only hard, bare, stony ground. There is no grass, no trees, nothing green." A fierce wind blew dust and sand and buffeted the children.[41]

Whom to choose? In the face of such misery, what criteria to apply? Marjorie reflected on her calculus of decision-making in a letter to Margaret Frawley on 22 April 1942. "It has all had to be done in a terrific rush," she wrote. "When your cable came announcing another convoy of fifty children and suggesting that I be given responsibility for selecting the children, it called for some deliberation." She "had hoped, originally, to spend several days in each colony ... observing the children at work and play, and talking to their teachers. In that way I had hoped to be able to make some sort of sound evaluation of the children, even though I was not able to give them intelligence tests, or make the selections on what could really be considered a sound psychological basis." But the sailing date shifted, and the children had to be in Marseille with their papers in order by 15 April. "The realities of my procedure were far different from my plans, because with the necessity for speed it was necessary for me to make a lightning tour of the colonies, choosing the children after only the most superficial consideration."

Marjorie set certain criteria. "I had in mind two basic considerations—the necessity for emigration and the desirability of immigration, of each child. I wished to satisfy myself (in so far as was possible under the circumstances) of the child's desirability as an immigrant to America—that he was a normal, at least averagely intelligent, adaptable child, who would be able to fit into an American family without too much difficulty." But life on the ground in Europe carried weight, too. "I also took into consideration the situation of the child here in France, for obviously not all cases were similar. I considered the children who had lost one or more parents, children whose parents had remained in Germany, or had been deported to Poland, children who were all alone without any family, have less future here and therefore have greater need for emigration [*sic*] to America than children of families who are all here."[42]

Thoughtful and rational as those considerations were, the essentially emotional nature of her decisions courses through short biographies she wrote about each of the children she selected for the convoy that left Marseille on 14 May 1942. Her descriptions of the

youngsters reveal that she chose children who appealed to her, priz-
ing the physically attractive, docile, and, if Jewish, not Orthodox.
Hannelore Berney, aged eleven, "is an attractive child, with lots of
personality." Henri Boleslavsky, twelve, "is obedient and coopera-
tive, very realistic and practical in the approach to life, and should
be easily adaptable." Twelve-year-old Savelly Chirman's "manners
and behavior show that he comes from a background of cultivation
and education." Doris Durlacher, aged eleven, was "a pretty, sweet-
looking girl" who "is obedient and docile, very easy to manage."
High-spirited children did not appeal, nor did the homely or plain,
and she did not choose them.[43]

In some instances, Marjorie picked children because she found
their mother sympathetic. Henri and Miriam Mass, aged six and
eight, respectively, were a case in point. Polish by nationality, Miriam and Henri were born in Antwerp, where their parents owned
a small restaurant. The family had fled to the south of France after

Marjorie McClelland holds Antoinette Steuer, a Jewish refugee
child, May 1942. *(United States Holocaust Memorial Museum, courtesy of
American Jewish Joint Distribution Committee).*

the Germans occupied the Low Countries in May 1940. The father, Samuel, was put to forced labor in January 1941. OSE placed the third and youngest child, four-year-old Hélène, with a French gentile family in Montpellier. The mother, Regina, and two older children were interned in Rivesaltes, where Marjorie met them. Regina Mass "seemed like a very nice, simple, earnest woman, very much concerned over her children. I thought it remarkable that she was so clean in the midst of the camp where cleanliness is so unbelievably difficult to achieve."[44] And what if Regina Mass had been disheveled?

Marjorie sympathized deeply with the victims. She cared about them, was sensitive to the assaults they had endured, and marveled at their resilience. "The thing that amazes me is how they can be so nearly normal children after the life histories they have gone through," she confided to Frawley. "Almost all of the group of Jewish children have passed through at least a year of concentration camp, have been uprooted from their homes, have seen their families separated, their parents die in camp, have had their existences robbed of all security, both emotional and physical." She worried if she "erred too much in my choices." And she passed on an exhortation: "As one gentleman from Ose remarked, 'Après tout, les enfants ne sont pas de la merchandise',—this was when we were having to decide who should go and who should not, practically on the spot."[45] The children certainly were not mere merchandise for Marjorie. "I have become very much attached to the children ... I'm fond of them," she confessed.[46] Yet she had to choose who would be granted the opportunity to escape. She was, as she said, "the formidable Dame Americaine who had the life and death power of deciding whether [a child] could have a future in America or must stay where he was with no future whatever to look forward to."[47]

At the safe distance of nearly a century, we assume that social workers such as she relied on a rationally developed rubric. We see the past, and the people who lived in that past, as two-dimensional and in black and white. We flatten them and what they did. Marjorie's record offers a fresh lens on the complexity of the decisions and choices she and others made. Age, gender, degree of religious observance, social class: all of these played a role in the calculus of selection. And so, too, did visceral reactions and connections to the people who sought help.

The May convoy included twenty-three Spanish children who were "among the best," as Kershner exulted to the Philadelphia office leadership. "I am sure you will be highly pleased with them. Many stand first in their classes."[48] Marjorie took a slightly different view. They were not selected by her, she explained to her family. "They are a very nice looking group," she acknowledged, "much prettier on the whole than the little Jewish [children], but I think not so bright."[49] Whether attractive or intelligent, the children constituted a mixed group, and USCOM, the Friends, the Joint, and OSE moved forward with a fifth convoy. Quickly organized, the group left Marseille at the end of June. Ernest and Richard Weilheimer were among those included. Their father Max wrote to Marjorie from internment at Gurs, and his words are a stark reminder of what was at stake in the selection process. Holding no hope of seeing his sons again, he thanked her "for what you have done for my boys." He cherished the thought that his sons "will go towards their happiness, free from perils, and that they will never in their lives have to submit again to so much unhappiness." And he concluded, "We had a family life of rare happiness and contentment—unfortunately it was too short! Again I thank you with all my heart."[50]

AN INITIATIVE to rescue children, the five USCOM convoys organized by the AFSC from May 1941 through June 1942 brought 336 youngsters to the United States.[51] The philanthropic organizations saw to most of their paperwork. By contrast, the masses of people desperate to emigrate faced the daunting prospect of navigating the obstacle course of affidavits, entry visas, exit visas, transit visas, train tickets, and ship tickets. Relief worker support was key to success. And here again spontaneous sympathy and other emotions spurred engagement. The social workers were aware of their fallibility, that their actions might be governed by visceral responses to their clients. Marjorie's predecessor in the Marseille office, Dorothy Bonnell, addressed this concern directly in a report upon her return to the United States. She urged delegates to "keep a sense of balance, proportion, and perspective." And she elaborated: "You have to ask yourself continuously am I giving too much time to X because he happens to have an attractive personality and is neatly dressed? Is Y getting too much attention simply because he has plenty of money? Do I tend to give Mrs. Z anything she asks for just because she brings her baby and it cries all the time till no one in the office can do any work until I get rid of her? (answer: Yes, I do!)"[52]

Bonnell's observations speak to the irrational motivations that spurred social workers to act on behalf of individual clients. But as we have seen, identifying the issue did not change the delegates' behavior with regard to their child clients—or, as the efforts to help an older couple, the Borchardts, reveal, with regard to adults. Marjorie opened the matter with an appeal to Margaret Jones to try to find affidavits for Adolphe Borchardt, aged sixty-six, and his wife Maria. Her interest in their case started in a conversation with her coworkers, she explained. "We were all bemoaning the fact that it so often happens that the undesirable people get the visas, while the ones you would like to see going to America are left behind. It is a phenomenon we all are familiar with, and we deeply regret that it is true that brassy, pushing people are the ones who manage to get the affidavits and the passage money, to become our fellow citizens, while the gentle, pleasant ones who do not know how to get the affidavits and the passage money, and how to put themselves forward properly, get left behind."[53]

Marjorie knew that Adolphe's age militated against success, but she found him such "a lovely old gentleman, very dignified and quiet," that she was moved to act. As the couple were evangelical Christians (of Jewish ancestry), Margaret Jones sent their file to Evelyn Hersey, at the American Committee for Christian Refugees in New York, where it got nowhere.[54] "I cannot turn this down now absolutely," Jones advised Marjorie, "neither can I hold out any real hope to you for them." Still, inspired by Marjorie's appeal, Jones wrote to

Dr. Robert Ehrenreich, listed by the Borchardts as someone willing
to recommend them. He did indeed recommend them, but he had
no affidavit of financial support to offer, nor did he feel able to pro-
cure one. What about the brother Alfred living in Switzerland or the
Baroness de Sinner (whom the Borchardts had listed as well)? Might
they be able to provide monetary help? Jones asked Ehrenreich. The
Philadelphia office did not leave it there. Adolphe Borchardt, a sci-
entist, had had contact with the Nobel laureate physicist Albert
Einstein, who had found refuge in the United States, and the AFSC
wrote to him too.[55] "I know that Dr. Borchardt is a very gifted man
who could—especially under present circumstances—be a valuable
asset to this country," Einstein replied. He suggested they "explain
the whole matter to Mr. Hiram J. Halle," inventor, philanthropist,
and part owner of the Gulf Oil Company, which they did. "I am
discussing it with several others some of whom may have personal
knowledge of Dr. Borchardt," Halle replied on 13 August 1942.[56]

By this point, the situation had changed on the ground in both
occupied and unoccupied France. The Germans introduced the star
marking on Jews in the northern zone in June 1942 and unleashed
ferocious roundups that swept through France that July and August.
The Holocaust had arrived in western Europe. Berlin planned to
deport forty thousand Jews: thirty-six thousand from the occupied
zone and four thousand from the free zone. Half would be French
nationals, half foreigners. To save face by protecting French Jews,
Vichy offered to increase the unoccupied zone quota with foreign
Jews. The Germans accepted happily. Less work for them: fewer
Jews to arrest and process in the occupied zone. The French did not
shoulder much extra work either; internment camps offered a ready
supply of alien Jews. French officials sorted and selected transit
camp inmates in a matter of weeks.

Well aware of these developments, Marjorie Page Schauffler,
who had taken over the correspondence in Philadelphia from Jones,
pressed Halle gently to help the Borchardts now that the Germans
were gathering up Jews. "I have not been neglectful," he responded.
Nor was he successful. Schauffler carried on, continuing to corre-

spond with an ever larger circle as each person sent her to others. Miraculously, a friend of the AFSC, Jean da Costa, a teacher at the Mary Wheeler School in Providence, Rhode Island, offered an affidavit of support. Only a secondary affidavit of support, an emergency backstop, was needed. Schauffler went back to Halle. Would he stand willing to furnish this financial guarantee? He was not. Schauffler found someone else who was. With all the paperwork in order, a successful conclusion to the quest Marjorie had set in motion seemed nigh. The scores of letters and unflagging attention were due to her championship of this couple's application, spurred by her warm appreciation of them. But while relief worker support was key to success, it was not necessarily sufficient. The situation in unoccupied France worsened and the Borchardts disappeared without a trace to this day.[57]

IF THE QUAKERS IN PHILADELPHIA grew alarmed that summer, the AFSC corps and all other aid organization personnel in France grew frantic. The aid organizations moved strenuously on two fronts: to intervene with the Vichy government and to accelerate the emigration of the regime's victims. Tracy Strong, general secretary of the World Alliance of the YMCA, secured an appointment with Pétain on 4 August and emphasized that deportations would have a negative effect on American public opinion. But Strong felt that Pétain was not able to absorb the import of the matter.[58] Donald Lowrie, a Quaker who worked for the YMCA and had joined forces with Strong on this matter, had an audience with Pétain and his secretary Jean Jardelle a few days later. Donald's wife Helen had worked with Martha Sharp on the first convoy in 1940, and he was emotionally as well as morally and professionally invested. In the meeting, Lowrie stressed that the Quakers and YMCA had operated in unoccupied France for two years and had helped ten thousand refugees to emigrate and wanted to continue with their work. He spoke, too, of his worries about their clients' changed status and its harmful effects on them. Seeking to put Lowrie off, Pétain asked whether he would remain in Vichy for a week or so for a response. "Monsieur le Marechal, the first train is leaving today," Lowrie shot back. "Well, then, I will speak to Laval this afternoon and you may telephone M. Jardelle tomorrow morning for my reply." Head of the Vichy government Pierre Laval, in the meantime, had got the same representations from Ross McClelland and his boss, Lindsley Noble, the interim director of the Marseille office. All to no avail. When Ross phoned Jardelle, the secretary told him that there was no reply because Laval had been called to Paris and that Pétain had much to do.[59] As these events unfolded, the first deportation train left for the East.

Still the aid workers did not give up. A concerted effort by representatives of USCOM, the AFSC, and the JDC pushed the State Department to grant one thousand visas for children.[60] By this time, deportation trains rolled regularly. "Between August 5 and 15 about 3500 inmates of internment camps . . . were seized and deported to occupied France and supposedly later to the vast ghetto the Nazis have set up in eastern Galicia," Donald Lowrie reported to Strong on 22 August. "We now learn that during the next three weeks 15,000 more foreign Jews are to be handed over to the Nazis."[61]

It was clear to all that emigration was the last best hope for rescue. The American consulate in Marseille prepared to issue fifty visas per day, and the AFSC grew confident that the one thousand visas would be increased to five thousand. Utterly intrepid, the Friends in France carried on without regard for their own safety, as Burritt Hiatt, newly arrived from the United States on 11 October 1942 to serve as the AFSC director, observed. His colleagues in Marseille "have for so long found life an affair of being frightened rather than being hurt that they have become inured to the danger of a situation that alarms me," Hiatt admitted in his logbook at the end of his first day. "They have an unconcern about French officials and about the power behind the French officials that I have not learned."[62]

The aid workers faced old dilemmas: which children were eligible and how to determine selection? Logistical problems beset them. With their eyes on the clock, they planned processing schedules against the calendar. How long would it take to bring the children to Marseille, photograph them, see to their medical examinations, and obtain American visas, Spanish and Portuguese transit visas, and French exit visas? How many children could the organization handle per day?[63]

Vichy officials raised the ante when they suddenly insisted that "only real orphans" might leave. And worried that the arrival of one thousand children in the United States would present an unflattering photo opportunity, Vichy insisted on a first convoy of five hundred. If it was met without fanfare, the second group would be permitted to depart.[64] Resolute, the aid workers carried on. A first group of 150 children arrived in Marseille on 8 November. But the unpredictable intervened; time was not with them. American and British forces launched Operation Torch that very day, invading Vichy-controlled Morocco and rupturing diplomatic relations between Vichy and the United States. "All exit visas were cancelled and the frontiers closed," Hiatt lamented in his diary. Still, the Friends staff continued to move forward until the German army occupied the free zone on 11 November and all Americans were ordered to leave the Departement Bouches-du-Rhône, in which Marseille sits, by 5:00 p.m.[65]

"Possibilities departure from unoccupied France practically non-existent now," a JDC representative in Lisbon cabled USCOM in New York the next day. "All emigration from France to the United States has now stopped and children will not be permitted to leave," a cable of 13 November announced. "Have cancelled all transportation arrangements." Later that day: "All telephone communication with Marseille now suspended."[66] Nazi German and Vichy French policy and practice were responsible for the deportation of the Jews. But on the ground during those days in November, the unpredictable factor of time prevented a greater number of rescues.

BURRITT HIATT had no idea when he arrived in Marseille to take charge of the Quaker office that the Germans would occupy Vichy France just one month later. He had been sent from Philadelphia to lead local operations. Success depended on the organization in

the head office (now grown from a staff of forty, when the McClellands had arrived fourteen months earlier, to fifty), its relationships
with its branch offices in Toulouse, Perpignan, and Montaubon,
and its ties with other philanthropic committees. Hiatt found that
there was much to be accomplished. As we have seen with regard
to other charitable institutions, AFSC intra-organizational fissures
abounded. "I sense administrative difficulties here after only one full
day in the office," Hiatt admitted in his diary.[67] Resolved to confront
the problems he found, he wondered how the operation functioned.
Who set priorities? How were initiatives financed? What fueled the
delegates to carry on with their relief and rescue activities?

Hiatt embarked on a tour of the Perpignan, Toulouse, and
Montaubon delegations. He expected a rational business model.
He found organizations structured on a very different and much
more intimate basis. "Both the offices at Perpignan and Toulouse
are the work of personalities rather than of systems and institutions," he observed. Yet both branches functioned effectively. Irish-
born Mary Elmes, head of the Quaker delegation in Perpignan, and
her staff ran an essential food program for children and provided
emigration information to Rivesaltes transit camp inmates. They
supervised four children's residence colonies, and they had instituted a slew of services for refugees: medical equipment, clothing
depots, milk distribution, a work room for women. Yet Elmes felt
"out of touch with the home office in Marseilles," Hiatt reported.
"She feels that important decisions affecting her work are not sent
to her rapidly enough for her to adapt her program to them." And
"when she makes proposals to the home office in Marseilles she
has difficulty in learning what has become of her suggestions." In
Hiatt's view, insufficient attention to personal relationships had
proved corrosive. Letters from the Marseille leadership, who held
greater authority and power than local personnel, had engendered
hurt feelings: "It was a case of a poor job of interpretation from the
main office—something that might have been cleared up during a
personal interview without leaving any aftermath of rancor such as
correspondence often leaves."[68]

Hiatt found the situation in Toulouse even worse. The local head, Helga Holbeck (a Dane), "creates in her staff a rivalry with Marseilles which leads them to feel that Toulouse is a unique delegation much hampered by being under the control of the Marseilles delegation. A great deal of her time and thought goes into this competitive effort to make the Toulouse office dominant and self-sufficient."[69] Still, the Toulouse operation, too, was successful. The staff ran feeding programs in the Gurs, Nexon, and Noé internment camps and organized money distribution to inmates who received funds through the Quakers from family or friends abroad. They helped hide Jews in Toulouse. And, when asked, staff stored deportees' valuables in the hope that they would return to claim them.

Like Elmes, "Helga Holbeck says that suggestions from the field to the Marseilles office meet with too much delay there while people are suffering." Holbeck went on to confess "that on one occasion the Toulouse office under her leadership established some relief activities independently and without the consent or knowledge of the office in Marseilles. She financed the projects with funds she herself had raised. . . . She was, of course, severely reprimanded for this by Marseilles but she still feels that the emergency needs of the situation and the lack of understanding on the part of Marseilles, justified the venture."[70]

Well aware that the heads were women and that all the Toulouse personnel were female, Hiatt ascribed his inability to intervene constructively to gender. "If the staff of the Toulouse office were men, I might feel that I had more chance to twit them about some of the complications or exaggerations of their position." But he also understood that he had misjudged the skills and competencies he needed to be effective. He had assumed he would need "endurance for physical hardship and courage to face the external dangers to the organization." He soon learned, however, that he needed the "ability to bring internal harmony among devoted and over-driven workers so that they will all be striving for the same objective and all will give each other credit for striving toward the same goal."[71]

Hiatt was correct. Like Kershner, his male predecessor in Mar-

seille, he did not have the managerial skills needed to improve relations between the head and branch offices. Nor did he have the time
to develop these competencies. In retrospect, however, what is amazing is not what the AFSC failed to do, but what it accomplished. Per-
severance, courage, commitment, the financial resources sent from
the home office in the United States—all of these counted. The
Quaker relief and rescue workers carried on, even as Vichy officials
grew obdurate, even as the Germans came an inch away.

And then the inch disappeared. The Germans swarmed over
the demarcation line on 11 November. The American Quakers were
caught unprepared. According to Hiatt, the Philadelphia office had
urged Marseille to obtain and store Swiss entry visas at the American consulate in case of just such an emergency. Ross was detailed
to this task but, absorbed by the unfolding tragedy of mass roundups and deportations and negotiating with Vichy officials to permit
children to emigrate, he had not attended to his colleagues' documents. By the time he contacted Bern, the French-Swiss border had
closed.[72] At that point, the US government deemed all American
activity in France as trading with the enemy, and communication
between Americans at home and in France was illegal. Permitted
by the Germans to live in seven *départements*, the ten American
Quakers remaining in France chose the nearest to Marseille, the
Vaucluse. They soon joined the diplomatic group in Lourdes, and by
mid-February, all, including Hiatt, had been sent to Baden-Baden,
Germany, where they were interned until released by a prisoner
exchange in February 1944.[73]

Marjorie and Ross were not among the American Quakers
in Marseille when the Germans occupied Vichy France. Having
delayed their departure for Switzerland through the terrible summer
of deportations and desperate attempts to secure Vichy agreement
on the USCOM convoys, they had moved to Geneva in September,
where they continued to deliver aid to refugees who had managed to
flee to that alpine state. The new AFSC posting, Ross explained to
his family, would "give us a chance to continue in the type of work
which we believe to be the only real solution to the problems created

by the hate & strife spreading over the world now." However firm their convictions had been when they set out for Italy from New York, however strongly they believed, as Marjorie had written to her family, that they both were "doing what we think is right to do," their resolve was even greater now.[74] As Ross maintained, "Someone must go on bearing a testimony to the power of simple goodwill, love & kindness & not abdicating his inner convictions to join in the general self-destruction & mutual slaughter."[75]

Without transition, Ross followed that very Quaker-inspired thought with a glance at his putative career. "It may also be possible for me to find time for a few hours of work a week at the Univ. of Geneva collecting material for my somewhat belated thesis."[76] It was just a nod to his former self, to their former aims. Their work had proved transformative—transformative for those they had helped and for themselves. Ross never returned to his thesis, nor did he pursue an academic life. Marjorie never again held a school leadership position. Ross went on to develop refugee relief programs in Switzerland; Marjorie gave birth to the first of the couple's four children in February 1943. When President Roosevelt established the War Refugee Board (WRB) in January 1944 to carry out a newly adopted (and very belated) American program of relief for and rescue of Nazi victims, Ross was selected as the WRB representative in Switzerland.[77] He commuted to Bern while Marjorie, then with a one-year-old and pregnant with their second child, ran the AFSC office in Geneva. Ross's appointment to the WRB was the beginning of a long career in government service. Marjorie's AFSC deployment in Geneva was her last.

Europe, 1 June 1943

German-occupied
and German-allied
territory

Norway

Swede

Denmark

Ireland

United Kingdom

Netherlands

Belgium

Germany

France

Switzerland

Pyrenees

MARSEILLE

Italy

Portugal

Spain

LISBON

Morocco

Algeria

Tunisia

0   250   500 miles

FIVE

LISBON, 1943

Elisabeth and Robert Dexter

LISABETH DEXTER[1] had recently returned to the United
States from Lisbon, Portugal, to help her daughter Harriet,
who was soon to give birth. A devoted mother, Elisabeth nevertheless would not remain long. "It is good to be home again, and
yet, almost immediately one starts thinking of getting back to one's
work," she wrote in the April 1943 issue of *Standing By*, the Unitarian
Service Committee's (USC) monthly bulletin.[2] Her husband, Robert Dexter, who as executive director of the USC's European operations had remained in Lisbon, needed her to manage their many
clients. A reported eighteen thousand refugees had fled across the
Pyrenees when the Germans occupied Vichy France in November
1942.[3] Many had found their way from Spain into Portugal, and more
had followed in their wake. These desperate people claimed Elisabeth's attention.

Neither Lisbon nor refugees were new to Robert or Elisabeth
by 1943. Head of the American Unitarian Association's (AUA)
Department of Foreign Relations since 1927, Robert had pressed
for denominational action when Britain and France undermined
Czechoslovakia by signing the Munich Pact on 30 September 1938.

Returning from a visit to Czechoslovakia in August, they were home only a few days when radio reports and newspaper articles broadcast Hitler's threats against that country. Robert was in New York when the Munich agreement was announced, and he recalled that he was stunned by it. He moved quickly, catching the overnight boat train to Boston to meet with AUA president Frederick M. Eliot the next morning. Robert had no definite plan. And indeed, as he reflected, "it took some faith to believe that a comparatively small religious body could be of use when great nations had failed." Still, eyeing the American Friends Service Committee (AFSC) as a model, the AUA sent Dexter to Prague on a fact-finding mission; he was joined by Robert Wood, a Philadelphia Quaker.[4] As we saw in chapter 1, their report had induced the AUA to establish the Commission for Service in Czechoslovakia and to appoint Martha and Waitstill Sharp as the first commissioners.

The Sharps had shipped home in September 1939. Encouraged by their success and faced with the Germans' invasion of Poland and the war that unleashed, the AUA embarked on a more comprehensive service initiative. The first meeting of what was initially called the International Unitarian Refugee Committee was held on 15 November; AUA treasurer Seth Gano was elected chair and Robert Dexter secretary. "It is the desire of the Board to build up in the Unitarian denomination a real organization of service to carry on the work so effectively accomplished by the Commission for Service in Czecho-Slovakia," Gano declared.[5] "Dr. and Mrs. Robert C Dexter" were soon appointed "accredited representatives" of the AUA, authorized to go to Europe to investigate the possibilities for and feasibility of humanitarian relief work.[6] Unpaid and untitled professionally ("Mrs. Robert C. Dexter" had earned a doctorate in history from Clark University in 1923 and chaired the history department at Skidmore College for some years), Elisabeth was nonetheless an authorized investigator.

The Dexters' three-month trip from 27 January to 29 April 1940 took them to nine countries and proved instructive about the refugee situation, they reported. A few general observations emerged from their exploratory tour. Most nations had closed their borders and, as emigration was thus far more difficult than before the war, the core task was to deliver short-term aid to refugees already living in each country. This included, as all relief organizations wherever they operated realized, the provision of food, clothing, shelter, medical care, help with individual problems, and opportunities for work and recreation. Unitarian policy privileged the political and cultural elite, and the Dexters found that "refugees, although of every type, have a disproportionately large number of intellectuals and leaders—teachers, clergymen, politicians, writers, and civic leaders of all sorts." These people's social networks opened possibilities for flight, and knowing they were at risk pushed them to act. "They, more than peasants and manual workers, have the contacts and the initiative to escape; and they are in far greater danger in a totalitarian country." As the Dexters saw it, "They are the people whose leadership will be sorely needed in the day of reconstruction." Noting that the scope for service was great, Elisabeth and Robert advised the Boston office to send a couple to Europe without delay, designate Paris as their headquarters, and pay "special attention to students and other intellectuals."[7]

The Unitarian officers again looked to the Sharps. After formally establishing the now-named Unitarian Service Committee in May and confirming Robert Dexter as its executive director, AUA president Eliot wrote to Waitstill "to invite you and Martha to go to France as our ambassadors extraordinary." Eliot warmly acknowledged the contribution of both wife and husband. "There just aren't words to express my feeling of admiration and deep respect for what you two people have done and for what you <u>are</u>," he beamed. "My dream for the Unitarian Service Committee centers in you, and it is a very big dream." Yet his letter was addressed to Waitstill alone.[8]

Martha and Waitstill accepted. They planned to go to Paris as the Dexters had recommended, but the city fell to the Germans on 14 June 1940 and they pivoted to Lisbon, the capital that had already gained the reputation of "Europe's sole window to the west."[9] Portugal, a neutral if fascist country run by the dictator António de

Oliveira Salazar, admitted refugees who offered proof of onward passage; ship tickets and valid entry visas for another country earned the harassed travelers a thirty-day transit visa. Opening an office in the Hotel Metropole in Lisbon's central Rossio Square, Martha and Waitstill undertook to relieve the bottleneck of endangered people in Marseille by moving them through Spain to Portugal, where they shipped out across the Atlantic or the English Channel.[10] Waitstill returned to the United States in September with the famous German Jewish novelist Lion Feuchtwanger, whom he and Martha had helped to spirit across the French-Spanish border and into Portugal.[11] Martha, working with YMCA operative Helen Lowrie on the first USCOM (United States Committee for the Care of European Children) convoy, brought that project to a successful close and accompanied twenty-seven children and five adults to the United States in December 1940.[12]

With Waitstill returned to America and Martha tied up in Marseille that fall of 1940, the AUA asked Charles Joy to take over the Lisbon operation. Joy was well known to the AUA leadership. An ordained Unitarian minister, he had held a number of positions in the Unitarian management, including serving as vice president from 1929 to 1937. Fluent in German, Spanish, and French, his linguistic competencies would help him communicate with clients, and his years in office had honed administration skills that would support running a relief and rescue initiative. Arriving in Lisbon in September 1940, Joy tackled the knotty problem of refugee aid. Some thirty to forty people sought help at the USC office every day. Joy's experiences and interactions with them helped him clarify a key difference between the Unitarian and Quaker rationale for engagement, which he explained to his colleagues in Boston. "We are not trying to help both friend and foe alike without distinction," he observed. Unlike the Quakers, the Unitarians did not espouse a neutral stance. On the contrary: "I conceive our work to be the strengthening of the side which we believe to be right." If the United States held a politically neutral position in the fall of 1940, the denomination did not. "I consider our committee to be an ally of all the forces of democracy and freedom and righteousness, and opposed to the subversive forces that would destroy our most precious heritage," Joy declared. The AUA leadership agreed unanimously and adopted his position as policy to shape where they would invest Unitarian money and delegate labor, and whom they would seek to save.[13]

Refugees continued to stream into Lisbon. The demands on Joy grew so arduous that eight months later Boston asked him to come home (April 1941) for a half-year respite and sent out Robert and Elisabeth Dexter. Robert went first, leaving on 12 April. According to Elisabeth, he found more work to be done than one person could handle. She yearned to join him; "I was crazy to go," she recalled. Politically and professionally committed to refugee aid, she longed to take part in the Lisbon project "but family affairs made it less easy" than when they had gone on their exploratory tour. Daughter Harriet had recently got engaged and planned a fall wedding. Son Lewis sought to join the armed services despite defective eyesight and was not yet settled in his personal life or his career. Bowing to the social convention that attending to such matters was maternal work and to the very real pull of her sense of responsibility to her children, Elisabeth remained in Massachusetts. Robert, for his part, "knew these complications and did not urge me to come." Happily, however, "my children told me of course not to stay home on their account, and so with divided feelings I agreed to go." Her ambivalence vanished: "As soon as the die was cast I felt better."[14]

Eager to engage the challenges of refugee assistance and the adventure of channeling her energies in fresh directions, Elisabeth took the next available Lisbon-bound ship and landed on 17 June. She went to work straight away, taking responsibility for a full roster of cases.[15] And she was hampered by the same problems American relief and rescue workers faced elsewhere: ever more restrictive visa regulations, government blocks on financial transfers, and a paucity of transport. Elisabeth faced the hurdles with equanimity. "There were of course difficulties," she acknowledged. "If the situation had been easy we would not have been needed."[16]

Refugees of no fewer than twenty-seven nationalities sought

USC help in July and August alone. Few were Jews. Two Jewish agencies operated in Lisbon, the Joint (American Jewish Joint Distribution Committee) and HICEM. These organizations served most of the Jewish refugees except, Elisabeth explained, for "what we called 'politicals,' people who were offensive to the Gestapo on account of their political activities or prominence." The Joint, HICEM, and the AFSC, which also was active in Lisbon, sent "politicals" to the USC. "These were the hardest to help, but we felt they were the most worthwhile, and were glad to take charge of them."[17]

The Heinrich family was among Elisabeth's German political refugee clients. Profession, social class, political affiliation, and age shaped their history—as did the irrational element of emotional response. In Germany, Dr. Heinrich had been a professor of modern history and Mrs. Heinrich (as Elisabeth called her; no first names given for either) a newspaper reporter, and both opposed the Nazi regime. Their daughter Ilse went to school, where she refused to raise her arm in the obligatory "heil Hitler" salute. The family soon found themselves in trouble and fled together to Paris. Father and daughter arrived; by a quirk of fate Mrs. Heinrich was caught and subsequently imprisoned. Released after some months, she managed to join her husband and Ilse. The fall of France pushed them to flee again, this time over the Pyrenees into Spain. There the three were arrested. Incarcerated, the parents fell ill; Ilse did not, and the authorities, presumably taking pity on a child but possibly because they saw no gain in holding her, let her go.

Ilse somehow made her way to Lisbon. And there, "quite on her own initiative she wrote a letter in halting English to an American official of whom she had heard in Spain, asking if he would please try to get her parents out of prison," Elisabeth recounted. "It was not his business," she explained. Indeed, "technically he ought not to have had anything to do with it; but he was touched by the letter." The emotional response Ilse's note triggered proved pivotal; it prompted him to inquire about the family, who had come to the Dexters' attention as political refugees worthy of USC help. Assured by Elisabeth's

attestation that "they were excellent people," he took action and succeeded in gaining their release.[18]

A charming story about a helpless child's imperfect appeal to a
powerful adult, it also illuminates the role of the irrational. The official acted because he was touched. Had he not engaged emotionally,
he would not have pursued the matter. Logical reasoning, rational
discourse, did not dictate his actions; sentiment did.

While the Heinrichs' story speaks to the role of emotions, the
Pollacks' speaks to the unpredictable: luck, timing, and fortuitous
circumstances. As Elisabeth related, Dr. and Mrs. Franz Pollack
were an older couple who had fled from Vienna to Geneva, which
served as a resting point while they assembled their papers to go to
the United States, where they had two sons and many friends. The
Pollacks turned up at the Lisbon USC office, weary from their journey through Spain and in despair: they had tickets on a ship that had
postponed sailing until 25 July, but their American visa would expire
on 14 July. Time was not with them. To no avail, Robert Dexter tele-
phoned the American consulate to request an extension. Worse still,
the Pollacks had another son who remained in German-occupied
territory. The newly instituted "close relative clause" applied as of
1 July and, as Elisabeth observed, the Pollacks "could not hope for
a new visa."

Elisabeth and Robert took another tack. They called the American Export Line office; one of its ships was to sail the following
day, but it was fully booked with a long waiting list. Still, they
phoned again the next morning. This time the agent, a Mr. Trautman, suggested that the Pollacks go directly to his office at the harbor. When they arrived, however, he declared that "the boat was
really sold out, and unless someone dropped dead. . . ." And then
Mr. Trautman changed course abruptly. Telling the Pollacks he did
not "think there is a prayer," he nevertheless said he'd check once
more. And without explanation or a bribe, space was found. With
USC staff help, the Pollacks completed the passenger paperwork,
collected their belongings, tied up loose ends, and arrived at the

Jewish refugee children and youth at the port of Lisbon just before
their departure for the United States on 17/18 April 1943. (*United
States Holocaust Memorial Museum, courtesy of Ike Bitton.*)

dock on time for their departure at four o'clock that afternoon.[19]
Luck was with them.

The Pollack case shows, too, that Elisabeth and Robert,
unschooled in the particulars of refugee casework in Portugal when
they arrived in spring 1941, proved resourceful and tenacious. They
learned on the job, quickly adapting to the rhythm of the city and
developing robust office systems. Perhaps more important, they
soon appreciated the precariousness of their clients' lives. They realized, for instance, that simply getting married posed numerous complications. Few refugees had all their papers in order, which meant
that they could not obtain a marriage license. More dire: "for such
a one and for a 'wanted' refugee, even with perfectly correct papers,
the attempt would involve considerable risk." The German presence
hovered, even in Portugal. Refugees, Elisabeth observed, "cannot
afford to make their whereabouts a matter of public record, lest the

ever-watchful Gestapo hunt them out." Involving the state bureaucracy, "being born, getting married, or dying, bring extra danger."[20]

THE DEXTERS' term of service in Lisbon ended in fall 1941; they
returned to the United States in October, and Charles Joy took over
in Portugal. Robert estimated that there were some three thousand
refugees in Lisbon at that time, but no one had a precise figure.[21]
Portugal's thirty-day transit visas and policy of admitting only people with valid entry visas elsewhere and ship tickets to get to those
destinations meant that the numbers fluctuated as the transients
arrived and departed. Then, too, those who overstayed the thirty-
day limit or who had never got a transit visa and had slipped into the
country clandestinely were not included in the count.

The Japanese attack on Pearl Harbor and America's entry into the
war changed the situation on the ground in Lisbon. As Joy reported,
the trickle of refugees in fall and winter 1941 "bore no resemblance
to the turbulent stream of fall and winter 1940." With little to be
accomplished in Portugal, he suggested closing the Lisbon office.[22]
Robert Dexter disagreed vehemently. Indeed, as we shall see, Joy's
position became a core complaint in what grew into Dexter's bitter brief against Joy in the years to come. At the time, however, the
two were still on speaking terms, and Dexter remonstrated with
his colleague in no uncertain terms. "It is absolutely essential that
we carry on in Portugal as long as we can," he insisted. Very practically, their Lisbon work appealed to supporters and was key to
raising the funds the USC needed. More significant, "it is our one
toehold on the continent of Europe for the sort of work that we are
best equipped to do." Writing from Boston, Dexter implored Joy to
improve relations with the Portuguese authorities and to impress
upon American officials the importance of helping the democratic
peoples of Europe.[23] It seemed to Dexter that Joy had lost focus; that
he was more engaged with the medical service the USC provided for
thousands of inmates in the transit camps of southern France than

"what has been our major aim from the very beginning . . . the salvaging of worthwhile people who are in danger in Europe because of their democratic attitudes."[24] That, too, fed Dexter's unremitting ire. "Joy's interest has always been the big showy things rather than in the details of helping individuals," he fumed in a letter to Seth Gano (then vice-chair of the USC's board of directors) a year later.[25]

By the time he wrote that letter in December 1942, the situation on the ground had changed once again. The Germans had swept across the demarcation line into the free zone in November and, as we saw, had occupied Marseille, a hub for Unitarian, Quaker, and other aid organization operations. Elisabeth and Robert had taken over the Lisbon office from Joy in August 1942 and were thus on site as a wave of undocumented refugees streamed into Portugal. They strained to respond to this humanitarian crisis. Seeking safety, Jews and other desperate people crossed the French-Spanish border "with

Jewish refugees wait to board the SS *Serpa Pinto*, Lisbon, September 1941. (*United States Holocaust Memorial Museum, courtesy of Milton Koch.*)

forged passports or none at all. They hid themselves in freight trains, vegetable carts, etc.; in fact all sorts of devices were used," Robert recalled. Elisabeth "estimated that as many people passed the frontier from France into Spain every day in 1943 as during each month in 1941." Many remained in Spain, "but a very considerable number were constantly getting through to Lisbon, and became each month an increasingly large number of people for whom we and the other agencies were responsible."[26]

The Dexters had experience with undocumented refugees during their previous Lisbon stint in the summer of 1941, when the USC was the main agency to help these "illegals." They knew the Portuguese authorities surveilled their operations: "We always carried on this work under the fear that the police might seize them and descend upon us because we had helped them." They had developed strategies to reduce risk, to which they returned in 1943. They instructed their clients to destroy papers with the USC office address and to

Left to Right: Robert Dexter, Elisabeth Dexter, Charles Joy, and a Mr. Hoffman. The original typed caption fails to identify Dr. Elisabeth Dexter with her academic title. (*Unitarian Service Committee, bMS 16076/11, Harvard Divinity School Library, Harvard Divinity School. Cambridge, Massachusetts.*)

avoid going to the premises in person. They also cautioned against using the telephone except from a booth that offered privacy. Most important, the Dexters exhorted the "illegals" to live as quietly and discreetly as possible. The USC would secure them a place to live; they needed to maintain a shadowy existence.[27]

Fueled by principle and passion, Elisabeth and Robert were unfazed by their clients' lack of documentation. Caring for them carried great risk, absorbed a lot of time, and claimed a significant portion of the Lisbon office budget. However, the Dexters held, "they were the people in the most desperate need and often the most worthwhile."[28] Robert maintained this view when he wrote his unpublished history of the USC in 1954, and Elisabeth affirmed that position in an oral history she recorded in 1962. They "specialized in illegals" because, she said, "the illegals on the average were outstanding people—people that because of their leadership in some field or another would be in more danger than the ordinary person." Then, too, as in 1941, the Unitarians cared for the undocumented because neither the Joint nor the Friends wished to do so. As Moses Beckelman had observed with regard to the JDC and Waitstill Sharp with regard to the AFSC, those organizations felt, as Elisabeth Dexter noted, that they could help more people in the long run if they followed all applicable laws and regulations.[29] The USC, however, did not aspire to mass emigration initiatives; "more" did not inspire them. Their key criteria were "distinction of the refugee in such fields as science, art, literature, social work, politics, religion" and the "danger to which the refugee is exposed."[30]

If undocumented refugees were primarily helped by the USC, they were hounded by a zealous political police force. The PVDE (Polícia de Vigiláncia e Defesa do Estado, the State Surveillance and Defense Police) was founded in 1933, a year after Salazar became the prime minister of Portugal. It remained in operation until 1945, when it was renamed the PIDE (the International and State Defense Police). Charged with state security, the PVDE was responsible for border control, immigration regulation, and surveillance of all foreigners in Portugal. Always hostile, there were "times when they were cracking down on everybody, when they'd watch our office and see if any illegals came in," Elisabeth recalled.[31] Danger lurked for the USC operatives and for those on the run.

Caught by the PVDE, refugees without papers were sent to prison where, to the foreigners' chagrin, inmates were responsible for their own food. Ability to pay determined first-, second-, or third-class status. "The third-class food was quite inadequate for anyone; the second-class for which payment was fairly high, would do; and the first-class was not bad at all," Robert explained.[32] The USC provided second-class food to its jailed clients. Accommodations, too, were assigned by ability to pay. But as Robert noted in his report to Boston on the Lisbon office's activities in 1943, the USC ceased to cover the cost of private quarters at the prisons as the price had climbed too high. Prison visits remained a major staff task, however, claiming significant time and attention.[33]

MAINTAINING "ILLEGAL" REFUGEES was not Elisabeth and Robert Dexter's sole clandestine activity in 1943. At age fifty-six (both were born in 1887), they were agents for the Office of Strategic Services (OSS). A wartime intelligence agency that grew out of the Office of the Coordinator of Information (COI), it was formally established by presidential military order on 13 June 1942. The decorated World War I veteran and prominent lawyer William Donovan, appointed by President Roosevelt in July 1941 to head the COI, soon recruited his friend and fellow lawyer Allen Dulles to open the agency's New York office: room 3663 in the International Building at Rockefeller Plaza. Dulles was the Dexters' first point of contact.

The attitude of the American government in general, and the State Department and COI/OSS in particular, toward nongovernmental relief agencies shifted when the United States entered the war. Originally persuaded that the Red Cross could manage all American relief activities abroad, intelligence service officials realized after Pearl Harbor that philanthropic relief operatives were well placed to gather information. As Robert observed, "Most of the people in the field and many of the officials in Washington began to recognize the fact that the various refugee agencies were getting information and indeed personnel of the utmost importance."[34]

Learning that the Dexters were to take over the Lisbon office in summer 1942, Allen Dulles invited Robert to meet with him in New York in June. Assessing his potential as an agent, Dulles appreciated Robert's perspective on the situation in Europe. And as he told his colleague John Hughes, he also appreciated that Robert stood ready to be of service.[35] Elisabeth did not lag far behind, although initially OSS interest in her was prompted by her status as Robert's wife. Planning to go to New York shortly before they left for Lisbon, the couple met with Dulles and Hughes. "Mr. Dulles and I look forward to seeing you and Mrs. Dexter at 3:30 PM next Monday afternoon, July 20, in Room 3670 of 630 Fifth Avenue, N.Y.C.," Hughes wrote to Robert. And he added, perhaps to signal that this was not a routine appointment, "Though you will find the door locked. There will be someone there to open it for you at that time."[36]

Dulles and Hughes sought to use the USC to gain an intelligence foothold in Europe, with the Dexters, among others, serving as informants. And Elisabeth and Robert, like several of their Unitarian colleagues, understood that as a philanthropic organization the USC could gain information from people and entrée into places closed to government operatives. Indeed, the USC promoted the advantages of their delegates working as spies for the government. As William Emerson, USC president, explained to assistant secretary of state Breckinridge Long, "It should be pointed out that American relief workers, moving freely about in unoccupied France, are able to gather a great deal of important information." By "American relief workers" he meant *Unitarian* relief workers, as the USC "has never been a neutral committee. It has always been committed to the victory of the United Nations," as the Allies called themselves.[37]

Emerson wrote just a week before unoccupied France was no more and American philanthropic operatives were forced to leave. But what held true in Vichy before 11 November 1942 remained the case in Lisbon thereafter. And the Dexters did not give up on maintaining contact with French sources. They found a way to continue to gather intelligence from Dr. René Zimmer, an Alsatian Jewish refugee who ran the USC's Marseille medical clinic, which they passed on to Dulles and Hughes.[38]

For Robert and Elisabeth, working with the intelligence branch spoke to their fervent anti-Nazi, anti-fascist politics and appealed to their ethic of civic responsibility. It also offered a welcome opportunity to flirt with risk in the service of doing good, which they enjoyed. When their mission neared the end in December 1942, Robert staked out their claim to remain in a letter to Gano sent by diplomatic pouch, to which their relationship with OSS gave them access. Mail and telegrams were censored and slow; the diplomatic pouch was exempt from the censors' prying eyes, and delivery was quicker and more reliable. "We were asked to do certain things for certain departments of our government, which our position made possible," Robert began. "We were asked in confidence and naturally respected that confidence." These activities were undertaken in France and Portugal, and in Robert's view the relationship has been "beneficial to the committee's work" and "helpful to the national effort."[39]

Many of the eighteen thousand people who had fled to Spain when the Germans took control of Vichy France made their way into Portugal, bringing fresh information about the occupation and conditions of daily life. The Dexters' constant contact with refugees provided an efficient and innocuous way to gain this useful intelligence. "The major portion of our new cases are escaped politicals from Spain and France who are here without proper papers," Robert reminded Gano. "Our friends in the U. S. service are very helpful; and these people in turn give to our U.S. officials all sorts of valuable information which we are able to secure." The whole web rested on personal contacts and grew through amicable relationships. Intelligence work was fueled by these close networks of trust, and thus "a change of personnel now would be exceedingly serious," Robert argued. Most especially, he insisted, Charles Joy should not take over the Lisbon post; he did not have those ties and in any case the Germans already suspected him.[40]

Hughes and Dulles agreed and intervened with the Boston leadership to keep Robert in Portugal. They did not need to press; the officers concurred unanimously, Gano reassured Hughes. Undoubtedly, "his services there will be of the greatest value to all concerned."[41] Although the entire committee realized that Elisabeth was integral to the European operation, she was not officially included. Robert alone was identified. Writing to both Dexters two days later on 21 December, Gano reiterated that Hughes "emphasized the desire of Washington to have you remain in Lisbon."[42] The offer was directed at Robert; that Elisabeth would work without pay at her husband's side was assumed.

John Hughes, who had taken over the OSS New York office from Allen Dulles, continued to value Robert Dexter's contribution.[43] Elisabeth's return to the United States to be on hand when their grandchild was born proved an opportunity for the OSS to recruit her in her own right. Her first meeting on 20 April 1943 with Toni Sender, the agent who became her handler, sparked a mutual confidence. Formerly a Social Democratic deputy to the Reichstag (the German parliament), Sender had fled Nazi Germany in 1933 and immigrated to the United States in 1935. European labor had claimed her interest before she emigrated and it remained her focus as an OSS operative, which resonated with Elisabeth. "Discussed with her [Elisabeth] possibilities of getting information through their contacts abroad," Sender reported. "She is ready to help us as much as it is possible."[44] Elisabeth was pleased that Sender did not let the connection fade. "Did I tell you that Toni Sender . . . is most anxious for a real talk with me before I go back?" Elisabeth chortled to Robert.[45] Sender detailed their meeting in New York a month later, telling her colleagues that she (Sender) had "asked in a more specific way for her [Elisabeth's] cooperation." She hoped Elisabeth and Robert would provide information to OSS that they got from their contacts in Lisbon and elsewhere. And would they identify people they thought OSS should debrief, "informing us of the arrival here of persons having information of European labor (date of their sailing from Lisbon)?" Elisabeth assured Sender of her cooperation and "promised to let us [OSS] have all information pertaining to European labor which she will be able to obtain from persons she gets in contact with in Portugal. She was understanding and willing to help in every way possible."[46]

AS TONI SENDER was taking advantage of Elisabeth's visit to the United States to tap her for OSS intelligence gathering, Gano used the opportunity to prevail upon her to attend a June meeting with USC senior leadership, including Charles Joy, to address the contention between the Dexters and Joy. "It was intended that all subjects of dispute should be explored," Elisabeth wrote to Robert. "That was not done, and perhaps just as well."[47]

Robert's charges against Joy (with which Elisabeth concurred) had festered since January when the prospect of Joy's possible appointment as the USC executive director spurred him to detail his grievances. Robert could not forget that Joy had suggested closing the Lisbon office. "You don't know how many times I shudder when I think of what might have happened, had we accepted Charles Joy's recommendation of a year ago," he seethed to Gano. "All the services which were and are rendered to people in need would have disappeared over night with the occupation of France if we had not had an office here." That egregious error in judgment spoke against Joy as a candidate. Worse still, Robert accused Joy of dereliction of duty and of embarrassing the denomination. "Last year, in order to diminish the importance of the work here, he turned away a great many people who came to us for assistance who desperately needed it and who were most valuable individuals." This reflected poorly on the Unitarians' reputation. Many who were denied help were political cases who then turned to the Quakers, thus creating an awkward situation for everyone.[48]

Spurred by his recollections, Robert wrote to President Emerson

too that day, asserting that Joy had never embraced the true mission of the USC. He was particularly neglectful of the USC's prime
concern, "the saving and helping of individuals who could make a
contribution either in America or in their own countries, towards
building up a free and democratic society." In closing, he repeated
his core complaint, emphasizing how wrong Joy had been to suggest
shuttering the Lisbon operation.[49]

Robert continued unrelenting in the weeks that followed.[50]
Weary of his tirades and anxious about the effect of the tensions on
the USC's operations, Gano told Robert that his "misapprehensions"
were "misunderstandings" on Robert's part and that he needed to
put the Lisbon issue behind him and move forward. Furthermore,
he argued, even if Joy were more interested in mass programs to feed
and provide medical care, as the Unitarians had undertaken in the
camps of Vichy France, than in individual casework, he proved a
loyal, energetic, and effective partner in the Dexters' refugee operation. Gano urged generosity. "If we all pull together on a coopera-
tive basis and seek to avoid misunderstandings rather than cultivate
them, and if each gives the other credit for honest intentions . . . we
shall get somewhere."[51]

Robert understood Gano's letter as an admonishment, but it
inspired little self-reflection. On the contrary: he attributed the
rebuke to Joy's machinations. "Apparently, Charles has got everybody over there pretty much on his side," he grumbled to Elisabeth. Elisabeth took umbrage at many things Joy did and advocated
against him. Robert agreed but realized that sentiment in the home
office ran in Joy's favor. "I think it is rather time for folding in our
horns for the time being," he allowed to her. Recognizing that his
irritation flowed from antipathy, he admitted, "It is certainly too bad
that personalities have to interfere." He went on to acknowledge,
grudgingly, "I don't doubt that I have been too censorious."[52]

But he could not let go; he had taken against Joy and no rational argument could persuade him to mitigate his stance. Thus,
when Elisabeth told him she had learned that various people had
been prepared to give money to support the Lisbon work but Joy

had discouraged them, Robert promptly shifted ground with Gano. Starting on a conciliatory note, he soon turned to Elisabeth's claim that Joy had declined offers of financial assistance to Lisbon. This spoke to Joy's lack of enthusiasm for refugee aid and perhaps to an aim to undermine it.[53] Gano remonstrated with him yet again, urging greater forbearance. "It is not a question of whether the criticism is justified or not but a question more of avoiding personalities," he observed.[54] Gripped by irrational hostility, however, Robert could not interpret his colleague's actions through a more benign lens.

Although Elisabeth had returned to the United States to help her daughter, she remained preoccupied by both Joy's shortcomings and the Lisbon operation. Writing to Robert frequently, she discussed work questions in great detail and family news cursorily. Two packed single-spaced pages about office matters and advice on how to handle the difficulties created by Joy were followed by fewer than seven lines about Harriet and baby Margaret that began "But I shd say something about the chn" and ended with an abrupt segue to a speaking engagement on behalf of the USC in Chicago: "I had an invitation from Preston Bradley!!! to speak in his church."[55] Glad as she was to perform her ascribed maternal and grandmotherly roles, to mix formulas and give bottles, Elisabeth was clear: "I . . . want to be back," she ended one letter. "I am certainly eager to get back, my dear," she closed another.[56] Speaking of her love for her husband, her worry that he worked too much, her analysis of the meeting with the leadership, and follow-up on various refugee cases, she lamented, "I am crazy to get back."[57]

Elisabeth returned to Lisbon in June 1943 and resumed the many tasks the Lisbon office handled. Like Robert, however, she could not let go of her grievances against Joy and wrote a memo for her husband elaborating on the charge that Joy had redirected funds that could have gone to support general Lisbon work and had curtailed philanthropic gifts to the Lisbon office.[58] These were tired issues, and it is possible that the Dexters' animosity might have abated with time but for reports Robert heard while on a trip to London that October and November to meet with Sir Herbert Emerson, the

League of Nations High Commissioner for Refugees and director of the Inter-Governmental Committee on Refugees (IGC).[59] Joy had visited London in July 1942 at the request and at the expense of the High Commissioner's office, or so he had told Boston. Assuming good relations, Robert requested a meeting with Sir Herbert and was chagrined when the assistant High Commissioner, Dr. Gustave G. Kullmann, told him that the appointment might be declined. Robert was surprised and noted that Joy had been invited to London by the High Commissioner the previous year. It was Kullmann's turn to be amazed. Yes, Joy had come, but not at the invitation or expense of the High Commissioner's office. Kullmann understood that Joy had come to London at the invitation of Jack Brent, a communist who had fought in the Spanish Civil War and who had become the Honorary Secretary of the International Brigade Association.[60] Joy did indeed secure an appointment with Sir Herbert and had brought Brent with him, uninvited and unannounced. It was a diplomatic error, as Sir Herbert had previously refused to see Brent officially, which Joy knew. The move was "not good form," Robert noted with disdain, "and it was very embarrassing for all concerned." It took extensive repair work and "a basis of mutual liking" between Robert and Kullmann, as well as "respect for the work we are doing," to persuade Kullmann to open Emerson's door to Robert.[61]

The story spooled through Robert's letters from London to Elisabeth in Lisbon, a consistent narrative thread.[62] He spoke about the food (and his indigestion), the blackout (which he found daunting), his love for her and his loneliness on his own, and the significance of his meetings. And in every letter, he expressed his contempt for Joy. Whatever subject he addressed—whether the important appointments Kullmann secured for him or refugee conditions in Spain—was introductory to his main theme: denigration of Joy. And self-congratulation. "The chief [Emerson]—a crusty old codger—who K[ullmann] tells me is not given to compliments said I gave him as clear a picture as he had had anywhere. He also did not like Charles.... I think we'll get on well with the old boy, if Charles keeps away."[63]

Searching the office files upon his return to Lisbon, Robert found letters corroborating Brent's invitation and Joy's acceptance if Brent paid his expenses, as well as a letter from Joy to Boston saying the High Commissioner had invited him to London and would cover the cost, followed by a letter a month later advising the USC leadership that Jack Brent's association had paid his expenses. His revised account did not garner much attention and the original understanding prevailed. "The whole thing . . . completely destroyed what confidence I had left in Dr. Joy's integrity," Robert reflected later.[64]

Still in England, however, Robert was irked further by the home office's plan for Joy to meet with him in London to resolve their differences and discuss developments in Boston. The USC's operations had doubled in volume and more than doubled in complexity since Robert had left the United States in August 1942, and little of this growth could be explained adequately by mail or cable.[65] Robert waited as Joy negotiated the usual travel impediments of obtaining the necessary papers and securing transport. First he waited for Joy to arrive. Then he waited for information from Joy. Finally, he became choleric. "Still no word from Charles Joy," he bristled to Elisabeth. "I'm just waiting around to hear from that s.o.b."[66] By mid-November it had become clear that Joy would not join Robert in London, and Boston urged him to return to the United States for consultations. This increased his fury. "I shall not go even if I have to resign," he raged. "I'm sick of being a pawn and I quite agree the time has come for some plain speaking. I'm going to do some as soon as I get back to Lisbon, I've been patient and conciliatory long enough."

Robert did not hesitate to present a blunt analysis to Gano. Speaking for Elisabeth as well as himself, he repeated his pattern of apology (or concession) followed by complaint. "I am sorry to return to the painful theme of our criticisms of Charles, but . . . the fact remains that we consider him: 1. A bungler . . . 2. So inaccurate in his reporting . . . that one cannot believe him. If he said a white horse went by, I should believe something moved, but it might have been a black cat or a jeep."[67] Once again Gano pressed his friend to return to the United States for consultations. Persuaded of the value of direct communication, Gano aimed to reestablish a harmonious relationship which, he was sure, would prove more productive than the current discord.[68] Separated by an ocean, each had the possibility of a visit on his mind the same day. "Frankly, I don't want to go home," Robert declared. "There are too many things developing here." These included clandestine work for the OSS. The situation was unsettled; "no one knows when developments of major importance will occur," and Robert felt that he should be on the spot. Having raised his objections, he acquiesced. He closed with his conclusion: he felt rather guilty because, he reminded Gano, he was responsible for selecting Joy in 1940. "He is a good man, a hard worker, but he is a bungler," Robert declared. He should not be sent to Europe or occupy a position that authorized him to shape policies. As for Robert, he insisted that he sought "to think all the time what was in the best interest of the work itself."[69]

THE WORK, most especially émigré casework, certainly claimed the Dexters' full attention—when not incensed about their colleague. And they readily put aside their disdain for Joy when he could help, even expressing warm appreciation for his efforts, as they did when they needed it for the Hussareks. As a couple, Friedrich (Fritz) and Helga Hussarek accounted for one of the 728 cases that the Lisbon office had in its care in 1943.[70] Indeed, they occupied a special position, as Fritz was on staff. The son of Baron Maximilian Hussarek von Heinlein, Austria's prime minister in the final months of World War I, Fritz (who also carried the title of baron) and his wife lived in Vienna until his father died in 1935. Maintaining legal residency in that city, the couple moved to Paris, where Fritz established a small radio factory and, in 1937, took on the position of consulting engineer for a French company, working on the Défense Nationale Française to protect the country against armed aggression.[71]

The annexation of Austria by Germany in March 1938 found the Hussareks in Davos, Switzerland, where they had stopped on their way to Vienna to vote against any such merger in a plebiscite called by the Austrian prime minister, Kurt von Schuschnigg. "Now our difficulties started," Fritz explained to Elisabeth a few years later. Trying to reenter France, they learned that Austrians now needed a visa. This they soon obtained, and they returned to Paris, where they changed their official country of residence from Austria to France. That triggered a decrease in the duration that their passports would remain valid, cutting the time to three months. In fact, their Austrian passports would soon no longer be valid at all. Austria had ceased to exist; there was no Austrian state to renew documents. With German passports their only legal option when their Austrian papers expired, Fritz inquired at the German consulate in Paris. "Knowing my father's name, the officials wanted to give us right away German passports." But Helga and Fritz would not accept Nazi documents. Choosing not to live in Austria under German rule, they sacrificed their money, estate, and fortune. They opted to remain in France, where Fritz could continue to work for the Défense Nationale. In the end, the French police forced them to accept German passports by threatening to deport Helga. She (and Fritz) needed a valid passport (which in their case meant a German passport) to obtain a French identity card, which allowed her to live in France. [72]

Fritz and Helga's hard-won stability was short-lived. Enemy aliens, they were sent to internment camps after war was declared.[73] The fall of France in June 1940 brought their release, and they fled to Marseille in the unoccupied zone. But they had lost their investments, the radio factory, and Fritz's consultancy. And, as they had given their passports for safekeeping to the now evacuated Austrian anti-Nazi émigré group, the Ligue Autrichienne, they had lost their documents. Fritz was caught by the police in August 1940 in a passport control raid and sent to an internment camp once again. They were stuck: without passports, they could not apply for exit visas from France or entry visas elsewhere. Helga turned to friends for help. They did not disappoint; they gave her two Dutch passports, off the books and "therefore without knowledge of the Dutch authorities in Marseille," Fritz reported to the American consul general in Lisbon nearly a year later. Traveling on these purloined papers, the couple crossed the Pyrenees in October 1940 and made their way from Spain to Portugal, where they applied to the USC for assistance; Joy ran the Lisbon office at the time. The help became mutual when Fritz joined the staff.[74]

The Hussareks remained at risk, however. Portuguese policy aimed at onward emigration. Prison or the lesser punishment of forced residence in the towns of Ericeira or Caldas loomed for those who overstayed their welcome. And by March 1943, Fritz worried that he could not remain in Lisbon much beyond August on the passports they held. "I hope he is wrong," Robert wrote to Elisabeth in the United States, "but this gives you a deadline at which to shoot."[75] The weeks passed and pressure mounted. Alarmed by the prospect that the Hussareks might be incarcerated, Robert cabled Joy the details of the situation.

They all were right to worry. Fritz was remanded to Aljube prison at the end of April. And Robert was right to turn to Joy. When the State Department advisory panel hearing the Hussarek case was moved up from 16 May to 8 May, Joy stepped in with alacrity to attend. Elisabeth had planned to appear on the Hussareks' behalf, but notified of the changed date eighteen hours in advance, she could not get to Washington, DC, from her daughter's home in Perry, Georgia, a twenty-four-hour journey, in time. She too turned to Joy, who by chance was in New York. "I said at once that I would go," he recalled. Having no files on hand, he phoned Elisabeth, who provided him with the information he needed. And off he went to Washington the next morning, arriving at 11:30 to attend the meeting at 1:30.[76] "Charles has been fine on this," Elisabeth reported to Robert. "I really am hopeful as far as the visa goes."[77]

Happily, the hearing went well. The Boston office learned a week later that the visa had been approved. But Fritz was still in prison and threatened with deportation. Eager to ensure that finances did not stand in the Hussareks' way, Elisabeth offered to put up a personal bond or establish a trust fund if either would help. And she urged Robert to "pay their transportation from any fund on hand; for that I am sure Charles would go to bat." Relying on Joy's emotional ties to Helga and Fritz and his investment of time and effort, she observed, "It is fortunate that he is really fond of them and he has worked hard."[78] If she understood that the same sentiments and engagement fueled her own offers and actions, she did not say.

The Hussareks were fortunate. They had secured the goodwill of key USC officers who sought to advance their application through the American bureaucracy and who stood willing to help financially. But as Robert worried to Joy, there were "several rather difficult hurdles left." Although Joy had successfully argued for advisory approval of the Hussareks' visas from the State Department, George Miller, the person who handled visas at the American consulate in Lisbon, was not persuaded. Why did Fritz and Helga get German passports in Paris before the war? he fretted. And why did they leave France on false papers? Then, too, Fritz needed to obtain a certificate of good conduct from the Lisbon police, which, as he sat in prison, they might not be willing to issue. Even if they got visas, the Germans had prevailed upon the Portuguese government to forbid men of military age from Germany and all occupied countries to travel on Portuguese ships, which sharply limited their options for passage out of the country. Born in 1900, Fritz fell just under the upper boundary age of forty-five. But if they did not leave, they would be deported. In their case in particular, "a great deal of German pressure" had been brought to bear, Robert confided to Joy. "I am convinced that they want Fritz in Germany and if he gets there, he will be lucky if he gets shot. He might get treated far worse."[79]

Robert hoped and pushed. He appreciated Joy's help and expressed his gratitude unstintingly. "No one except you and Elisabeth can possibly realize the worries we have had with this case," he confessed. "It has literally been a matter of life and death, and still is. You have certainly done more than your share," he thanked Joy. "May I tell you how deeply grateful Fritz and Helga are, and how immensely I and all the others in the office who know these people appreciate what you have done."[80] Their efforts proved successful. Fritz was released from Aljube on 28 May, probably on the strength of the authorization of his visa, although Miller had not yet issued it. Fritz's discharge papers allowed him only ten days to leave the country, but he managed to elude deportation and, having obtained an exemption from the age rule, he and Helga set sail toward the end of June.[81] A few months later, the phone rang on Charles Joy's desk. "Over the wire came a familiar voice which I had last heard in Europe, the voice of a man who had served us well when working in our Lisbon office. . . . He was speaking now as the man we had saved from imprisonment, deportation, and probable death, and then, in the face of extraordinary difficulties, brought to freedom and safety." They were, Joy noted, "members of two of Austria's most distinguished families," and they had given up position, comfort, and possessions and endured "concentration camps, prisons and exile" to elude Nazi rule. "Now at last . . . they were actually in America."[82]

IF THE DEXTERS and Joy's united efforts yielded a successful outcome, it did nothing to resolve their discord. Indeed, as we have seen, Elisabeth was summoned to a leadership meeting to discuss "all subjects of dispute" on 7 June, while they were still in the thick of overcoming the Hussareks' emigration challenges. Notwithstanding the appreciation their collaborative work generated, the passions that fueled the quarrel between the Dexters and Joy prevailed. By the end of the year—in the wake of Robert's trip to England and the damage he found Joy had done to key USC relationships there, not to mention the falsities in his letter—Robert took his London tale to Gano. Robert had kept Elisabeth informed letter by letter. Now he brought what he had learned to Gano. Of all the many complaints about Joy that Robert had lodged with Gano, this was the most damning in his view. And the most threatening to the USC. He and Elisabeth were "very much concerned for the good name and continuing good work of our Committee," he warned.[83]

Howard Brooks, USC associate director and at the time Robert's assistant in Lisbon, was alarmed by the infighting. Acknowledging that the point he wished to draw to Gano's attention was "extremely delicate," he went on to address the conflict between the USC act-ing executive director (Joy) and the executive director (Robert). "It is absolutely essential that the misunderstandings between the two top people on the Committee's staff be cleared up," he declared. He was "more worried than I can possibly tell you," he confided. "I am afraid that the Committee's work will suffer terribly." Brooks recognized that Gano had "struggled with these problems"; he sought merely "to underline what you already know and to indicate to you that I think they are more urgent than they have ever been before."[84]

Joy agreed. Referencing Brooks's letter (which Gano had shown him), he asked William Emerson for a definitive ruling on the issue of authority: did it reside in Boston with him, or with Robert in Lisbon? Either Robert had to remain in America to fulfil his duties as executive director, or he had to give up the title, Joy argued. For his part, "If my resignation is thought necessary to restore harmony, it is at your disposal." Possibly because he knew what to say and to whom, and perhaps out of conviction, Joy continued, "The work is too important to be sacrificed, or even weakened, because of personal considerations."[85]

The heart of the problem was personal, however. The Dexters and Joy surely differed regarding the best use of USC resources: relief initiatives versus rescue actions; large-scale programs versus retail casework. But the core issue was irrational antipathy. They did not trust or admire each other. They could not resolve their differences because there was no resolving their mutual dislike.

Quarreling marked many operatives' relationships. Born, perhaps, from the unremitting stress of their work, the constant uncertainty about the outcome of their efforts, or a fierce conviction about the value of one's own priorities in the face of dire need as opposed to one's colleague's, these antipathies took root and colored relations. In the case of the Dexters and Joy, Robert had returned to the United States in February 1944, as Gano had urged, for consultations, but talking could not forge a bridge between them. The AUA leadership had to act.

AUA president Frederick Eliot suggested (22 March 1944) the establishment of a subcommittee to examine the previous six months of correspondence between Boston and Lisbon, as well as all correspondence relating to Joy's 1942 trip to London. The sub-committee, comprised of two men, Alfred Whitman, then USC secretary, and Leslie Pennington, a prominent Unitarian minister in Cambridge, was to look for misrepresentations by Joy and Dexter and to assess the tone of the communications. Dexter and Joy agreed to accept the subcommittee's findings as final, and both submitted voluminous files to be reviewed.[86] In the interim, they continued to complain about each other yet to work together. Indeed, they had a new project in view; they were in a group that developed plans for the Roosevelt administration's nascent War Refugee Board (WRB). Recently established (January 1944), the WRB needed the help of experienced operatives to imagine relief and rescue initiatives for Nazi victims and to actualize them on the ground. As we have seen, Ross McClelland was tapped to serve as the WRB representative in Switzerland. Robert Dexter was chosen as the representative in Portugal.[87] Returning to Lisbon in April, he was seconded to the American embassy, where he worked for the WRB; Elisabeth continued to run the USC's Lisbon office.

Whitman and Pennington rendered their judgment in June. Despite the Dexters' spirited and detailed offensive, the report exonerated Joy in full. The committee found "many evidences of kindness, pleasantness and appreciation" on Joy's part and no evidence of misrepresentation or distortion. Robert Dexter's behavior, by contrast, was marked by "issues of judgment, criticism, irritation and barbed thrusts at Dr. Joy." But the real culprit was Elisabeth. The woman who, until spring 1944, had shouldered full-time work for the USC at no pay, was the spoiler. "It seems to us possible that the increase in [Robert's censorious stance] may be related to a more extreme attitude in Mrs. Dexter," Whitman and Pennington suggested. "Several of her communications and reports show an extreme hostility and suspicion." Moving from general observations to an analysis of the Dexters' contentions, the report raised the question of the couple's "future relationships with the Unitarian Service Committee." Pennington and Whitman claimed to be sensitive to "the emotional strain our foreign representatives are under" and to understand, too, the complications of communication between the home and field offices. But they lived and worked in Massachusetts; they had no experience of dictatorships or of asylum seekers running for their lives. And in their analysis, again the woman was to blame. Consistently stripping Elisabeth of her academic title while using it for the male protagonists, they opined, "Mrs. Dexter has been particularly difficult, emotional, and unjust; and it seems possible that her presence in Lisbon may have contributed to the growth of this attitude in Dr. Dexter."[88] Deploying a lexicon of traditionally misogynist terms, they denigrated Elisabeth and emasculated Robert.

They were correct on one point: Robert respected Elisabeth's analyses and opinions. He relied on her for her clarity and judgment. On the Unitarian Service Committee Lisbon letterhead Robert was identified as the executive director and Elisabeth as the associate director but, as their correspondence reveals, their working relationship was not hierarchical. For example, writing to her in the midst of a wave of unsettling political rumors, he noted his inability to decipher current events. "There are several serious messes here which frankly my feeble intelligence does not understand," he regretted. "I wish that your wiser brain were here. At any rate I could talk things over with you and we might, between us, find some raison d'etre for what is happening. It is just beyond me."[89] Come back, he implored her when she had been in the United States for some weeks. "I fear that it means another month or so before you can get here, and I'll be a raving maniac by that time." The workload was too heavy; he needed her help. "I'm doing the best I can but I cannot handle scores of accounts, look after people whose lives are threatened, get the information our friends [OSS] want and need, and keep everything straight," he confessed. And to make sure she took his point, he switched to capitals: "DO GET A CLIPPER IF YOU CAN—IF NOT THE EARLIEST POSSIBLE BOAT."[90] Robert consistently looked to Elisabeth for ideas to advance casework, for advice about practical matters, and for her counsel regarding his quarrel with Joy and his relations with the USC leadership. "This was one of the days

I needed you terribly," he lamented from London on 29 October 1943 upon receipt of a cable from the Boston office to which he took umbrage; he just wanted her help composing his reply.[91]

Embracing the USC mission, Elisabeth undertook both the myriad tasks of casework and her role in the professional partnership with her husband. "I really do something here which seems to be worthwhile," she explained to her son Lewis.[92] She felt it had "a symbolic value far beyond anything that figures can show." The refugees were not abandoned; "someone is standing by <u>willing</u> to help." Then, too, the USC's rescue initiatives were part of the fight for democracy and against Nazism. In the refugees "lies the hope of a free Europe," she declared. "If they are allowed to perish now, no matter who wins the war there will be no one to build the peace."[93] Committed to these principles, Elisabeth also enjoyed the adventure of their life in Lisbon. Her letters to her children speak of the many people with whom she interacted, the foods she ate, weddings and parties she attended, and the local customs she learned.

Unpaid, Elisabeth was perceived as a professional volunteer by

Young Jewish refugees play outside the Colonia Balnear Infantil Do Seculo building, their home in the Lisbon area. 1941. (NY_03618, Courtesy of JDC Archives, New York.)

the Boston leadership. The couple's living expenses were covered, but only Robert was salaried. It was an arrangement that held until the War Refugee Board asked Robert if, upon his return to Lisbon from his visit to the United States in spring 1944, he would serve as the WRB representative in Lisbon with the rank of attaché at the embassy. The USC accorded him a leave of absence to do so, and as Elisabeth would take over the Lisbon office, they offered her a salary of $4,000 a year.[94] Robert had earned $9,000.[95]

Elisabeth was thus running the USC mission in Portugal and Robert working for the WRB when the Pennington/Whitman sub-committee rendered its decision. Mindful of censorship and anxious to avoid embarrassment to anyone, the Boston leadership did not send the Dexters the whole report. They learned only that "the Committee's report vindicates Dr. Joy in full."[96] And that Joy was offered the position of executive director of the USC. The news reached them in October. Both responded with letters of resignation, to take effect on 1 December 1944. With the end of the war in sight, the WRB's Lisbon work decreased and Robert urged Washington to close its operations in Portugal. Their OSS responsibilities ended too, as a coded message to John Hughes advised. "110 [Allen Dulles] does not feel Dexters are particularly secure and that Mr. Dexter is inclined to be temperamentally indiscreet." The Allies' victory was assured, and the Cold War gained purchase. OSS's needs—the intelligence the agency sought and the personnel to pursue it—was shifting. 110 "feels they [the Dexters] are better suited for welfare work than for our type operations. Suggest therefore that we forget them. 109 [William Donovan] agrees."[97] The Dexters' wartime assignments concluded, Elisabeth and Robert accepted the invitation of the Church Peace Union (now the Carnegie Council for Ethics in International Affairs) to serve as European representatives. Martha Sharp, appointed USC's area director for Spain and Portugal, took charge of the Lisbon office.

Eager as the Dexters were to assume new responsibilities and, as their positions required extensive travel, embark upon new adventures, the breach with the USC grieved them. "I do not know anything in my life, before or since, that has caused me, personally, such a heartbreak," Robert admitted. Speaking for Elisabeth and for himself, he continued, "The Unitarian Service Committee and its predecessor were both largely our brain children. We had worked and fought for them and the result on the whole, we had reason to be proud of."[98]

Still, his colleagues' confidence in Joy over him continued to rankle after the war. If Robert did not have the last word with the subcommittee or on its verdict, he claimed it in his history of the USC. Not two years later, the USC "had to accept Dr. Joy's resignation under very compromising circumstances," he noted. Robert did not specify that Joy's offense was an extramarital affair. Rather, he pointed to additional evidence that he had been right: the USC then engaged the well-respected Unitarian minister Raymond Bragg, "whom I had suggested for the position when I was home in 1944."[99]

Robert enjoyed a five-year stint with the Church Peace Union. He seems not to have quarreled with any of his coworkers; in any case, the record is silent on the subject. He retired in 1950 and suffered from an unspecified serious illness as well as depression until his death in 1955 at age sixty-eight. Elisabeth left her position with the Church Peace Union before Robert, returning to scholarship in 1948. Focusing on women, she published *Career Women of America, 1776–1840* in 1951 and went on to research and write an unpublished biography of Sir Walter Scott's wife, Charlotte Carpenter. Elisabeth outlived Robert by sixteen years; she died in 1971 at age eighty-four.

EPILOGUE

WITH THE END of the war in sight, the JDC, founded in 1914, took the opportunity of its thirtieth anniversary to recount its history and relate its achievements. The past decades had seen "a 30-year global war for survival," chairman Paul Baerwald declared in his preface. That struggle had begun in 1914 "with the clash of contending armies" and now was coming to a close with "the scorched residue of the extermination camps." Among the "heroes" of that war for survival were the JDC representatives "who sought out the victims, snatched them from danger, gave them shelter and healing." The report granted that the organization originally "represented three distinct, diverse groups"—The American Jewish Relief Committee, founded by the well-established Jewish community; the Central Relief Committee, supported by more recent, Orthodox immigrants; and the People's Relief Committee, organized by newly arrived immigrant labor groups—but that situation no longer held. The "experience of working harmoniously [had] led to a change. The divisions gave way; the lines of demarcation faded, J.D.C. became the master solvent for differences." Indeed, the "J.D.C. was the great meeting ground, the complete expression of the philanthropic urge . . . that sought to help Jews in need whoever they were, whatever their views in religion, politics, Jewish and general life." Turning to the JDC's wartime operations, the author asserted, "Obstacles did not halt the work. In addition to relief, resettlement and refugee aid, J.D.C. took on the problem of sheer rescue." The mission on the ground was supported by the organization's robust machinery: a national council, an advisory board of directors, an executive committee, administration officers and staff, donors, budget development, and expenditure reconciliation.[1]

A USC pamphlet published soon after the war struck a similarly heroic note: "The Committee financed escape and refuge for scores of writers, scholars, artists, and professional men—leaders marked by the enemy for extermination," the writer declared. "All told, in the past six years the Committee has reached half a million destitute and shattered people—mainly the most intelligent and sensitive, the first to suffer."[2]

Results oriented, these are celebratory accounts, and the main points they convey are correct. Indeed, all three committees—USC, JDC, and AFSC—aided "destitute and shattered people." They instituted feeding programs and clothing depots, and saw to the provision of medical care, living quarters, and an array of educational and training courses. Offering emigration advice and essential assistance to help desperate people obtain the papers and permissions they needed to flee, committee staff wrote scores of letters and sent dozens of telegrams every day. In an era before easy electronic communications, and in the midst of wartime postal regulations, disruptions, and mail censorship, operatives produced an astonishing volume of correspondence.

JDC, Unitarian, and Quaker operatives were indeed heroes, people of improbable courage and fortitude. They were heroes, too, in their tenacious engagement with relief and rescue work. Their commitment shines bright in their letters, diaries, and memoirs: the long hours they worked; their unflagging attention to the problems at hand. And if danger frightened them, it did not stop them.

Yet postwar accounts such as those by the JDC and USC do not capture the messiness of rescue and relief efforts on the ground;

they elide the irrational, the emotional pulls that spurred organizational decisions and determined operatives' actions; they ignore the unpredictable, the role of luck, chance, fortuitous circumstances, and timing; and they hide the operatives' little notice of policies and rules. The stories they tell are partial and lean.

Our Americans were, at one and the same time, saints and liars. Martha and Waitstill Sharp and Elisabeth and Robert Dexter undertook illicit activities to achieve their goals, including clandestine rescue, illegal currency exchange, and aiding undocumented refugees. Laura Margolis bent rules and regulations without a qualm to obtain needed supplies, equipment, and funds to keep the Jewish refugee community in Shanghai afloat. Moses Beckelman insisted on joining a delegation to no-man's-land to assess the unfolding tragedy in the Suwalki district himself. And Marjorie and Ross McClelland continued to try to save targeted victims even as deportation trains rolled from France to annihilation camps in the East.

Telescoping into specific situations and mapping our Americans' efforts as they unfolded, another, richer narrative emerges. We learn, for instance, that in addition to the ominous data yielded by exploratory visits to Europe, ties of kinship and friendship, as well as denominational rivalry with the Quakers, spurred the Unitarians to found a Commission for Service in Czechoslovakia, which they then grew into a more comprehensive Unitarian Service Committee. We learn, too, that while operatives such as Martha and Waitstill Sharp relished the chance to make a difference, they also relished the dangers they risked. As Waitstill put it, "Yankees like to skate on thin ice."[3] Moses Beckelman, even as he was committed to relief and rescue initiatives, was also fueled by professional rivalry and his desire for career advancement. And far from "the master solvent for differences . . . the great meeting ground," the JDC proved a battlefield for intra-denominational jousts for rescue priority, with each sector of the community claiming the primacy of its adherents.

As we have seen, intra-communal wrangling marked relief efforts in Shanghai, too—as did the acrimony between Laura Margolis and the Jewish community's lay leaders. Many entangled issues led to the impasse between them, including personal antipathies and gendered power conflicts, with Margolis needing the authority of the JDC to prevail in her effort to institute rational aid systems. She also had to rely on earlier relationships even when it came to a current enemy: the Japanese official charged with Jewish affairs in Shanghai, Captain Koreshige Inuzuka.

If personal relations shaped relief work in Shanghai, they proved equally powerful in Marseille. Training our lens on AFSC delegates Marjorie and Ross McClelland's efforts in unoccupied France, we see that such sentiments, amid a welter of rational considerations, made a lifesaving difference. And while the Unitarians had a clear policy as to whom they sought to rescue—"leaders marked by the enemy for extermination"—Elisabeth and Robert Dexter's experience in Lisbon reveals that their rescue activities, too, were shaped by their emotional connections.

Zooming in on the rescue and relief activities of one person or couple in one city during one year, the role of unpredictable factors and irrational triggers surfaces. The chance occurrence, for example, of a fountain pen filled with green ink; the fortuitous circumstance of two of a specific type of steam boiler available for use when none other would serve; the sheer luck that berths materialized on an already overbooked ship; the pull of spontaneous sympathy in the rescuer's choice of people to help emigrate; the sting of ambition.

SEEKING TO PRESENT a logical account of American operatives' relief and rescue initiatives, Nazi-era and postwar narratives cut through the quotidian mayhem the delegates experienced. The aim of such accounts was to discern order in the chaos that obtained. Then, too, assessments written after the war were grounded in the knowledge of what these Americans had achieved. At the time, however, no one knew what the outcome would be, nor the best way to secure the goals the committees envisioned. The delegates functioned in a fog of uncertainty. They negotiated constantly changing regulations, transport possibilities, and financial arrangements; the

shifting military developments; the capricious whims of multiple lay-
ers of authorities and officials. And they dealt with an endless stream
of people in constant stress. Reclaiming the perplexity of the American operatives and the pressure under which they functioned—lives
were at stake—offers a key to the constant quarreling that emerges
from contemporary accounts. Certainly, the fights were the result
of clashing perspectives on the problems they faced and how best to
handle them. Equally certainly they were the result of competition
over power and authority. Most of all, however, the wrangling was
an expression of the operatives' ardent wish to provide relief and to
effect rescue, and the murkiness of the path forward to do so. At
the time each situation unfolded, the aid workers confronted an as
yet undetermined future; its horizon was the decisions they would
make. Every moment was the *now* of responsibility, the *now* of decision. Foregrounding the role of the unpredictable and the irrational
infuses the black-and-white narratives that present history as if logical and orderly with color, transforming a story with a predictable
outcome into an open-ended tale, vivid and complex.

The operatives' external reality was shaped by a wide array of
baffling factors. Their internal world was marked by turmoil and
loneliness, as they acknowledged to themselves, their spouses, and
their supervisors, but neither wartime nor postwar accounts mention this.[4] These narratives elide their sentiments and strip them of
their passions; they emerge as, for instance, "the angelically patient
Beckelman."[5] The American aid workers did not buckle under
the emotional strain of their assignments, but they surely were
affected by them. "Somehow I seem to have dried up emotionally
spiritually—and every other good way," Martha, in Prague, wrote
(16 July 1939) to Waitstill, in Paris. "I am terribly lonely without you,"
she confessed a week later.[6] Beckelman, ruminating in his diary on
his career in conjunction with his request for a secretary, weighed
the benefits of marriage: "If I'm going to stay here for several years
I might as well get married—the present business is getting on my
nerves." By "the present business" Beckelman may have meant "sex
starvation," which exacerbated his isolation.[7] As we saw, Margolis, a

thirty-eight-year-old single woman without friends or congenial colleagues, lamented that she was as "lonesome as can be" and admitted, "I hate Shanghai."[8] Corresponding by letter and telegram when separated, Elisabeth and Robert Dexter consistently expressed their love and yearning for one another. "I'm lonely and rather fed up," Robert wrote from London to Elisabeth in Portugal. "If I could only get my job done and come home to you and Lisbon." And he closed, "I surely miss you; if you were here I shouldn't mind things half so much. We do things together. Much love, my dear."[9] Marjorie McClelland's letters to her family in Connecticut express a similar message from a different perspective. Rather than loneliness when apart, she remarked on the bonds created by her joint mission with Ross. "Our work, our new experiences shared, and our sense of aloneness in a world somewhat alien, draw us even closer together."[10] These sentiments open a fresh perspective on the operatives' lives at the time, adding another dimension to our understanding of the delegates and the responsibilities they assumed.

Their loneliness when on their own suggests that relief and rescue was desolate work. Operatives appear to have craved partnership, including Americans like Beckelman, who, as we know, contemplated marriage, and Margolis, who insisted that the JDC send her colleague Manny Siegel, whom she trusted and liked, to Shanghai.[11]

Still, however integral spouses were to their partners' morale, and however valuable their contribution to relief and rescue initiatives, wives (in contrast to husbands) did not enjoy fully fledged roles. A disconnect obtained between expectations at headquarters and experience in the field. Indeed, wives' roles emerge as a basso continuo of discord, a specific structural problem. Much was entwined: recognition, respect, pay.

Many women operatives shared Martha Sharp's frustration with her home office's lack of respect for her work and inadequate pay. "I gave my report to the Service Committee yesterday—and only got to Spain & Portugal," Martha fumed to Waitstill on 14 November 1945. "As usual the agenda was crowded with minutiae until 4:20 when I was allowed to begin." The committee put her off to the following week, but that meeting proved equally disappointing. Promised the afternoon to present her report, Martha got a half hour at the end of the day. If the Service Committee did not value what she had to say, others did. She "had 18 speaking engagement requests to-day alone," she informed Waitstill. These presentations paid. "Hadassah is offering me $50.00 and expenses per speech and 8 were for them." And AmRelCzech (American Committee for Relief in Czechoslovakia) offered her a job. Sidelined and silenced by the USC executive, Martha "went ahead and accepted the new assignment . . . they want me badly."[12]

Martha's abbreviated report, Laura Margolis's repeated requests for JDC endorsement of her project to rationalize relief, Boston's assessment of Elisabeth Dexter's role in the antagonism that had developed with Charles Joy and their failure to pay her at all until she took over the Lisbon office, and then she got less than half the salary Robert had earned in the same position: all speak to a disjuncture between the women's scope for action on the ground and remuneration for or even recognition of their achievements.

Yet women operatives relished their work; they gloried in the opportunities to undertake tasks and shoulder responsibilities they never would have at home. If their respective committee leaderships did not fully appreciate what they achieved or its worth, the women did. Offering them a chance to exceed their own expectations of themselves, to engage in a mission they valued, their work, as we have seen, proved transformative—transformative for those they helped and transformative for them, too.

ACKNOWLEDGMENTS

ONE OF THE GREAT PLEASURES of finishing a book is that it gives the author the opportunity to thank those who helped the project become a product. I could not have garnered the information, collected the photographs, or even afforded the research costs without the assistance and support of others.

Saints and Liars is about Americans who went abroad to offer relief to victims of Nazi Germany and other racist regimes and, when the persecution turned lethal, remained to rescue as many as they could. Vanishingly few of the people they helped remembered their names. Not many recalled the names of the organizations that aided them. But they knew they got help, and that help saved them. My first and greatest debt is thus to the women and men who recounted their personal histories to me. I am grateful for their time and for the care they devoted to the enterprise. I do not forget for an instant the searing nature of such recollection.

Hearing from a number of survivors about philanthropic organization operatives prompted me to wonder who those Americans were, what they had done, and what had spurred them to act. It was from survivors, too, that I learned about the role of unpredictable factors such as luck, timing, and fortuitous circumstances, and of the irrational: sympathies, antipathies, drives, and impulse. Nearly every survivor referenced unpredictable and irrational factors in their life narratives, yet it took me years to absorb the message they sought to convey. I finally did so with this project.

IF ORAL HISTORIES pointed me in fresh directions, archival documents underpinned those life narratives. It is a pleasure to acknowledge the help offered by staff at the myriad collections through which I sifted as I pursued American relief and rescue workers. Most especially, I thank Joanna Sliwa (then at the JDC, now historian at the Claims Conference) for introducing me to the JDC archive and its amazing archivists, Abra Cohen and Misha Mitsel. I am grateful to the United States Holocaust Memorial Museum librarian and archivist Ron Coleman and historian and archivist Rebecca Erbelding for their endless generosity of spirit and with documents. And I remain indebted to long retired American Friends Service Committee archivist Jack Sutter, whose help years ago has stood me in good stead.

Key individuals supported my work in archival collections in the United States and abroad. Believing in the project (and in me), philanthropist Cathy Cohen Lasry funded my research munificently; I was and continue to be deeply grateful. Sidney and Rosalie Rose and Ralph and Shirley Rose endowed the chair I held at Clark University and I thank my Four Roses for the research fund attached to the professorship. And David Strassler, founding donor of the Strassler Center at Clark, championed my endeavors in multiple ways.

I was honored to be invited to serve as the J. B. and Maurice C. Shapiro Senior Scholar-in-Residence at the Jack, Joseph and Morton Mandel Center for Advanced Holocaust Studies at the United States Holocaust Memorial Museum for a miraculous year of scholarly discoveries and unending conversations with the Fellows. And I was privileged to be the Bildner Visiting Scholar at Rutgers University, where I taught a course on this subject to schoolteachers, whom I found inspirational.

I have been fortunate to enjoy the kindness of my colleagues— staff and faculty—at Clark University, where I served as director of the Strassler Center and as Rose Professor for much of the time I researched this subject, and at the Graduate Center of the City University of New York, where I am now the director of the Center for the Study of the Holocaust, Genocide, and Crimes Against Humanity, and where I wrote *Saints and Liars*. I have been equally fortunate to enjoy the support and good cheer of my wonderful graduate students. I count myself among the luckiest of *doktormutters* and MA supervisors.

The long COVID-19 years would surely have proved intellectually isolating but for the encouragement of enthusiastic friends: Betsy Anthony, Sara Brown, Beth Cohen, Sarah Cushman, Mikal Eckstrom, Susan Fischer, Marion Kaplan, Debra Kessler, Michal Goldberg, Amos Goldberg, Tracey Petersen, Carolyn and Richard Rampton, Claire Rosenson, Christine Schmidt, Raz Segal, Miriam Starkman, Irena Sumi, Sylvia Urbach, Susan Weingast. Indeed, just living through that pandemic would surely have proved isolating but for their virtual companionship.

In the transformation of project to product, I thank Betsy Anthony for her help identifying images and securing the permissions to use them, and for introducing me to geographer Maël Le Noc, whose gorgeous maps add much to this book. And I thank Alexandra Kramen, who served as the notes editor, shifting from paper to digitized document citations and ensuring that all conformed with numerous style and archival guidelines. It is she, too, who identified and addressed quotation permissions questions. I happily acknowledge my deep debt to both Betsy and Ali. I am also happily indebted to Norton editor Amy Cherry for her astute advice, assistant editor Huneeya Siddiqui for her patience, and copyeditor Janet Greenblatt for her keen eye.

Finally, I thank my parents, aunts, and uncles (all of blessed memory) for nourishing my interest in the past with family stories. Surely those tales inspire my work, which I bequeath to my daughters and grandchildren in the hope that it will light their path into the future.

DD
New York and Wellfleet
2025

NOTES

ABBREVIATIONS

People

EAD – Elisabeth Anthony Dexter

LLM – Laura Leah Margolis, later Laura Margolis Jarblum

MAL – Moses A. Leavitt

MDS – Martha Dickie Sharp

MMC – Marjorie McClelland

MWB – Moses W. Beckelman

RCD – Robert Cloutman Dexter

RMC – Roswell McClelland

WHS – Waitstill Hastings Sharp

Organizations/Institutions

AFSC – American Friends Service Committee

AUA – American Unitarian Association

CFA – Committee for the Assistance of European Jewish
Refugees

CUNY – City University of New York

ICJ – The Avraham Harman Institute of Contemporary Jewry,
Hebrew University

IGC – Inter-Governmental Committee on Refugees

JDC – American Jewish Joint Distribution Committee

OSE – Oeuvre de Secours aux Enfants (Children's Aid Society)

OSS – United States Office of Strategic Services

UJA – United Jewish Appeal

USC – Unitarian Service Committee

USCOM – United States Committee for the Care of European Children

USHMM – United States Holocaust Memorial Museum

UUSC – Unitarian Universalist Service Committee

Collections

MWS Collection – Martha and Waitstill Sharp Collection

RED Papers – Robert Cloutman and Elizabeth Anthony Dexter Papers

RMM Papers – Roswell and Marjorie McClellan Papers

Archives

AFSCA – American Friends Service Committee Archives, Philadelphia, PA

HDSL – Harvard Divinity School Library, Cambridge, MA

JDCA – Archives of the American Jewish Joint Distribution Committee, New York/Jerusalem

JDCTA – Georgette Bennett and Leonard Polonsky Digitized JDC Text Archive, Archives of the American Jewish Joint Distribution Committee, New York/Jerusalem

JHL – John Hay Library, Brown University, Providence, RI

NARA – National Archives and Records Administration, College Park, MD

PRO – Public Record Office, National Archives (UK), Kew, Richmond

USHMMA – United States Holocaust Memorial Museum Archives, Washington, DC

INTRODUCTION: *Americans to the Rescue*

1. See USCOM, "Plan for the Evacuation of Children from France in Relation to the Problem of Securing Admission of Such Children into the United States," n.d., p. 3, box: General Files, 1941, Committees and Organizations (Spanish Refugee Relief to War Resisters League), file: Committees and Organizations 1941, USCOM, AFSCA. In May 1941 one camp alone, Rivesaltes, counted 3,200 child inmates.

2. Isaac Chomski, "Children in Exile," *Contemporary Jewish Record* 4 (1941): 522.

3. Chomski, "Children in Exile," 526.

4. Chomski, "Children in Exile," 527.

5. Chomski, "Children in Exile," 527–28.

6. Chomski, "Children in Exile," 523.

7. Hanna Kent-Sztarkman, oral history interview by Debórah Dwork, 13 December 1985, Stamford, CT, transcript (in possession of author), 8.

8. Dorothy Bonnell, "Annual Report on Counselling and Camp Department, 1940–1941, AFSC in France," n.d., https://www.afsc.org/document/1941-annual-report-counselling-and-camp-department-1940-1941 (last accessed 31 December 2022).

9. EAD, "Mrs. Dexter's 14 Points," *Standing By. Monthly Bulletin of the USC*, no. 23 (April 1944), images 0056–0059 (RG-67.012/box 01/folder 0008), UUSC Records, ca. 1935–2006, RG-67.012, USHMMA.

10. EAD, "Mrs. Dexter's 14 Points."

CHAPTER 1: *Prague, 1939*

1. Report on MDS's activities in Europe, n.d. (probably late January 1941), image "Series 1_01_01_030" (RG-67.017/series 1/folder 01/subfolder 01), MWS Collection, RG-67.017, USHMMA. For an overview of Martha and Waitstill Sharp's activities, see the documentary by their grandson Artemis Joukowsky and filmmaker Ken Burns. It was my good fortune to serve as the historian of record on and off film. Artemis Joukowsky and Ken Burns, *Defying the Nazis: The Sharps' War* (Walpole, NH: Florentine Films, 2016), DVD, 90 min. See, too, Joukowsky's book by the same name: Artemis Joukowsky, *Defying the Nazis: The Sharps' War* (Boston: Beacon Press, 2016).

2. Čapek's daughter Bohdana and her husband Karel Haspl had graduated from the Pacific Unitarian School of Religion in Berkeley (CA). Charlotte Masaryk, the deceased wife of Tomas Masaryk, the beloved president of Czechoslovakia (1918–1935), was an American Unitarian.

3. Letter from Howard Matson to Frederick Eliot, n.d., seq. 31–32 (16003/1(3)), https://nrs.lib.harvard.edu/urn-3:div.lib.usc:2961809?n=31, USC. Records on relief work in Czechoslovakia, 1938–1946, bMS 10063, HDSL. These ties and the

responsibility they engendered were adduced to persuade Unitarians to provide financial support. See, for example, AUA and AFSC, "An Appeal for Service to Czecho-Slovakia," January 1939, box 2, folder 3, RED Papers, Ms.2005.029, JHL.

4. AUA Board of Directors, "Discussion Regarding Refugee Problem," 5 October 1938, images "Series 1_03_18_006"–"Series 1_03_18_007" (RG-67.017/series 1/folder 03/subfolder 18), MWS Collection, RG-67.017, USHMMA.

5. See RCD, "Report. Czechoslovakian Mission," November 1938, box 2, folder 1, RED Papers, Ms.2005.029, JHL.

6. "Preliminary and Confidential Report from Robert C. Dexter to the American Unitarian Association," 16 November 1938, images "Series 1_03_18_011" and "Series 1_03_18_013" (RG-67.017/series 1/folder 03/subfolder 18), MWS Collection, RG-67.017, USHMMA.

7. AUA, Exploratory Committee on Czechoslovakian Relief meeting minutes, 21 October 1938, image "Series 1_05_38_068" (RG-67.017/series 1/folder 05/subfolder 38), MWS Collection, RG67.017, USHMMA.

8. WHS, oral history interview by Ghanda DiFiglia, 18–19 October 1978, Greenfield, MA, transcript, images "Series 4_43_103_009"–"Series 4_43_103_010" (RG-67.017/series 4/folder 43/subfolder 103), MWS Collection, RG-67.017, USHMMA.

9. USC, "Minutes of Executive and Campaign Committees," 31 January 1939, seq. 32–33 (16004/25(12)), https://nrs.lib.harvard.edu/urn-3:div.lib.usc:3202384?n=32, USC. Case Files, 1938–1951, bMS 16004, HDSL.

10. MDS, "Church Mouse in the White House," n.d. (unpublished memoir draft), image "Series 4_30_02_29" (RG-67.017/series 4/folder 30/subfolder 02), MWS Collection, RG-67.017, USHMMA.

11. The United States fielded a legation headed by a minister rather than an embassy with an ambassador at that time.

12. Letter from WHS to RCD, 13 March 1939, images "Series 1_03_18_053"–"Series 1_03_18_056" (RG-67.017/series 1/folder 03/subfolder 18), MWS Collection, RG-67.017, USHMMA. See also: "Joint Report by the Two Commissioners of the Commission for Service in Czechoslovakia and the Two Agents for the Committee for Relief in Czechoslovakia," 4 February–4 September 1939, image "Series 1_09_76_071" (RG-67.017/series 1/folder 09/subfolder 76), MWS Collection, RG 67.017, USHMMA.

13. Letter from Brackett Lewis to RCD, 30 January 1939, seq. 73–74 (16003/1(13)), https://nrs.lib.harvard.edu/urn-3:div.lib.usc:2961940?n=73, USC. Records on relief work in Czechoslovakia, 1938–1946, bMS 10063, HDSL; "Joint Report," 4 February–4 September 1939, image "Series 1_09_76_071."

14. MDS, "Church Mouse," images "Series 4_30_02_050"–"Series 4_30_02_051" (RG-67.017/series 4/folder 30/subfolder 02).

15. US Department of State, *Documents on German Foreign Policy, 1918–1945,* Series D, Vol. 4 (Washington, DC: US Government Printing Office, 1956), 270–85.

16. "Report on Prague," n.d., images "Series 1_09_83_017"–"Series 1_09_83_020"

(RG-67.017/series 1/folder 09/subfolder 83), MWS Collection, RG-67.017, USHMMA. No author; probably WHS. First line reads: "The writer who was in Prague from the last part of February until the middle of April." Possibly written to be passed to the US government.

17. MDS, "Church Mouse," images "Series 4_30_02_081"–"Series 4_30_02_084" (RG-67.017/series 4/folder 30/subfolder 02).

18. MDS, "Church Mouse," image "Series 4_30_02_091" (RG-67.017/series 4/folder 30/subfolder 02).

19. Commission for Service in Czechoslovakia, "Secretary's Report," n.d., image "Series 1_03_18_086" (RG-67.017/series 1/folder 03/subfolder 18), MWS Collection, RG-67.017, USHMMA; "Joint Report," 4 February–4 September 1939, image "Series 1_09_76_072."

20. Letter from RCD in Boston to Charles Joy in Lisbon, 17 March 1942, seq. 40 (16024/6(7)), https://nrs.lib.harvard.edu/urn-3:div.lib.usc:3317362?n=40, USC. Records on relief work in Czechoslovakia, 1938–1946, bMS 10063, HDSL.

21. WHS, *The Liberation of the Human Spirit*, ed. Ghanda DiFiglia (Sherborn, MA: Journey to Freedom, 2016), loc. 312 of 939, Kindle.

22. MDS, "Church Mouse," images "Series 4_30_02_099"–"Series 4_30_02_104" (RG-67.017/series 4/folder 30/subfolder 02).

23. MDS, "Church Mouse," image "Series 4_30_02_105" (RG-67.017/series 4/folder 30/subfolder 02).

24. MDS, "Church Mouse," images "Series 4_30_02_104"–"Series 4_30_02_107" (RG-67.017/series 4/folder 30/subfolder 02).

25. Convoy (24–26 March 1939) group note, n.d., image "Series 1_03_23_056" (RG-67.017/series 1/folder 03/subfolder 23), MWS Collection, RG-67.017, USHMMA.

26. Letter from MDS to Brackett Lewis, 31 March 1939, images "Series 1_02_14_014"–"Series 1_02_14_017" (RG-67.017/series 1/folder 02/subfolder 14), MWS Collection, RG-67.017, USHMMA.

27. Letter from MDS to Brackett Lewis, 31 March 1939, images "Series 1_02_14_014"–"Series 1_02_14_017."

28. Telegram from MDS to Seth Gano, 27 March 1939, seq. 109 (16003/1(6)), https://nrs.lib.harvard.edu/urn-3:div.lib.usc:2961813?n=109, USC. Records on relief work in Czechoslovakia, 1938–1946, bMS 10063, HDSL.

29. Letter from Brackett Lewis to WHS, 31 March 1939, images "Series 1_03_19_002"–"Series 1_03_19_004" (RG-67.017/series 1/folder 03/subfolder 19), MWS Collection, RG-67.017, USHMMA.

30. Letter from Brackett Lewis to Malcolm Davis, 4 April 1939, images "Series 1_02_17_005"–"Series 1_02_17_006" (RG-67.017/series 1/folder 02/subfolder 17), MWS Collection, RG-67.017, USHMMA.

31. Memorandum from MDS to Malcolm Davis, 14 June 1939, image "Series 1_03_21_045" (RG-67.017/series 1/folder 03/subfolder 21), MWS Collection, RG-67.017, USHMMA.

32. Letter from Brackett Lewis to WHS, 10 May 1939, images "Series 1_03_

24_013"–"Series 1_03_24_015" (RG-67.017/series 1/folder 03/subfolder 24), MWS Collection, RG-67.017, USHMMA.

33. Letter from WHS to Brackett Lewis, 20 July 1939, images "Series 1_08_64_13"–"Series 1_08_64_14" (RG-67.017/series 1/folder 08/subfolder 64), MWS Collection, RG-67.017, USHMMA.

34. Letter from Brackett Lewis to WHS, 3 August 1939, image "Series 1_05_36_034" (RG-67.017/series 1/folder 05/subfolder 36), MWS Collection, RG-67.017, USHMMA.

35. Letter from WHS to associate dean, 20 June 1939 (copy), and letter from WHS to Malcolm Davis, 20 June 1939, images "Series 1_02_17_021"–"Series 1_02_17_022" (RG-67.017/series 1/folder 02/subfolder 17), MWS Collection, RG-67.017, USHMMA.

36. "Joint Report," 4 February–4 September 1939, images "Series 1_09_76_071"–"Series 1_09_76_072."

37. WHS interview, images "Series 4_43_103_058"–"Series 4_43_103_060."

38. Letter from WHS to RCD, 24 April 1939, image "Series 1_08_64_004" (RG-67.017/series 1/folder 08/subfolder 64), MWS Collection, RG-67.017, USHMMA.

39. WHS interview, images "Series 4_43_103_060"–"Series 4_43_103_064."

40. WHS interview, image "Series 4_43_103_043." See, too, letter from WHS to RCD, 24 April 1939, images "Series 1_08_64_003"–"Series 1_08_64_006."

41. WHS interview, images "Series 4_43_103_044"–"Series 4_43_103_045."

42. WHS interview, images "Series 4_43_103_039"–"Series 4_43_103_050." See, too, WHS, *Human Spirit*, loc. 286–306 of 939.

43. Letter from WHS to Parker Marean, 13 June 1939, images "Series 1_07_60_017"–"Series 1_07_60_018" (RG-67.017/series 1/folder 07/subfolder 60), MWS Collection, RG-67.017, USHMMA.

44. Letter from WHS to RCD, 13 June 1939, images "Series 1_02_08_016"–"Series 1_02_08_017" (RG-67.017/series 1/folder 02/subfolder 08), MWS Collection, RG-67.017, USHMMA; letter from WHS to RCD, 24 April 1939, images "Series 1_08_64_003"–"Series 1_08_64_006."

45. Letter from WHS to RCD, 13 June 1939, images "Series 1_02_08_016"–"Series 1_02_08_017"; and letter from RCD to WHS, 21 June 1939, image "Series 1_03_18_071" (RG-67.017/series 1/folder 03/subfolder 18), MWS Collection, RG-67.017, USHMMA.

46. Report on "The Jewish Question," n.d. (probably August 1939), images "Series 1_05_42_013"–"Series 1_05_42_015" (RG-67.017/series 1/folder 05/subfolder 42), MWS Collection, RG-67.017, USHMMA.

47. Letter from WHS to RCD, 16 June 1939, images "Series 1_07_60_023"–"Series 1_07_60_024" (RG-67.017/series 1/folder 07/subfolder 60), MWS Collection, RG-67.017, USHMMA.

48. Letter from WHS to MDS, 17 July 1939, images "Series 1_04_25_019"–"Series 1_04_25_024" (RG-67.017/series 1/folder 04/subfolder 25), MWS Collection, RG-67.017, USHMMA.

49. Letter from MDS to WHS, 26 July 1939, images "Series 1_04_25_047"–"Series 1_04_25_050" (RG-67.017/series 1/folder 04/subfolder 25), MWS Collection, RG-67.017, USHMMA.

50. MDS, "Church Mouse," image "Series 4_30_03_025" (RG-67.017/series 4/folder 30/subfolder 03).

51. MDS, "Church Mouse," images "Series 4_30_03_031"–"Series 4_30_03_036" (RG-67.017/series 4/folder 30/subfolder 03). See, too, letter from WHS to Malcolm Davis, 10 August 1939, images "Series 1_10_94_009"–"Series 1_10_94_012" (RG-67.017/series 1/folder 10/subfolder 94), MWS Collection, RG-67.017, USHMMA.

52. WHS, *Human Spirit*, loc. 314–346 of 939.

53. Report on MDS's activities in Europe, image "Series 1_01_01_030."

54. Letter from WHS, on behalf of MDS, too, to Frederick Eliot, 14 May 1940, image "Series 1_07_54_003" (RG-67.017/series 1/folder 07/subfolder 54), MWS Collection, RG-67.017, USHMMA.

55. Letter from WHS to MDS, 1 June 1939, images "Series 1_10_91_022"–"Series 1_10_91_025" (RG-67.017/series 1/folder 10/subfolder 91), MWS Collection, RG-67.017, USHMMA.

56. Letter from MDS to WHS, 16 July 1939, images "Series 1_02_14_022"–"Series 1_02_14_029" (RG-67.017/series 1/folder 02/subfolder 14), MWS Collection, RG-67.017, USHMMA.

57. Letter from WHS to MDS, 19 July 1939, image "Series 1_04_25_031" (RG-67.017/series 1/folder 04/subfolder 25), MWS Collection, RG-67.017, USHMMA.

58. Letter from MDS to WHS, 23 July 1939, image "Series 1_03_20_034" (RG-67.017/series 1/folder 03/subfolder 20), MWS Collection, RG-67.017, USHMMA.

59. International Unitarian Refugee Committee [name subsequently changed], minutes of first meeting, 15 November 1939, images "Series 1_03_18_022"–"Series 1_03_18_024" (RG-67.017/series 1/folder 03/subfolder 18), MWS Collection, RG-67.017, USHMMA.

60. MDS, report on work for USC, n.d., images "Series 1_10_88_020"–"Series 1_10_88_022" (RG-67.017/series 1/folder 10/subfolder 88), MWS Collection, RG-67.017, USHMMA.

61. MDS, report on work for USC, images "Series 1_10_88_022"–"Series 1_10_88_024."

62. MDS, report on work for USC, image "Series 1_10_88_033."

63. Letter from WHS to MDS, 10 August 1940, images "Series 1_04_30_26"–"Series 1_04_30_27" (RG-67.017/series 1/folder 04/subfolder 30); letter from WHS to MDS, 14 August 1940, images "Series 1_04_29_016"–"Series 1_04_29_017" (RG-67.017/series 1/folder 04/subfolder 29); letter from WHS to RCD, 12 August 1940, images "Series 1_05_37_004"–"Series 1_05_37_006" (RG-67.017/series 1/folder 05/subfolder 37); and letter from WHS to MDS, 20 August 1940, images "Series 1_10_105_025"–"Series 1_10_105_026" (RG-67.017/series 1/folder 10/subfolder 105), MWS Collection, RG-67.017, USHMMA.

64. Cable from MDS to USC, 5 September 1940, image "Series 1_07_59_010"

(RG-67.017/series 1/folder 07/subfolder 59), MWS Collection, RG-67.017, USHMMA.

65. Letter from USCOM to RCD, 11 September 1940, seq. 136 (16185/1(22)), https:// nrs.lib.harvard.edu/urn-3:div.lib.usc:3442951?n=136, UUSC. Executive Director, RCD. Records, 1940–1941, bMS 16185, HDSL. Securing these immigration visas proved complicated. The State Department raised numerous objections. See full correspondence in this file. See, too, USC, Executive Committee meeting minutes, 7 October 1940, seq. 54–56 (16185/1(4)), https://nrs.lib.harvard .edu/urn-3:div.lib.usc:3442806?n=54, UUSC. Executive Director, RCD. Records, 1940–1941, bMS 16185, HDSL.

66. MDS, report on work for USC, images "Series 1_10_88_033"–"Series 1_10_ 88_035."

67. Letter to MDS and WHS, 14 September 1940, images "Series 1_07_56 _003"–"Series 1_07_56_004" (RG-67.017/series 1/folder 07/subfolder 56), MWS Collection, RG-67.017, USHMMA. The letter is unsigned, but the text and tone indicate that it was written by someone in the USC office.

68. Letter from MDS to WHS, 19 September 1940, images "Series 1_05_42_020"– "Series 1_05_42_024" (RG-67.017/series 1/folder 05/subfolder 42), MWS Collection, RG-67.017, USHMMA.

69. Child transport passenger lists, 22 November 1940, images "Series 1_02_ 03_ 005"–"Series 1_02_03_011" (RG-67.017/series 1/folder 02/subfolder 03), MWS Collection, RG-67.017, USHMMA.

70. MDS, report on work for USC, images "Series 1_10_88_035"–"Series 1_10_88_ 036" (RG-67.017/series 1/folder 10/subfolder 88), MWS Collection, RG-67.017, USHMMA.

71. Letter from MDS to Mlle. M. Willems, 5 November 1940, images "Series 1_04_26_018"–"Series 1_04_26_019" (RG-67.017/series 1/folder 04/subfolder 26), MWS Collection, RG-67.017, USHMMA.

72. Group transport passenger lists, 6 and 13 December (no year listed, 1940), image "Series 1_07_58_016" (RG-67.017/series 1/folder 07/subfolder 58), MWS Collection, RG-67.017, USHMMA.

73. Child transport passenger lists, 22 November 1940, images "Series 1_02_03_ 005" and "Series 1_02_03_007."

74. MDS, report on work for USC, images "Series 1_10_88_030"–"Series 1_10_88_ 032" and "Series 1_10_88_040."

75. USC, Executive Committee meeting minutes, 5 February 1941, seq. 87–89 (16185/1(3)), https://nrs.lib.harvard.edu/urn-3:div.lib.usc:3442805?n=87, UUSC. Executive Director, RCD. Records, 1940–1941, bMS 16185, HDSL.

76. Letter from MDS to WHS, 3 December 1945, images "Series 1_10_103 _006"–"Series 1_10_103_009" (RG-67.017/series 1/folder 10/subfolder 103), MWS Collection, RG-67.017, USHMMA.

77. Letter from MDS to WHS, 12 January 1946, images "Series 1_11_106_008"–"Series

1_11_106_010" (RG-67.017/series 1/folder 11/subfolder 106), MWS Collection, RG-67.017, USHMMA.

78. Letter from WHS to MDS, 23 February 1946, image "Series 1_11_106_023" (RG-67.017/series 1/folder 11/subfolder 106), MWS Collection, RG-67.017, USHMMA.

79. Letter from WHS to MDS, 23 February 1946, images "Series 1_11_106_024"– "Series 1_11_106_025."

80. Letter from WHS to MDS, 23 February 1946, images "Series 1_11_106 _026"–"Series 1_11_106_027."

81. Letter from MDS to WHS, 29 June 1946, images "Series 1_11_106_069"– "Series 1_11_106_073" (RG-67.017/series 1/folder 11/subfolder 106), MWS Collection, RG-67.017, USHMMA.

CHAPTER 2: *Vilna, 1940*

1. Telegram from JDC to Tovilas Zadeikis, 26 October 1939, item 416217, folder: Administration, EUREXCO, General, 1933–1940 February, NY_AR193344/1/2 / 1/172, JDCTA.

2. For a history of the JDC, see Avinoam Patt, Atina Grossman, Linda Levi, and Maud Mandel, eds., *The JDC at 100: A Century of Humanitarianism* (Detroit: Wayne State University Press, 2019).

3. Moses Beckelman has not yet claimed a biographer's attention, nor did he write his memoirs. His name pops up in books on other subjects: Yehuda Bauer, *American Jewry and the Holocaust: The American Jewish Joint Distribution Committee, 1939–1945* (Detroit: Wayne State University Press, 1981); David Crowe, *Oskar Schindler: The Untold Account of His Life, Wartime Activities, and the True Story Behind the List* (New York: Basic Books, 2007); Laura Jockusch, *Collect and Record! Jewish Holocaust Documentation in Early Postwar Europe* (New York: Oxford University Press, 2012); USHMM, *Flight and Rescue* (Washington, DC: The Museum, 2001); and Patt et al., *The JDC at 100*.

4. MWB, memorandum, 24 October 1939, item 489196, folder: Lithuania. Administration, General, 1937–1940 (May), NY_AR193344/4/41/1/730, JDCTA.

5. MWB, diary, 29 October 1939, images "RG-11.001M.0833.00001794"–"RG-11.001M.0833.00001795."

6. MWB, diary, 29 October 1939, image "RG-11.001M.0833.00001798."

7. MWB, diary, 29 October 1939, images "RG-11.001M.0833.00001787"–"RG-11.001M.0833.00001788."

8. MWB, "Account of Events in Vilna Tuesday October 31," 1939, item 489173, folder: Lithuania. Administration, General, 1937–1940 (May), NY_AR193344/4/41 /1/730, JDCTA.

9. MWB, diary, 3 November 1939, image "RG-11.001M.0833.00001827."

10. MWB, diary, 1 November 1939, images "RG-11.001M.0833.00001815"–"RG-11.001M.0833.00001817."

11. Telegram from MWB in Vilna to JDC Amsterdam office, 30 October 1939, item 489176, folder: Lithuania. Administration, General, 1937–1940 (May), NY_AR193344/4/41/1/730, JDCTA.

12. For a general discussion of Jewish refugees and aid efforts in Lithuania, see Bauer, *American Jewry and the Holocaust*, 107–17; Zorach Warhaftig, *Refugee and Survivor: Rescue Efforts during the Holocaust* (Jerusalem: Yad Vashem, 1988), 31–38.

13. MWB, "Memorandum Re Expulsions over the Lithuanian German Border," 8 November 1939, item 509242, folder: Poland. Subject Matter, Refugees, General, 1934; 1937–1939, NY_AR193344/4/49/3/874, JDCTA.

14. Telegram from MWB to Morris Troper, 4 November 1939, image "RG-11.001M.0832.00001684" (RG-11.001M/folder 0832), JDC. European Executive Bureau in Paris, France (Fond 722), RG-11.001M.97, USHMMA.

15. MWB, diary, 4 November 1939, images "RG-11.001M.0833.00001834" and "RG-11.001M.0833.00001836."

16. MWB, diary, 4 November 1939, images "RG-11.001M.0833.00001836"–"RG-11.001M.0833.00001837"; MWB, "Memorandum Re Expulsions over the Lithuanian German Border."

17. MWB, diary, 4 November 1939, images "RG-11.001M.0833.00001835" and "RG-11.001M.0833.00001837."

18. MWB, diary, 6 November 1939, image "RG-11.001M.0833.00001852."

19. MWB, diary, 5 November 1939, images "RG-11.001M.0833.00001843"–"RG-11.001M.0833.00001844."

20. MWB, diary, 8 November 1939, image "RG-11.001M.0833.00001861."

21. JDC, "Remarks on Budget for the Months of November and December 1939 for Vilna," stamped 15 December 1939, item 489120, folder: Lithuania. Administration, General, 1937–1940 (May), NY_AR193344/4/41/1/730, JDCTA.

22. Letter from MWB to Kazys Bizauskas, 7 November 1939, item 489125, folder: Lithuania. Administration, General, 1937–1940 (May), NY_AR193344/4/41/1/730, JDCTA.

23. Telegram from MWB to JDC Paris office, 25 November 1939, images "RG-11.001M.0832.00001646"–"RG-11.001M.0832.00001647" (RG-11.001M/folder 0832), JDC. European Executive Bureau in Paris, France (Fond 722), RG-11.001M.97, USHMMA.

24. JDC, "Remarks on Budget for the Months of November and December 1939 for Vilna."

25. MWB, diary, 13 November 1939, images "RG-11.001M.0833.00001889" and "RG-11.001M.0833.00001892."

26. MWB, diary, 14 November 1939, images "RG-11.001M.0833.00001901"–"RG-11.001M.0833.00001902."

27. MWB, diary, 28 November 1939, images "RG-11.001M.0833.00001928" and "RG-11.001M.0833.00001935."

28. MWB, diary, 12 November 1939, image "RG-11.001M.0833.00001884."

29. MWB, diary, 3 December 1939, images "RG-11.001M.0833.00001949"–"RG-11.001M.0833.00001951."

30. MWB, diary, 28–29 November 1939, images "RG-11.001M.0833.00001937"–"RG-11.001M.0833.00001940."

31. MWB, diary, 17 December 1939, images "RG-11.001M.0833.00001975"–"RG-11.001M.0833.00001976."

32. MWB, diary, 10–11 December 1939, images "RG-11.001M.0833.00001977"–"RG-11.001M.0833.00001981."

33. MWB, diary, 11–12 December 1939, images "RG-11.001M.0833.00001982"–"RG-11.001M.0833.00001984."

34. See, for example, letter from US Department of State to JDC, 15 December 1939, item 416207, folder: Administration, EUREXCO, General, 1933–1940 February, NY_AR193344/1/2/1/172, JDCTA; Joseph Hyman, report to JDC Executive Committee, 18 December 1939, item 401042, folder: Administration, Executive Committee, 1939, NY_AR193344/1/1/2/19, JDCTA.

35. Henrietta Buchman, JDC Administration Committee meeting minutes, 4 April 1940, item 402446, folder: Administration, Committees, Administration Committee, 1939–1940, NY_AR193344/1/1/2/59, JDCTA.

36. JDC, "Summary of Cable Information Received from Mr. Troper," 24 January 1940, item 401177, folder: Administration, Executive Committee, 1940, NY_AR193344/1/1/2/20, JDCTA; Joseph Schwartz, report to JDC Executive Committee, 27 December 1939, item ID 401036, folder: Administration, Executive Committee, 1939, NY_AR193344/1/1/2/19, JDCTA.

37. JDC, "Bulletin #5—War Relief Activities of J.D.C.," 11 January 1940, item 509512, folder: Poland. Subject Matter, Refugees, General, 1940–1944, NY_AR193344/4/49/3/875, JDCTA.

38. JDC, memorandum, 19 January 1940, item 498481, folder: Poland. Administration, General, 1940 (January–March), NY_AR193344/4/49/1/797, JDCTA.

39. JDC, memorandum, 19 January 1940.

40. Morris Troper, report to JDC board of directors meeting, 21 March 1940, p. 10, item 400488, folder: Administration, Board of Directors, 1940, NY_AR193344/1/1/2/7, JDCTA.

41. MWB, "The Refugee Problem in Lithuania," February 1940, item 509490, folder: Poland. Subject Matter, Refugees, General, 1940–1944, NY_AR193344/4/49/3/875, JDCTA.

42. Refugee Relief Committee of the Kehillah in Vilnius, report, January 1940, image "RG-11.001M.0832.00002092" (RG-11.001M/folder 0832), JDC. European Executive Bureau in Paris, France (Fond 722), RG-11.001M.97, USHMMA.

43. MWB, "The Refugee Problem in Lithuania."

44. JDC, "Summary of Recent Communications Regarding Overseas Developments," 20 May 1940, item 446901, folder: Refugees, General, 1938–1944, NY_AR193344/3/9/1/405, JDCTA; MWB, "Recent Developments in Government

Refugee Policy," 9 May 1940, item 489270, folder: Lithuania. Administration, General, 1937–1940 (May), NY_AR193344/4/41/1/730, JDCTA.

45. JDC, "Summary of Cables Received," 3 July 1940, item 402421, folder: Administration, Committees, Administration Committee, 1939–1940, NY_AR193344/1/1/2/59, JDCTA.

46. Cable from MWB to JDC, 8 August 1940, item 489429; cable from MWB to JDC, 18 August 1940, item 489415; and cable from MWB to JDC, 21 August 1940, item 489382, folder: Lithuania. Administration, General, 1940 (June–September), NY_AR193344/4/41/1/731, JDCTA; Henrietta Buchman, JDC Administration Committee meeting minutes, 21 August 1940, item 402405, folder: Administration, Committees, Administration Committee, 1939–1940, NY_AR193344/1/1/2/59, JDCTA.

47. Cable from MWB to JDC, 26 August 1940, item 489367, folder: Lithuania. Administration, General, 1940 (June–September), NY_AR193344/4/41/1/731, JDCTA.

48. Henrietta Buchman, JDC Administration Committee meeting minutes, 14 August 1940, item 402408, folder: Administration, Committees, Administration Committee, 1939–1940, NY_AR193344/1/1/2/59, JDCTA. See, too: MAL, report to JDC Executive Committee meeting, 18 September 1940, item 401113, folder: Administration, Executive Committee, 1940, NY_AR193344/1/1/2/20, JDCTA.

49. See, inter alia, Debórah Dwork and Robert Jan van Pelt, *Holocaust: A History* (New York: W. W. Norton, 2002), 325–26; Yukiko Sugihara, *Visas for Life*, trans. Hiroki Sugihara (San Francisco: Edu-Comm., 1995); Warhaftig, *Refugee and Survivor*.

50. JDC, Executive Committee meeting minutes, 21 May 1941, item ID 401240, folder: Administration, Executive Committee, 1941, NY_AR193344/1/1/2/21, JDCTA.

51. JDC, Administration Committee meeting agenda, 2 December 1940, item 402387, folder: Administration, Committees, Administration Committee, 1939–1940, NY_AR193344/1/1/2/59, JDCTA.

52. JDC, Executive Committee meeting minutes, 23 December 1940, item 401093, folder: Administration, Executive Committee, 1940, NY_AR193344/1/1/2/20, JDCTA.

53. JDC, Executive Committee meeting minutes, 15 January 1941, item 401264, folder: Administration, Executive Committee, 1941, NY_AR193344/1/1/2/21, JDCTA.

54. JDC, Executive Committee meeting minutes, 15 January 1941.

55. JDC, Executive Committee meeting minutes, 15 January 1941.

56. Letter from JDC to Moses Schonfeld, 8 June 1943, item 439728, folder: Vaad Hahatzala (Emergency Committee for War-Torn Yeshivot), 1943, NY_AR193344/3/3/1/361, JDCTA.

57. JDC, Executive Committee meeting minutes, 21 May 1941.

58. JDC, Executive Committee meeting minutes, 21 May 1941.
59. David Gurvitz and Nathan Guttman, "During World War II, U.S. Intelligence Targeted American Jews," *Forward*, 23 March 2016.

CHAPTER 3: *Shanghai, 1941*

1. Cable from JDC to CFA, 21 January 1941, item 455948, folder: China. Administration, General, 1941 (January–July), NY_AR193344/4/12/1/461, JDCTA.
2. Cable from Kobe to JDC, 19 March 1941, item 455940, folder: China. Administration, General, 1941 (January–July), NY_AR193344/4/12/1/461, JDCTA; cable from Kobe to JDC, 24 March 1941, item 455937, folder: China. Administration, General, 1941 (January–July), NY_AR193344/4/12/1/461, JDCTA.
3. Cable from MWB in Kobe to JDC, 4 April 1941, item 455928, NY_AR193344/4/12/1/461, folder: China. Administration, General, 1941 (January–July), JDCTA.
4. Zorach Warhaftig, *Refugee and Survivor: Rescue Efforts during the Holocaust* (Jerusalem: Yad Vashem, 1988), 208.
5. G. E. Miller, *Shanghai: Paradise of Adventurers* (New York: Orsay Publishing House, 1937), 38–41.
6. Miller, *Shanghai*, 254.
7. See Marcia Reynders, *Port of Last Resort: The Diaspora Communities of Shanghai* (Stanford: Stanford University Press, 2001).
8. Miller, *Shanghai*, 64–67. While visas were not required to enter Shanghai, the Chinese consul general in Vienna, Dr. Ho Feng Shan, issued such visas to Jews, notwithstanding an explicit order not to do so by the Chinese ambassador in Berlin. In the wake of the November Pogrom (9–10 November 1938, a wave of state-sponsored violence across Germany and Austria that started with the destruction of Jews' property and ended with mass arrests of Jewish men), these visas helped as many as a couple of thousand Jews obtain release from concentration camps, exit visas from Greater Germany, and transit visas to third countries. When war broke out in September 1939, most of these Shanghai visa holders had found refuge in these third countries; few of them actually went to Shanghai.
9. Minute from Frank Foley to George Ogilvie-Forbes, January 1939, FO 371/24079, PRO.
10. See Georg Armbrüster, *Leben im Wartesaal: Exil in Shanghai 1938–1947* (Berlin: Stiftung Stadtmuseum, 1997); Georg Armbrüster, Michael Kohlstruck, and Sonja Mühlberger, eds., *Exil Shanghai 1938–1947: Jüdisches Leben in der Emigration* (Teetz: Hentrich & Hentrich, 2000); Barbara Geldermann, "'Jewish Refugees Should Be Welcomed and Assisted Here!' Shanghai: Exile and Return," *Leo Baeck Institute Year Book*, vol. 44 (1999), 227–43; David Kranzler, *Japanese, Nazis & Jews: The Jewish Refugee Community of Shanghai 1938–1945* (New York: Yeshiva University Press, 1976); James Ross, *Escape to Shanghai: A Jewish Community*

in China (New York: Free Press, 1994). Memoirs include Ernest G. Heppner, *Shanghai Refuge: A Memoir of the World War II Jewish Ghetto* (Lincoln: University of Nebraska Press, 1993); Evelyn Pike Rubin, *Ghetto Shanghai* (New York: Shengold, 1993); Sigmund Tobias, *Strange Haven: A Jewish Childhood in Wartime Shanghai* (Urbana: University of Illinois Press, 1999). See, too, an excellent collection of documents: Irene Eber, ed., *Jewish Refugees in Shanghai: A Selection of Documents* (Göttingen: Vandenhoeck & Ruprecht Verlage, 2018).

11. JDC, Executive Committee meeting minutes, 21 May 1941, p. 15, item 401240, folder: Administration, Executive Committee, 1941, NY_AR193344/1/1/2/21, JDCTA.

12. LLM, "Race against Time in Shanghai," *Survey Graphic* 33 (March 1944): 168. See, too, Gao Bei, *Shanghai Sanctuary* (Oxford: Oxford University Press, 2013).

13. LLM, oral history interview by Menahem Kaufman (UJA), 26 April 1976, Tel Aviv, transcript, p. 11, box: China, JDCA. Laura Margolis's life awaits a biographer. Like Moses Beckelman, her name appears in Yehuda Bauer, *American Jewry and the Holocaust: The American Jewish Joint Distribution Committee, 1939–1945* (Detroit: Wayne State University Press, 1981), and her work claims a chapter, "Laura Margolis and JDC Efforts in Cuba and Shanghai," by Zhava Litvac Glaser, in Avinoam Patt, Atina Grossman, Linda Levi, and Maud Mandel, eds., *The JDC at 100: A Century of Humanitarianism* (Detroit: Wayne State University Press, 2019). Oddly, Margolis is discussed only glancingly in the literature on the wartime Jewish refugee community in Shanghai, whether scholarly or memoir, perhaps because while Jews sheltering in Shanghai benefited from her initiatives, few writing decades later may have known who was responsible for those activities. Happily, however, Margolis claimed the attention of an MA student, Julie Kerssen, and a doctoral candidate, Zhava Litvac Glaser (mentioned above). See Julie L. Kerssen, "Life's Work: The Accidental Career of Laura Margolis Jarblum" (master's thesis, University of Wisconsin-Milwaukee, 2000), *Theses and Dissertations*, https://dc.uwm.edu/etd/548; Zhava Litvac Glaser, "Refugees and Relief: The American Jewish Joint Distribution Committee and European Jews in Cuba and Shanghai, 1938–1943" (dissertation, CUNY, 2015), *CUNY Academic Works*, https://academicworks.cuny.edu/gc_etds/561.

14. LLM interview, 26 April 1976. See, too, LLM, oral history interview by Linda G. Kuzmack, 11 July 1990, transcript, USHMM Collection, RG-50.030.0149, USHMMA.

15. Less than six months into her tenure in Havana, Margolis became a key participant in negotiations on behalf of the 908 asylum-seeking *St. Louis* passengers as that now infamous ship hovered by Havana Harbor in May 1939. Forbidden to land, the Jewish refugees faced closed doors. Desperate negotiations yielded acceptance for delimited numbers into Belgium, Britain, France, and the Netherlands. Bitterly disappointed with the United States' refusal to admit any of the passengers, Margolis nevertheless took solace that the *St Louis* would not return to Germany. She thought the Jewish refugees were safe. Little did she imagine

that Germany would invade Poland three months later and that the refugees in Belgium, France, and the Netherlands would be caught in the Nazi net.

16. LLM interview, 26 April 1976. See, too, LLM interview, 11 July 1990; and LLM, oral history interview by Margalit Bejerano, 1 February 1987, Cassettes 2726A and 2726B, Oral History Department, Institute of Contemporary Jewry, Hebrew University.

People are complicated. A flaming antisemite, Avra Warren tapped every measure at his disposal to choke immigration, including squelching creative ideas that would have increased admission to the United States, like the plan to settle Jewish refugees in the territory of Alaska.

17. MAL, report to JDC Executive Committee meeting, 19 March 1941, item 401253, folder: Administration, Executive Committee, 1941, NY_AR193344/1/1/2/21, JDCTA.

18. Letter #4 from LLM to Robert Pilpel, 28 May 1941, item 455880, folder: China. Administration, General, 1941 (January–July), NY_AR193344/4/12/1/461, JDCTA.

19. Letter #4 from LLM to Pilpel, 28 May 1941.

20. Letter #4 from LLM to Pilpel, 28 May 1941.

21. Letter #4 from LLM to Pilpel, 28 May 1941.

22. For a discussion of Shanghai's diaspora communities, see Marcia Reynders, *Port of Last Resort* (Stanford: Stanford University Press, 2001).

23. Letter #4 from LLM to Pilpel, 28 May 1941.

24. Cable from Michel Speelman to JDC, 22 March 1941, item 455935, NY_AR193344/4/12/1/461, folder: China. Administration, General, 1941 (January–July), JDCTA.

25. Cable from EastJewCom to JDC, 24 March 1941, item 455936, folder: China. Administration, General, 1941 (January–July), NY_AR193344/4/12/1/461, JDCTA.

26. Cable from MWB to JDC, 4 April 1941, item 455928, folder: China. Administration, General, 1941 (January–July), NY_AR193344/4/12/1/461, JDCTA.

27. Cable from JEWCOM to JDC, 18 April 1941, item 455972, NY_AR193344/4/12/1/461, Folder: China. Administration, General, 1941 (January–July), JDCTA.

28. Letter #4 from LLM to Pilpel, 28 May 1941.

29. Letter #4 from LLM to Pilpel, 28 May 1941.

30. Letter #8 from LLM to Robert Pilpel, 11 June 1941, item 455854, folder: China. Administration, General, 1941 (January–July), NY_AR193344/4/12/1/461, JDCTA.

31. Letter #7 from LLM to Robert Pilpel, 9 June 1941, item 455863, folder: China. Administration, General, 1941 (January–July), NY_AR193344/4/12/1/461, JDCTA.

32. Letter #8 from LLM to Pilpel, 11 June 1941.

33. Letter #10 from LLM to Robert Pilpel, 18 June 1941, item 455850, folder: China. Administration, General, 1941 (January–July), NY_AR193344/4/12/1/461, JDCTA.

34. Letter #11 from LLM to Robert Pilpel, 2 July 1941, item 455847, folder: China. Administration, General, 1941 (January–July), NY_AR193344/4/12/1/461, JDCTA.

35. Letter #11 from LLM to Pilpel, 2 July 1941.

36. Letter from LLM to Robert Pilpel, 18 June 1941, item 455849, folder: China. Administration, General, 1941 (January–July), NY_AR193344/4/12/1/461, JDCTA.

37. Letter #10 from LLM to Pilpel, 18 June 1941.

38. Letter #10 from LLM to Pilpel, 18 June 1941.

39. Letter #16 from LLM to Robert Pilpel, 17 July 1941, item 455834, NY_AR193344/4/12/1/461, folder: China. Administration, General, 1941 (January–July), JDCTA.

40. Cable from LLM to JDC, 18 July 1941, item 455830, folder: China. Administration, General, 1941 (January–July), NY_AR193344/4/12/1/461, JDCTA.

41. Letter #18 from LLM to Robert Pilpel, 29 July 1941, folder: China. Administration, General, 1941 (January–July), NY_AR193344/4/12/1/461, JDCTA.

42. Letter #19 from LLM to Robert Pilpel, 2 August 1941, item 456067, folder: China. Administration, General, 1941 (August–December), NY_AR193344/4/12/1/462, JDCTA.

43. Letter from LLM to MAL, 29 July 1941, item 455815, folder: China. Administration, General, 1941 (January–July), NY_AR193344/4/12/1/461, JDCTA.

44. Cable from LLM to JDC, 28 July 1941, item 455820, folder: China. Administration, General, 1941 (January–July), NY_AR193344/4/12/1/461, JDCTA.

45. Letter #18 from LLM to Pilpel, 29 July 1941.

46. Cable from LLM to JDC, 28 July 1941.

47. Memorandum of telephone conversation between Joseph Hyman and Avra Warren, 30 July 1941, item 455818, folder: China. Administration, General, 1941 (January–July), NY_AR193344/4/12/1/461, JDCTA. See, too, cable from JDC to LLM, 30 July 1941, item 455813, folder: China. Administration, General, 1941 (January–July), NY_AR193344/4/12/1/461, JDCTA.

48. Letter #20 from LLM to Robert Pilpel, 11 August 1941, item 456061, folder: China. Administration, General, 1941 (August–December), NY_AR193344/4/12/1/462, JDCTA.

49. JDC, meeting minutes, 8 September 1941, item 456019, folder: China. Administration, General, 1941 (August–December), NY_AR193344/4/12/1/462, JDCTA.

50. Cable from JDC to LLM in Manila, 8 September 1941, item 456018, folder: China. Administration, General, 1941 (August–December), NY_AR193344/4/12/1/462, JDCTA. See, too, Edward M. M. Warburg, statement to JDC Executive Committee, 11 September 1941, item 401211, folder: Administration, Executive Committee, 1941, NY_AR193344/1/1/2/21, JDCTA.

51. Letter #22 from LLM to MAL, 14 September 1941, item 456007, folder: China. Administration, General, 1941 (August–December), NY_AR193344/4/12/1/462, JDCTA.

52. Letter #23 from LLM to Robert Pilpel, incorrectly dated 29 July 1941 (probably 29 September 1941), item 455814, folder: China. Administration, General, 1941 (January–July), NY_AR193344/4/12/1/461, JDCTA.

53. Letter #27 from LLM to Robert Pilpel, 26 October 1941, item 456147, folder: China. Administration, General, 1941 (August–December), NY_AR193344/4/12/1/462, JDCTA.

54. Memorandum from Koreshige Inuzuka to A. Herzberg, 17 September 1941, item 456149, folder: China. Administration, General, 1941 (August–December), NY_AR193344/4/12/1/462, JDCTA.

55. Letter #27 from LLM to Pilpel, 26 October 1941.

56. Letter #27 from LLM to Pilpel, 26 October 1941.

57. Letter #27 from LLM to Pilpel, 26 October 1941.

58. Letter from A. Herzberg to LLM, 15 October 1941, item 456170, folder: China. Administration, General, 1941 (August–December), NY_AR193344/4/12/1/462, JDCTA.

59. Letter #29 from LLM to Robert Pilpel, 5 November 1941, item 456139, folder: China. Administration, General, 1941 (August–December), NY_AR193344/4/12/1/462, JDCTA.

60. Letter from LLM to A. Herzberg, 15 October 1941, item 456171, folder: China. Administration, General, 1941 (August–December), NY_AR193344/4/12/1/462, JDCTA.

61. Letter from Michel Speelman to LLM, 16 October 1941, item 456174, folder: China. Administration, General, 1941 (August–December), NY_AR193344/4/12/1/462, JDCTA.

62. Letter from LLM to Michel Speelman, 17 October 1941, item 456173, folder: China. Administration, General, 1941 (August–December), NY_AR193344/4/12/1/462, JDCTA.

63. Letter from LLM to Speelman, 17 October 1941.

64. Letter #29 from LLM to Pilpel, 5 November 1941.

65. A. Herzberg, memorandum, 7 November 1941, item 456135, folder: China. Administration, General, 1941 (August–December), NY_AR193344/4/12/1/462, JDCTA; LLM, memorandum, 9 November 1941, item 456126, folder: China. Administration, General, 1941 (August–December), NY_AR193344/4/12/1/462, JDCTA.

66. Letter #30 from LLM to Robert Pilpel, 9 November 1941, item 456130, folder: China. Administration, General, 1941 (August–December), NY_AR193344/4/12/1/462, JDCTA. NB: Page 2 of letter #30 is incorrectly cataloged as page 2 of item 456126 in same folder.

67. Cable from JDC to MWB in Paraguay, 15 December 1941, item 456079, folder: China. Administration, General, 1941 (August–December), NY_AR193344/4/12/1/462, JDCTA.

68. LLM, "Report of Activities in Shanghai, China, from December 8, 1941, to September 1943," 2, n.d., Box: China, JDCA.

69. LLM interview, 26 April 1976, p. 18; LLM, "Report of Activities in Shanghai," 3; LLM, "Race against Time," 169; LLM interview, 11 July 1990, p. 8.

70. See: LLM interview, 26 April 1976, p. 18.

71. LLM, "Report of Activities in Shanghai," 4, 5–6.
72. Affidavit signed by LLM and Manuel Siegel, 26 March 1942, item 456218, folder: China. Administration, General, 1942–1944, NY_AR193344/4/12/1/463, JDCTA.
73. For an account of the boiler acquisition, see LLM interview, 26 April 1976, pp. 19–20; LLM, "Report of Activities in Shanghai," 8–9; LLM, "Race against Time," 171; and LLM interview, 11 July 1990, p. 10. According to these accounts, the boilers had not been used in many years, or had never been used, or had arrived the day before the Pearl Harbor attack.
74. LLM, "Report of Activities in Shanghai," 9–11.
75. LLM, "Report of Activities in Shanghai," 7, 12.
76. LLM interview, 26 April 1976, pp. 20–21. See, too, inter alia: MAL, "Memorandum on the Refugee Situation in Shanghai," 17 June 1942, item 456277, folder: China. Administration, General, 1942–1944, NY_AR193344/4/12/1/463, JDCTA; memorandum dated 20 July 1942, containing excerpt of memorandum dated 22 July 1942, item 456259, folder: China. Administration, General, 1942–1944, NY_AR193344/4/12/1/463, JDCTA.
77. LLM, "Report of Activities in Shanghai," 14–17.
78. LLM interview, 26 April 1976, pp. 24–25.
79. LLM, "Report of Activities in Shanghai," 20.
80. LLM interview, 26 April 1976, p. 25.
81. LLM, "Report of Activities in Shanghai," 23, 1.
82. Letter from LLM to MAL, 3 November 1943, item 456377, folder: China. Administration, General, 1942–1944, NY_AR193344/4/12/1/463, JDCTA.
83. Letter from MAL to LLM on the *Gripsholm*, 30 November 1943, item 456374, folder: China. Administration, General, 1942–1944, NY_AR193344/4/12/1/463, JDCTA.
84. LLM interview, 26 April 1976, p. 27.
85. Pontus Rudberg, *The Swedish Jews and the Holocaust* (New York: Routledge, 2017), 241–8.
86. LLM interview, 26 April 1976, pp. 27–33.

CHAPTER 4: *Marseille, 1942*

1. Letter from MMC to family, 28 July 1940, image 8 (series 4/file 1), RMM Papers, 2014.500.1, USHMMA. See, too, Kirk McClelland, "Roswell Dunlop McClelland (25 January 1914 to 6 May 1995): The Early Years," n.d., images 11–17 (series 2/file 1), RMM Papers, 2014.500.1, USHMMA.
2. Letters from MMC to family, 3, 17, and 31 August and 20 October 1940, images 16–21, 27–29, 52–55 (series 4/file 1), RMM Papers, 2014.500.1, USHMMA.
3. Letter from MMC to family, 20 October 1940, images 54–55.
4. Letter from MMC to family, 20 October 1940, image 55.

5. Letters from MMC to family, 18 November and 7 December 1940, images 63–64, 62, 65 (series 4/file 1), RMM Papers, 2014.500.1, USHMMA.

6. Letters from MMC to family, 18 November and 7 December 1940, images 68, 62, 64.

7. Letter from MMC to family, 11 March 1941, image 21 (series 4/file 2), RMM Papers, 2014.500.1, USHMMA.

8. Letter from MMC to family, 12 and 21 June 1941, and letter to Mary Hoxie Jones, 11 July 1941, images 38–41 (series 4/file 2), RMM Papers, 2014.500.1, USHMMA.

9. Letter from MMC to family, 15 July 1941, images 42–43 (series 4/file 2), RMM Papers, 2014.500.1, USHMMA.

10. Letter from MMC to family, 17 August 1941, image 46 (series 4/file 2), RMM Papers, 2014.500.1, USHMMA.

11. Denis Peschanski, *La France des camps: L'internement, 1938–1946* (Paris: Gallimard, 2002), 42–45.

12. D. E. Wright, "Brief Report on Trip to Perpignan, January 21–25, 1941," n.d., box: General Files 1941, Foreign Service, file: France-Relief, Internment Camps, AFSCA.

13. Christian Eggers, *Unerwünschte Ausländer: Juden aus Deutschland und Mitteleuropa in französchen Internierungslagern, 1940–1942* (Berlin: Metropol Verlag, 2000), 48–55, 216–23; Peschanski, *La France des camps*, 72–79.

14. Eggers, *Unerwünschte Ausländer*, 54–61, 216–23; Peschanski, *La France des camps*, 152–9.

15. As quoted in Eggers, *Unerwünschte Ausländer*, 336.

16. See Hanna Schramm, *Menschen in Gurs* (Worms: Georg Heintz, 1977), 371.

17. AFSC, Annual Report, 1940, pp. 9–12, https://www.afsc.org/sites/default/files/documents/1940%20Annual%20Report.pdf (last accessed 30 August 2023).

18. Report from RMC to Howard Kershner on social workers resident in each camp, 12 January 1942, image 00004 ("RG-67.007M"/"Box 57 of 84"/"Box 57_Folder 017 of 100"), AFSC records relating to humanitarian work in France, RG-67.007M, USHMMA (originals held at AFSCA).

19. See Debórah Dwork, *Children with a Star* (New Haven: Yale University Press, 1991), 121.

20. Letter from MMC to family, 17 August 1941, image 50.

21. Letter from MMC to Mary Rogers, 29 November 1941, image 93 (series 4/file 2), RMM Papers, 2014.500.1, USHMMA.

22. Burrit Hiatt, activities log, n.d. (handwritten title page, log itself typed by Dorothy Lang Hiatt), p. 27, box: General Files 1942, Foreign Service France, file: Relief of refugees, Marseille, AFSCA. See also, "The Camp Situation in Unoccupied France," 21 July 1941, box: General Files 1941, Foreign Service, file: France-Relief, Internment Camps, AFSCA.

23. AFSC, Annual Report, 1941, pp. 6–7, https://www.afsc.org/sites/default/files/documents/1941%20Annual%20Report.pdf (last accessed 30 August 2023).

24. Delegation in Perpignan, "Camp of Rivesaltes: Report for December 1941," n.d.,

box: General Files 1941, Foreign Service, file: France-Relief, Internment Camps, AFSCA.

25. Letter from RMC to Mary Elmes, 20 January 1942, image 00079 ("RG-67.007M"/ "Box 11 of 84"/"Box 11_Folder 027 of 134"), AFSC records relating to humanitarian work in France, RG-67.007M, USHMMA (originals held at AFSCA).

26. See USCOM, "Plan for the Evacuation of Children from France in Relation to the Problem of Securing Admission of Such Children into the United States," n.d., p. 3, box: General Files, 1941, Committees and Organizations (Spanish Refugee Relief to War Resisters League), file: Committees and Organizations 1941, USCOM, AFSCA.

27. Ernst Papanek, report, 26 December 1940, box: General Files 1940, Foreign Service, file: France-Relief, Children's Camps, 1940, AFSCA.

28. Letter from USCOM to Howard Kershner, 7 February 1941, p. 4, box: General Files, 1941, Committees and Organizations (Spanish Refugee Relief to War Resisters League), file: Committees and Organizations, 1941, USCOM, AFSCA.

29. OSE Montpellier to AFSC, "Children's Immigration to the USA," n.d., p. 1, box: General Files 1941, Foreign Service, file: France-Relief, Children Transports, 1941, AFSCA.

30. Letter #114 from Howard Kershner to John Rich, 14 February 1941, box: General Files 1941, Foreign Service, file: France-Relief, Letters and Cables to and from Marseille, January–April 1941, AFSCA.

31. Margaret Frawley, "Confidential Memorandum USCOM," 9 May 1941, p. 2, box: General Files, 1941, Committees and Organizations (Spanish Refugee Relief to War Resisters League), file: Committees and Organizations, 1941, USCOM, AFSCA.

32. See Debórah Dwork and Robert Jan van Pelt, *Flight from the Reich* (New York: W. W. Norton, 2009), 236–7.

33. Letter #319 from Margaret Frawley to Allen Bonnell, 18 July 1941, box: General Files 1941, Foreign Service, file: France-Relief, Letters and Cables to and from Marseille, May–August 1941, AFSCA.

34. Letter #322 from Margaret Frawley to Lindsley Noble, 28 July 1941, box: General Files 1941, Foreign Service, file: France-Relief, Letters and Cables to and from Marseille, May–August 1941, AFSCA.

35. Letter from RMC to Mary Elmes, 8 September 1941, image 00008 ("RG-67.007M"/"Box 11 of 84"/"Box 11_Folder 027 of 134"), AFSC records relating to humanitarian work in France, RG-67.007M, USHMMA (originals held at AFSCA).

36. Elke Fröhlich, ed., *Die Tagebücher von Joseph Goebbels: teil II, Diktate 1941–1945*, Vol. 2 (Munich: Saur, 1996), 498–501.

37. Letter from Max Gossels to AFSC, 16 September 1941, box: General Files 1941, Foreign Service France, file: Relief and Refugees, Children's Transports 1941, AFSCA.

38. Letter from MMC to Margaret Jones, 2 January 1942, images 1–5 (series 4/file 3), RMM Papers, 2014.500.1, USHMMA.

39. Letter from MMC to Walter Miles, 15 March 1942, image 12 (series 4/file 3), RMM Papers, 2014.500.1, USHMMA.

40. Letter #5 from MMC to Catharine Cox Miles, 20 March 1942, image 14 (series 4/file 3), RMM Papers, 2014.500.1, USHMMA.

41. Letter from MMC to Margaret Jones, 14 April 1942, box: General Files 1942, Foreign Service France, file: Relief and Refugees, Marseille, Letters and Cables, January–May 1942, AFSCA.

42. Letter #137 from MMC to Margaret Frawley, 22 April 1942, box: General Files 1942, Foreign Service France, file: Relief and Refugees, Marseille, Letters and Cables, January–May 1942, AFSCA.

43. Case histories for Hannelore Berney (#1), Henri Boleslavsky (#2), Savelly Chirman (#3), and Doris Durlacher (#4), box: General Files 1942, Foreign Service Refugee Services, file: Refugee Services, June–August 1942, Children, USCOM–AFSC Cooperation, Case Histories, AFSCA.

44. Case histories for Henri and Miriam Mass (#26/7), box: General Files 1942, Foreign Service Refugee Services, file: Refugee Services, June–August 1942, Children, USCOM–AFSC Cooperation, Case Histories, AFSCA.

45. Letter #137 from MMC to Margaret Frawley, 22 April 1942.

46. Letter #140 from MMC to Margaret Frawley, 9 May 1942, box: General Files 1942, Foreign Service Refugee Services, file: Refugee Services, June–August 1942, Children, USCOM–AFSC Cooperation, AFSCA.

47. Letter from MMC to family, 4 May 1942, image 27 (series 4/file 3), RMM Papers, 2014.500.1, USHMMA.

48. Letter #134 from Howard Kershner to Clarence Pickett et al., 14 April 1942, box: General Files 1942, Foreign Service France, file: Relief and Refugees, Marseille, Letters and Cables, January–May 1942, AFSCA.

49. Letter from MMC to family, 4 May 1942, image 27 (series 4/file 3), RMM Papers, 2014.500.1, USHMMA.

50. Letter from father [Max Weilheimer] of two USCOM children to MMC, 5 July 1942, box: General Files 1942, Foreign Service France, file: Relief and Refugees, Concentration Camps, 1942, AFSCA.

51. USCOM, "Report of the Executive Director to the Board of Directors," 12 May 1943, pp. 11–12, https://afsc.org/sites/default/files/documents/1943%20 Annual%20Report%20European%20Children%20Care.pdf.

52. Dorothy Bonnell, "Annual Report on Counselling and Camp Department, 1940–1941, American Friends Service Committee in France," n.d., https://www .afsc.org/document/1941-annual-report-counselling-and-camp-department -1940-1941 (last accessed 31 December 2022).

53. Letter from MMC to Margaret Jones, 1 December 1941, box 285, file 8207, AFSC Refugee Assistance Case Files, 1933–1963, 2002.296, USHMMA.

54. Letters from Margaret Jones to Evelyn Hersey, 4 December 1941 and 28 January 1942, box 285, file 8207, AFSC Refugee Assistance Case Files, 1933–1963, 2002.296, USHMMA.

55. Letter from Margaret Jones to MMC, 12 June 1942; letters from Margaret Jones to Robert Ehrenreich, 16 June and 6 July 1942; and letter from Annelise Thieman to Albert Einstein, 14 July 1942, box 285, file 8207, AFSC Refugee Assistance Case Files, 1933–1963, 2002.296, USHMMA.

56. Letter from Albert Einstein to Annelise Thieman, 18 July 1942; letter from Marjorie Page Schauffler to Hiram J. Halle, 30 July 1942; and letter from Hiram J. Halle to Marjorie Page Schauffler, 13 August 1942, box 285, file 8207, AFSC Refugee Assistance Case Files, 1933–1963, 2002.296, USHMMA.

57. Letter from Marjorie Page Schauffler to Hiram J. Halle, 3 September 1942; letter from Hiram J. Halle to Marjorie Page Schauffler, 8 September 1942; letter from Jean Da Costa to Marjorie Page Schauffler, 9 September 1942; letter from Marjorie Page Schauffler to Hiram J. Halle, 25 September 1942; and letter from Hiram J. Halle to Marjorie Page Schauffler, 28 September 1942, box 285, file 8207, AFSC Refugee Assistance Case Files, 1933–1963, 2002.296, USHMMA.

58. Donald Lowrie, memorandum, 10 August 1942, p. 1, box: General Files 1942, Foreign Service France, file: Relief and Refugees, General 1942, AFSCA.

59. Lowrie, memorandum, 2.

60. For the negotiations in Washington, DC, see "Statement by Mr. George L. Warren," 14 September 1942, box: General Files 1942, Foreign Service France, file: Relief and Refugees, Children's Transports 1942, AFSCA.

61. Donald Lowrie, "Second Memorandum re Measures Applied to Foreign Jews in Non-Occupied France," 22 August 1942, box: General Files 1942, Foreign Service France, file: Relief and Refugees, Marseille, Letters and Cables, June–August 1942, AFSCA.

62. Hiatt, activities log, p. 5.

63. Lindsley Noble, "Children's Emigration," 27 October 1942, box: General Files 1942, Foreign Service, file: Refugee Jews, September–December 1942, AFSCA.

64. Donald Lowrie, "Conversation with Mr. Bousquet, Secretaire-General de la Police. Vichy, October 16th," 1942, box: General Files 1942, Foreign Service, file: Refugee Jews, September–December 1942, AFSCA.

65. Hiatt, activities log, p. 112.

66. "Agenda Board Meeting USCOM," 24 November 1942, box: General Files 1942, Foreign Service, file: Refugee Jews, September–December 1942, Children, USCOM–AFSC Cooperation, AFSCA.

67. Hiatt, activities log, pp. 4, 11.

68. Hiatt, activities log, pp. 46, 15, 22.

69. Hiatt, activities log, p. 47.

70. Hiatt, activities log, p. 39.

71. Hiatt, activities log, pp. 48, 46.

72. Hiatt, activities log, pp. 112–13.

73. AFSC, "1942 Activities in France (Baden-Baden Report)," 13 June 1943, https://www.afsc.org/sites/default/files/documents/1942_Activities_in%20France_Baden%20Baden%20Report_0.pdf.

74. Letter from MMC to family, 28 July 1940, image 8 (series 4/file 1), RMM Papers, 2014.500.1, USHMMA.
75. Letter from RMC to mother, 4 May 1942, image 23 (series 4/file 3), RMM Papers, 2014.500.1, USHMMA.
76. Letter from RMC to mother, 4 May 1942.
77. For more on the War Refugee Board and RMC's role, see: Rebecca Erbelding, *Rescue Board: The Untold Story of America's Efforts to Save the Jews of Europe* (New York: Doubleday, 2018).

CHAPTER 5: *Lisbon, 1943*

1. It gives me great pleasure to acknowledge an undergraduate honors thesis and an MA thesis by Nora Newhard, then a student at Clark University. Her scholarship shed new light on Elisabeth and Robert Dexter. "The Unitarian Service Committee: Under the Direction of Dr. Robert C. Dexter, 1938–1944" was submitted on 5 May 2009. "Altruism in the Nazi Era: The Unitarian Service Committee's Medical Program" was submitted on 21 April 2010.
2. EAD, "Around the Corner," *Standing By. Monthly Bulletin of the USC*, no. 12 (April 1943), box 2, folder 3, RED Papers, Ms.2005.029, JHL.
3. Letter from Seth Gano to RCD and EAD, 21 December 1942, entry 160A, box 12, folder 99, Records of the OSS 1940–1946, RG 226, NARA.
4. RCD, "History of the USC. Chapter 1. In the Beginning," n.d. (unpublished manuscript), pp. 3–5, box 2, folder 6, RED Papers, Ms.2005.029, JHL.
5. International Unitarian Refugee Committee [name subsequently changed], minutes of first meeting, 15 November 1939, image "Series 1_03_18_022" (RG-67.017/series 1/folder 03/subfolder 18), MWS Collection, RG-67.017, USHMMA.
6. "Voted by the American Unitarian Association," 10 January 1940, box 2, folder 1, RED Papers, Ms.2005.029, JHL.
7. EAD and RCD, "Report on Trip to Europe, January 27–April 29, 1940," n.d., pp. 2, 12–13, box 2, folder 1, RED Papers, Ms.2005.029, JHL.
8. Letter from Frederick Eliot to WHS, May 1940, image "Series 1_07_54_050" (RG-67.017/series 1/folder 03/subfolder 54), MWS Collection, RG-67.017, USHMMA.
9. Seth Gano, "'With Good Will Doing Service': The Story of the Unitarian Service Committee in World War II," *Christian Register* (January 1946): 1.
10. Charles Joy moved the USC office out of the Hotel Metropole when the Japanese naval attaché took rooms on an upper floor and a Portuguese policeman stood guard at the officer's door. Joy chose a fourth-floor walk-up at Rua Castilho 15/4. Upon the Dexters' arrival in August 1942, they moved the office again to the first floor of Rua Marquês de Fronteira 111. "Many of the people who came to us were elderly, had small children, or were ill, as they had just come out of concentration

camps," Robert Dexter explained; they could not negotiate so many flights of stairs. Then, too, the Dexters wanted an office with two exits to allow "illegals" to slip away if necessary. RCD, "Chapter IX. Stormy Weather," n.d. (unpublished manuscript), p. 15, box 2, folder 12, RED Papers, Ms.2005.029, JHL.

11. A number of accounts detail the escape of Lion and Marta Feuchtwanger and the key roles played by Varian Fry, of the Emergency Rescue Committee; the American vice-consuls in Marseille, Hiram Bingham and Myles Standish; and Martha and Waitstill Sharp. See, inter alia, Varian Fry, *Surrender on Demand* (Chicago: Johnson Books, 1997); Sheila Isenberg, *A Hero of Our Own* (New York: Random House, 2001); MDS, "Church Mouse in the White House," n.d. (unpublished memoir), images "Series 4_30_04_082"–"Series 4_30_04_091" (RG-67.017/series 4/folder 30/subfolder 04), MWS Collection, RG-67.017, USHMMA; WHS, oral history interview by Ghanda DiFiglia, 18–19 October 1978, Greenfield, MA, transcript, images "Series 4_43_103_118"–"Series 4_43_103_136" (RG-67.017/series 4/folder 43/subfolder 103), MWS Collection, RG-67.017, USHMMA; MDS, oral history interview by Ghanda DiFiglia, 16 April 1979, New York, transcript, images "Series 4_43_106_064"–"Series 4_43_106_073" (RG-67.017/series 4/folder 43/subfolder 106), RG-67.017, MWS Collection, USHMMA.

12. See chapter 1.

13. USC, meeting minutes, 21 January 1941, seq. 106–107 (16185/1(3)), https://nrs .lib.harvard.edu/urn-3:div.lib.usc:3442805?n=106, UUSC. Executive Director, RCD. Records, 1940–1941, bMS 16185, HDSL.

14. EAD, "Introduction to Port of Freedom," n.d. (unpublished manuscript), box 2, folder 12, RED Papers, Ms.2005.029, JHL.

15. EAD, "Lisbon: Last Port of Freedom," n.d. (unpublished manuscript), p. 9, box 2, folder 12, RED Papers, Ms2005.029, JHL.

16. EAD, "Lisbon: Last Port of Freedom. Chapter Two. Full Steam Ahead," n.d. (unpublished manuscript), p. 1, box 2, folder 12, RED Papers, Ms.2005.029, JHL.

17. EAD, "Lisbon: Last Port of Freedom," p. 12. The World Jewish Congress also had a representative in Lisbon. Dr. Yitzhak Weisman worked collaboratively with the USC while, according to Elisabeth, "relations were not fully friendly" between Weisman and the other Jewish organizations. See EAD, oral history interview by Yehuda Bauer, 20 August 1962, images 0015–0016 (RG-67.012/box 03/folder 0035), UUSC Records, ca. 1935–2006, RG-67.012, USHMMA.

18. EAD, "Lisbon: Last Port of Freedom. Chapter Two. Full Steam Ahead," 5–7.

19. EAD, "Lisbon: Last Port of Freedom. Chapter Two. Full Steam Ahead," 20–24. EAD uses two surnames for the refugee couple: Pollack and Rosenblatt.

20. EAD, "Lisbon: Last Port of Freedom. Chapter Two. Full Steam Ahead," 8–9.

21. AFSC, "Conference with Dr. and Mrs. Dexter," 14 November 1941, box: General Files, 1941. Committees and Organizations (Spanish Refugee Relief to War Resisters League), file: Committees and Organizations 1941, USC, AFSCA.

22. Charles Joy, "Report of Activities in Europe, 1941–1942," 14 September 1942,

seq. 3 (16081/15(1)), https://nrs.lib.harvard.edu/urn-3:div.lib.usc:3429151?n=3, USC. Executive Director. Records, 1941–1951, bMS 16081, HDSL.

23. Letter from RCD to Charles Joy, 27 January 1942, seq. 9 (16024/6(7)), https://nrs.lib.harvard.edu/urn-3:div.lib.usc:3317362?n=9, USC. Executive Director. Records, 1941–1953, bMS 16024, HDSL.

24. Letter from RCD to Charles Joy, 17 March 1942, seq. 40 (16024/6(7)), https://nrs.lib.harvard.edu/urn-3:div.lib.usc:3317362?n=40, USC. Executive Director. Records, 1941–1953, bMS 16024, HDSL.

25. Letter from RCD to Seth Gano, 8 December 1942, p. 2, box 1, folder 23, RED Papers, Ms.2005.029, JHL.

26. RCD and EAD, "USC History. Chapter XII. The Long Haul in Lisbon: August 1942–December 1944," n.d. (unpublished manuscript), pp. 11–12, box 2, folder 7, RED Papers, Ms.2005.029, JHL.

27. RCD and EAD, "USC History. Chapter XII," 11–12.

28. RCD and EAD, "USC History. Chapter XII," 11.

29. EAD interview, 20 August 1962, images 0013–0014.

30. USC, "Memorandum from the Case Work Committee," 26 March 1943, seq. 25 (16003/1(1)), https://nrs.lib.harvard.edu/urn-3:div.lib.usc:2961807?n=25, USC. Records on relief work in Czechoslovakia, 1938–1946, bMS 16003, HDSL.

31. EAD interview, 20 August 1962, images 0013–0014.

32. RCD and EAD, "USC History. Chapter XII," 13.

33. USC, Case Committee report, 29 February 1944, seq. 6 (16003/1(1)), https://nrs.lib.harvard.edu/urn-3:div.lib.usc:2961807?n=6, USC. Records on relief work in Czechoslovakia, 1938–1946, bMS 16003, HDSL.

34. RCD and EAD, "USC History. Chapter XII," 2.

35. Memorandum from Allen Dulles to John Hughes, 17 June 1942, image 0008 (RG-67.012/box 06/folder 0103), UUSC Records, ca. 1935–2006, RG-67.012, USHMMA.

36. Letter from John Hughes to RCD, 16 July 1942, seq. 110 (16004/25(13)), https://nrs.lib.harvard.edu/urn-3:div.lib.usc:3202385?n=110, USC. Case Files, 1938–1951, bMS 16004, HDSL.

37. Letter from William Emerson to Breckenridge Long, 4 November 1942, seq. 155, 152 (16004/22(8)), https://nrs.lib.harvard.edu/urn-3:div.lib.usc:3200626?n=152, USC. Case Files, 1938–1951, bMS 16004, HDSL.

38. Letter from RCD to Seth Gano, 4 December 1942, box 1, folder 23, RED Papers, Ms.2005.029, JHL.

39. Letter from RCD to Seth Gano, 8 December 1942.

40. Letter from RCD to Seth Gano, 8 December 1942.

41. Letter from Seth Gano to John Hughes, 19 December 1942, image 0012 (RG-67.012/box 06/folder 0104), UUSC Records, ca. 1935–2006, RG-67.012, USHMMA.

42. Letter from Seth Gano to RCD and EAD, 21 December 1942, pp. 1, 3.

43. Memorandum from John Hughes to Mr. Shapiro, 15 March 1943, image 0036

(RG-67.012/box 06/folder 0104), UUSC Records, ca. 1935–2006, RG-67.012, USHMMA.

44. T[oni] S[ender], "Interoffice Report," 22 April 1943, entry A1-210, box 242, folder 10520, Records of the OSS 1940–1946, RG 226, NARA.

45. Letter from EAD to RCD, 9 May 1943, box 1, folder 28, RED Papers, Ms.2005.029, JHL.

46. T[oni] S[ender], "Interoffice Report," 15 June 1943, entry A1-210, box 242, folder 10520, Records of the OSS 1940–1946, RG 226, NARA.

47. Letter from EAD to RCD, 8 June 1943, box 1, folder 29, RED Papers, Ms.2005.029, JHL. See, too, letter from Seth Gano to RCD (20 May 1943), in which he bruits the prospect of this meeting. Box 1, folder 28, RED Papers, Ms.2005.029, JHL.

48. Letter from RCD to Seth Gano, 25 January 1943, box 1, folder 24, RED Papers, Ms.2005.029, JHL.

49. Letter from RCD to William Emerson, 25 January 1943, box 1, folder 24, RED Papers, Ms.2005.029, JHL.

50. Letter from RCD to Seth Gano, 9 February 1943, box 1, folder 25, RED Papers, Ms.2005.029, JHL.

51. Letter from Seth Gano to RCD, 27 April 1943, box 1, folder 27, RED Papers, Ms.2005.029, JHL.

52. Letter from RCD to EAD, 10–13 May 1943, box 1, folder 28, RED Papers, Ms.2005.029, JHL.

53. Letter from RCD to Seth Gano, 11 May 1943, box 1, folder 28, RED Papers, Ms.2005.029, JHL.

54. Letter from Seth Gano to RCD, 16 June 1943, box 1, folder 29, RED Papers, Ms.2005.029, JHL.

55. Letter from EAD to RCD, 27 April 1943, box 1, folder 27, RED Papers, Ms.2005.029, JHL.

56. Letters from EAD to RCD, 8 and 9 May 1943, box 1, folder 28, RED Papers, Ms.2005.029, JHL.

57. Letter from EAD to RCD, 8 June 1943.

58. EAD, memorandum, July 1943, box 1, folder 30, RED Papers, Ms.2005.029, JHL.

59. The Inter-Governmental Committee on Refugees (IGC) was established at the Evian Conference, held in July 1938 at President Roosevelt's invitation. The purpose of the meeting, which was attended by representatives of thirty-two countries, was to facilitate the emigration of "political refugees" (not Jews) from Germany and Austria. The IGC, like the Evian Conference, achieved little.

60. The international brigades were military units comprised of volunteer troops from many nations who fought (1936–1938) on behalf of Republican Spain. Formed at the end of the Spanish Civil War in 1939, the International Brigade Association aimed to continue the defense and advance of democracy against fascism in Britain.

61. See RCD, "Insert to Chapter XII," n.d. (unpublished manuscript), pp. 17g–17i, box 2, folder 7, RED Papers, Ms.2005.029, JHL; and letter from RCD to Seth

Gano, 17 December 1943, box 1, folder 35, RED Papers, Ms.2005.029, JHL. See, too, "Report of Sub-Committee on Relationships between Dr. Dexter and Dr. Joy as Revealed from an Analysis of Correspondence and Documents 1943–44, and Special Study of Evidence Concerning Dr. Joy's Trip to London, July, 1942," n.d., with supporting documentation "Data re Auspices and Expenses Joy's Trip to London," 20 December 1943; "An Answer by Mr. Joy to the Charges Made by Dr. Dexter," 3 April 1944; and "Supplementary Statement by Mr. Joy," 19 April 1944, seq. 7–11, 44–45, 13–19, 20 (16024/6(8)), https://nrs.lib.harvard.edu/urn -3:div.lib.usc:3317368?n=7, USC. Executive Director. Records, 1941–1953, bMS 16024, HDSL.

62. See, for instance, letters from RCD to EAD, Sunday 17 and Monday 18 [incorrectly dated 17] October 1943, box 1, folder 33, RED Papers, Ms.2005.029, JHL.

63. Letter from RCD to EAD, 20 October 1943, box 1, folder 33, RED Papers, Ms.2005.029, JHL.

64. RCD, "Insert to Chapter XII," pp. 17g–17i.

65. Memorandum from Robert Joy to USC Executive Committee, 29 November 1943, box 1, folder 34, RED Papers, Ms.2005.029, JHL.

66. Letter from RCD to EAD, 28 October 1943, box 1, folder 33, RED Papers, Ms.2005.029, JHL.

67. Letter from RCD to Seth Gano, n.d. (October or November 1943), box 1, folder 33, RED Papers, Ms.2005.029, JHL.

68. Letter from Seth Gano to EAD and RCD, 17 December 1943, box 1, folder 35, RED Papers, Ms.2005.029, JHL.

69. Letter from RCD (with addenda by EAD) to Seth Gano, 17 December 1943, box 1, folder 35, RED Papers, Ms.2005.029, JHL.

70. USC, Case Committee report, 29 February 1944, seq. 6.

71. Letter from Fritz Hussarek to EAD, 26 March 1943, box 1, folder 28, RED Papers, Ms.2005.029, JHL. Hussarek went by the surname "Holtberg" in Lisbon until spring 1943, presumably to reduce the risk of unwanted German attention. See letter from RCD to EAD, 1 June 1943, box 1, folder 29, RED Papers, Ms.2005.029, JHL.

72. Letter from Fritz Hussarek to EAD, 26 March 1943.

73. Fritz Hussarek was incarcerated in an internment camp shortly after the war began and let out nine weeks later. See Jewish Telegraphic Agency, "156 Noted Refugees Listed as Released from French Isolation Camps," 22 January 1940.

Released to continue his work on the Défense Nationale project, Fritz was reinterned in May 1940; Helga was incarcerated at the same time. Both were released in June 1940 and fled to the south of France, the free zone, where they found each other in July. See Fritz Hussarek, statement to the American Consul-General in Lisbon, 10 June 1941, box 1, folder 28, RED Papers, Ms.2005.029, JHL.

74. See letter from Fritz Hussarek to EAD, 26 March 1943. See, too, Fritz Hussarek, statement to the American Consul-General in Lisbon, 10 June 1941.

75. Letter from RCD to EAD, 29 March and 1 April 1943, box 1, folder 26, RED Papers, Ms.2005.029, JHL.

76. Letter from Charles Joy to RCD, 21 May 1943, box 1, folder 28, RED Papers, Ms.2005.029, JHL.

77. Letter from EAD to RCD, 8 May 1943, box 1, folder 28, RED Papers, Ms.2005.029, JHL.

78. Letter from EAD to RCD, 9 May 1943.

79. Letter from RCD to Charles Joy, 24 May 1943, box 1, folder 28, RED Papers, Ms.2005.029, JHL.

80. Letter from RCD to Charles Joy, 24 May 1943.

81. See letter from RCD to EAD, 29 May 1943, box 1, folder 28, RED Papers, Ms.2005.029, JHL. See, too, letter from RCD to EAD, 13 June 1943, box 1, folder 29, RED Papers, Ms.2005.029, JHL.

82. Charles Joy, "Thank you! Thank you! Thank you!" *Standing By. Monthly Bulletin of the USC*, no. 17 (October 1943). In the possession of the author.

83. Letter from RCD to Seth Gano, 17 December 1943, box 1, folder 35, RED Papers, Ms.2005.029, JHL.

84. Letter from Howard Brooks to Seth Gano, 3 February 1944, seq. 6 (16024/1(14)), https://nrs.lib.harvard.edu/urn-3:div.lib.usc:3314016?n=6, USC. Executive Director. Records, 1941–1953, bMS 16024, HDSL.

85. Letter from Charles Joy to William Emerson, 11 March 1944, seq. 57 (16004/25(14)), https://nrs.lib.harvard.edu/urn-3:div.lib.usc:3202386?n=57, USC. Case Files, 1938–1951, bMS 16004, HDSL.

86. Frederick Eliot, memorandum, 22 March 1944, seq. 34–36 (16004/25(14)), https://nrs.lib.harvard.edu/urn-3:div.lib.usc:3202386?n=34, USC. Case Files, 1938–1951, bMS 16004, HDSL. On the documents each submitted, see, for example, RCD, "Data Re Auspices and Expenses of Joy's Trip to London," 20 December 1943, seq. 44–45 (16024/6(8)), https://nrs.lib.harvard.edu/urn-3:div .lib.usc:3317368?n=44, and "Mr. Joy's Visit to London, July 1942. An Answer by Mr. Joy," 3 April 1944, seq. 13–18 (16024/6(8)), https://nrs.lib.harvard.edu/urn -3:div.lib.usc:3317368?n=13, USC. Executive Director. Records, 1941–1953, bMS 16024, HDSL.

87. On the Refugee War Board, see Rebecca Erbelding, *Rescue Board: The Untold Story of America's Efforts to Save the Jews of Europe* (New York: Doubleday, 2018).

88. "Report of Sub-Committee on Relationships between Dr. Dexter and Dr. Joy as Revealed from an Analysis of Correspondence and Documents 1943–44, and Special Study of Evidence Concerning Dr. Joy's Trip to London, July, 1942," n.d., seq. 7, 9 (16024/6(8)), https://nrs.lib.harvard.edu/urn-3:div.lib.usc:3317368?n=7, USC. Executive Director. Records, 1941–1953, bMS 16024, HDSL.

89. Letter from RCD to EAD, 17–21 May 1943, box 1, folder 28, RED Papers, Ms.2005.029, JHL.

90. Letter from RCD to EAD, 13 June 1943, box 1, folder 29, RED Papers, Ms.2005.029, JHL.

91. Letter from RCD to EAD, 29 October 1943, box 1, folder 33, RED Papers, Ms.2005.029, JHL.

92. Letter from EAD to Lewis Dexter, 22 October 1943, box 1, folder 33, RED Papers, Ms.2005.029, JHL.

93. EAD, "Heavy Weather," n.d. (unpublished manuscript), pp. 21, 25, 21, box 2, folder 13, RED Papers, Ms.2005.029, JHL.

94. RCD, "Chapter XII," n.d. (unpublished manuscript), p. 40, box 2, folder 7, RED Papers, Ms.2005.029, JHL.

95. On salaries, see letter from Charles Joy to Frederick Eliot, 19 March 1944, seq. 40 (16004/25(14)), https://nrs.lib.harvard.edu/urn-3:div.lib.usc:3202386?n=40, USC. Case Files, 1938–1951, bMS 16004, HDSL.

96. USC, "Executive Session of the Executive Committee," 8 June 1944, with additional note dated 13 June 1944, seq. 12 (16024/6(8)), https://nrs.lib.harvard.edu/urn-3:div.lib.usc:3317368?n=12, USC. Executive Director. Records, 1941–1953, bMS 16024, HDSL.

97. Message from OSS London office to NY Secret Service Intelligence Branch, 22 May 1945, entry 160A, box 12, folder 98, Records of the OSS 1940–1946, RG 226, NARA.

98. RCD, "Chapter XII," n.d. (unpublished manuscript), p. 17i, box 2, folder 7, RED Papers, Ms.2005.029, JHL.

99. RCD, "Chapter XII," n.d. (unpublished manuscript), p. 17i, box 2, folder 7, RED Papers, Ms.2005.029, JHL.

EPILOGUE

1. JDC, "30 Years. The Story of the JDC," 1945, pp. 2, 8, 10, item 402220, folder: Administration, National Council, Minutes of Meetings, 1944, NY_ AR193344/1/1/2/34, JDCTA.

2. USC, "Half a Million Now Have Hope," n.d., seq. 18–19 (16004/25(16)), https://nrs.lib.harvard.edu/urn-3:div.lib.usc:3202388?n=18, USC. Case Files, 1938–1951, bMS16004, HDSL.

3. Letter from WHS to RCD, 13 June 1939, images "Series 1_02_08_016"–"Series 1_02_08_017" (RG-67.017/series 1/folder 02/subfolder 08), MWS Collection, RG-67.017, USHMMA.

4. The entire run of *Standing By*, the monthly bulletin of the Unitarian Service Committee, from its first publication in May 1942 through its thirty-sixth in July/August 1945, is silent about delegates' sensibilities.

5. Yehuda Bauer, *American Jewry and the Holocaust: The American Jewish Joint Distribution Committee, 1939–1945* (Detroit: Wayne State University Press, 1981), 113.

6. Letter from MDS to WHS, 16 July 1939, images "Series 1_02_14_022"–"Series 1_02_14_029" (RG-67.017/series 1/folder 02/subfolder 14); and letter from MDS to WHS, 23 July 1939, images "Series 1_03_20_034"–"Series 1_03_20_040" (RG-67.017/series 1/folder 03/subfolder 20), MWS Collection, RG-67.017, USHMMA.

7. MWB, diary, 3 December 1939, images "RG-11.001M.0833.00001949"–"RG-11.001M.0833.00001951" (RG-11.001M/folder 0833), JDC. European Executive Bureau in Paris, France (Fond 722), RG-11.001M.97, USHMMA.

8. Letter from LLM to Robert Pilpel, 18 June 1941, item 455849, folder: China. Administration, General, 1941 (Jan.–July), NY_AR193344/4/12/1/461, JDCTA.

9. Letter from RCD to EAD, 3 November 1943, p. 4, box 1, folder 34, RED Papers, Ms.2005.029, JHL.

10. Letter from MMC to family, 18 November 1940, image 64 (series 4/file 1), RMM Papers, 2014.500.1, USHMMA.

11. The precise nature of their relationship remains unclear.

12. Letter from MDS to WHS, 14 November 1945, images "Series 1_02_10_037"–"Series 1_02_10_039" (RG-67.017/series 1/folder 02/subfolder 10); letter from MDS to WHS, 18 November 1945, images "Series 1_02_10_040"–"Series 1_02_10_041" (RG-67.017/series 1/folder 02/subfolder 10); and letter from MDS to WHS, 3 December 1945, images "Series 1_10_103_006"–"Series 1_10_103_009" (RG-67.017/series 1/folder 10/subfolder 103), MWS Collection, RG-67.017, USHMMA.

INDEX

Page numbers in italics indicate a figure on the corresponding page.

ABOUT THE AUTHOR

DEBÓRAH DWORK is the director of the Center for the Study of the Holocaust, Genocide, and Crimes Against Humanity at the Graduate Center—CUNY. The author of award-winning books, she is also a leading authority on university education in this field. Dwork is the recipient of the Distinguished Achievement Award in Holocaust Studies from the Holocaust Educational Foundation, the Annetje Fels-Kupferschmidt Award bestowed by the Dutch Auschwitz Committee, and the Lifetime Achievement Award from the International Network of Genocide Scholars.